FROM FASTING SAINTS TO ANOREXIC GIRLS
THE HISTORY OF SELF-STARVATION

From Fasting Saints to Anorexic Girls

The History of Self-Starvation

WALTER VANDEREYCKEN
& RON VAN DETH

NEW YORK UNIVERSITY PRESS
Washington Square, New York

First published in the U.S.A. in 1994 by
NEW YORK UNIVERSITY PRESS
Washington Square New York, N.Y. 10003

© Walter Vandereycken and Ron van Deth 1994
© 1990 by Biermann Verlag GmbH, D-5352 Zülpich.
Published in German as *Hungerkünstler, Fastenwunder, Magersucht:
eine Kulturgeschichte der Ess-störungen*

Library of Congress Cataloging-in-Publication Data

Vandereycken, Walter, 1949–
    [Hungerkünstler, Fastenwunder, Magersucht. English]
    From fasting saints to anorexic girls: the history of self
–starvation / Walter Vandereycken & Ron van Deth.
        p.   cm.
    This translation is based on the German edition, which was an
adapted and shortened version of the original Dutch.
    Includes bibliographical references and index.
    ISBN 0-8147-8783-5 — ISBN 0-8147-8784-3 (pbk.)
    1. Anorexia nervosa—History.   I. Deth, Ron van, 1955–
II. Title.
RC552.A5V36313   1994
616.85′262′09—dc20   94-2859
                                                            CIP

Typeset by
Datix International Limited, Bungay, Suffolk
Printed and bound in Great Britain by
Bookcraft (Bath) Limited

Contents

Preface

Originally this book was published in Dutch in 1988 (*Van vastenwonder tot magerzucht: anorexia nervosa in historisch perspectief*, Amsterdam: Boom). An adapted and shortened version in German appeared in 1990 (*Hungerkünstler, Fastenwunder, Magersucht: eine Kulturgeschichte der Ess-störungen*, Zülpich: Biermann Verlag); of this edition a pocketbook was published in 1992 (Munich: Deutscher Taschenbuch Verlag). The present English adaptation has been based mainly on the German edition, with some new material added.

Many friends and colleagues have contributed to the writing of this book by their advice, criticism or help with documentation:

From Australia: P. J. V. Beumont (Sydney).

From Austria: G. Rathner (Innsbruck).

From Belgium: C. Coolen-Perednia (Louvain), F. Depestele (Aarschot), A. Gielis (Turnhout), S. Joos (Louvain), J. Rolies (Louvain), S. Thomas (Tienen), G. Vandendriessche (Louvain), P. Vandermeersch (Louvain), M. Van Moffaert (Ghent), J. Van de Wiele (Ghent).

From Canada: Z. J. Lipowski and E. Shorter (Toronto).

From Finland: R. Fried (Jyväskylä).

From France: J. Bullerwell-Ravar (Paris), P. Aimez (Paris), N. Duval (Paris), J. L. Vénisse (Nantes).

From Germany: U. Geisselbrecht-Capecki (Kleve), T. Habermas (Berlin), R. Meermann (Bad Pyrmont), J. E. Meyer (Göttingen), K. M. Pirke (Munich), H. Schadewaldt (Düsseldorf), H. U. Ziolko (Berlin).

From Great Britain: A Cockett (Ipswich), C. G. Fairburn (Oxford), I. A. D. Hohberger (London), J. H. Lacey (London), E. Miller (Cambridge), B. and W. Parry-Jones (Glasgow), G. F. M. Russell (London), J. M. Tanner (London).

From the Netherlands: R. Deckers (Haarlem), M. Gielis (Tilburg), M. Gijswijt-Hofstra (Amsterdam), R. Hemel (Klazienaveen), A. de Knecht-Van Eekelen (Malden), G. A. Lindeboom (Amsterdam), L. McCaw (Zoeterwoude), R. Sieders (Arnhem), W. Spies (Amsterdam), J. H. van den Berg (Woudrichem), G. van der Veer (Leyden), A. van de Wege (Utrecht), H. de Waardt (Diemen), W. Weeda-Mannak (Amsterdam), G. Zwarts (Zoeterwoude).

From Norway: J. Rosenvinge (Oslo).

From Sweden: H. Fries (Ljungbyhed), S. Espmark (Stockholm), S. Theander (Lund).

From the USA: R. Bogdan (Syracuse), D. M. Garner (East Lansing), K. A. Halmi (White Plains), J. Kroll (Minneapolis), E. L. Lowenkopf (New York City), J. A. Silverman (New York City), J. Wortis (Brooklyn).

Despite their help, omissions and mistakes in this book are not excluded, for which only we are responsible. Last but not least, we would like to thank our house-mates who for some years have accepted the considerable distraction from family life due to the preparation of this book. What this has meant to us cannot be expressed in a few clichéd words.

1
A Mirror of Time and Culture

An illness known until recently to only a small circle of physicians grew into a 'modern' illness, for which even lay people are more or less able to use the Latin term. Anorexia nervosa has become a fashionable disorder: television producers smell sensation, women's magazines see a subject for their advisory columns, publishers dream of autobiographical bestsellers. Often the illness is presented as 'mysterious': physicians are desperately seeking an ultimate explanation and self-help organizations do not know which therapy to recommend. The specialist literature is interminable: an immense number of scientific papers, a growing pile of books and even some specialized journals are devoted specifically to the phenomenon. Before analysing this particular and growing interest against a sociocultural background, we will briefly outline the disorder which has moved us to write this book.

A current view of anorexia nervosa

In general, every description of anorexia nervosa begins with the fact that the Latin term is misleading. Literally it denotes a lack or absence of appetite of nervous origin. But the patients – the anorexics – do not suffer from a lack of appetite: partly the term refers to a desired or deliberate suppression of appetite and hunger, partly to a disturbed eating behaviour from a deeply rooted pursuit of thinness. Therefore *self-starvation* would be a better term. Although there are many definitions, the following criteria are usually considered essential for the diagnosis:

(a) an intense fear of becoming fat, even though under-weight;
(b) disturbance in the way in which one's body weight, size, or shape is experienced, e.g. the person claims to 'feel fat' even when emaciated;
(c) refusal to maintain body weight over a normal minimum

weight for age and height, e.g. weight loss leading to a body weight of 15 per cent below that expected.

In addition, the following characteristics often occur: absence of menses (amenorrhoea); a striking physical and often intellectual hyperactivity (a strange endurance despite emaciation); unusual handling of food, in particular the selection of low-calorie food and/or avoidance of regular meals.[56] (This number refers to the corresponding source listed at the end of this book.)

Although anorexia nervosa mostly occurs in adolescence, it may also be found in adulthood. Boys may also suffer from anorexia nervosa, though more than 90 per cent of the cases are girls or women. The essence of the syndrome is the abnormal attitude towards eating and weight, which may be expressed in several ways. Often anorexics deny that something is wrong; they even claim to feel well or fit and deny hunger or tiredness. They do not suffer from their weight loss or refusal of food; on the contrary, it even seems to offer them some satisfaction. Many are proud of their self-discipline and resistance to the temptation of food ('asceticism'). Non-eating and emaciation have become part of their achievement-oriented stance or perfectionism, which often marks their general pattern of life. To the outside world they want to present themselves as energetic, tireless and impervious. Yet being obsessed by thinness, they tend to become increasingly narrow-minded and their social environment progressively dwindles. Finally, they seem to live on an island where eating is surrounded by rituals and secrecy. Social eating is avoided more and more, but total food abstinence is exceptional. Mostly they live on a minimal and calculated diet, often accompanied by surreptitious eating. This 'pigheaded' life-style does not offer them real satisfaction, nor do they feel themselves more self-assured. A paralysing sense of helplessness and a low self-esteem or negative self-image seriously impede their psychosocial functioning, despite the 'successful' emaciation.[47]

The most characteristic form of anorexia nervosa is marked by self-induced starvation, but additionally there is a group of anorexics who realize their pursuit of thinness by regular self-induced vomiting or abuse of laxatives. In the latter binge eating is frequently observed: this rapid and mostly secret intake of large amounts of food in a short period of time is known nowadays as bulimia ('voracity'). For a growing number of patients frequent bingeing, followed by vomiting or purging, is the dominant feature of their disturbed eating behaviour. This variant of anorexia nervosa, for this reason labelled *bulimia nervosa*, is increasingly considered a distinct syndrome. It attracted attention only in the early 1980s and thus seems to be a 'new' phenomenon.[23] Perhaps its arrival marks the end of 'classical' anorexia nervosa? This question is beyond the scope of this study, the more so as this development is still too recent to see from a historical viewpoint.

More than a century of scientific interest in anorexia nervosa has given rise to a host of hypotheses and speculations on the cause and meaning of anorexia nervosa.[42] There are many theories which attempt to provide an explanation and promote a particular corresponding therapy. From a biological point of view one is particularly fascinated by the several metabolic and hormonal disturbances in anorexia nervosa, but the question remains unanswered whether the established physiological disturbances are the causes or the consequences of the disorder. The psychodynamic point of view, which states that anorexics are in fact afraid of their sexual maturation and female growth, is also significant. By means of emaciation their growth and development are hampered in order to lead, physically and mentally, a childish, asexual life. But where does this fear come from and how is such a theory proved? The same holds for the learning-theory perspective of anorexia nervosa as a kind of weight-phobia which is 'rewarded' in two ways: by losing weight fear of overweight is avoided and at the same time the anorexic is paid a great deal of attention, particularly by her parents. The latter view is linked with the systems theory, which regards anorexia nervosa as a sign of disturbed structures and interactions within the family. But questions arise such as whether a disturbed family system is the cause or effect of the self-starvation, and why does the eating disorder occur in this form and in this particular member of the family. Finally, the increase of anorexia nervosa in Western women has led to sociocultural views often inspired by feminist ideas: anorexia nervosa is a sign of a (male) society submitting women amidst abundance to an ever more emphatic ideal of slenderness. But why do only certain individuals fall 'victim' to these societal influences while the majority seem to 'escape'?

Comparing these and other explanations of anorexia nervosa, each model does clarify specific aspects of the illness, yet none of the distinct theories offers a full explanation. For this reason many researchers are inclined to consider anorexia nervosa the outcome of a complex interaction of various predisposing, precipitating and perpetuating factors. The resulting affliction is the outcome of a multitude of influences which may vary for each anorexic patient, but which mutually interact in an extensive roundabout way until cause and effect cannot be clearly distinguished.[42] This interaction of biological, psychological and social factors – the *biopsychosocial model* – implies that there is no simple and uniform treatment. The therapies put forward for anorexia nervosa are as numerous as the available explanations. The biopsychosocial complexity of anorexia nervosa consequently requires mostly a combination of therapies, which should pay attention to the bodily aspects (the emaciation and its consequences) as well as the psychosocial aspects: body-image, self-experience, development in family and society.[56]

Anorexia nervosa as a culture-bound syndrome

May anorexia nervosa be called a 'new' disorder? This is one of the main questions this book is trying to answer. Our curiosity about the history of self-starvation was aroused by recent findings. Research has repeatedly stressed that anorexia nervosa has become more frequent in the Western world during the last decades. According to a tentative estimate, 1 per cent of girls between 12 and 18 years of age present evident signs of anorexia nervosa. If diagnostic criteria are applied less rigorously, however, eating disorders occur in about 5 per cent of the female adolescents and young adults. Furthermore, it is evident that, in general, anorexic patients show a higher educational level than peers and come more frequently from middle and upper social classes. Beyond this, it is striking that anorexia nervosa occurs almost exclusively in prosperous countries marked by the socio-economic characteristics of Western (post-)industrial society. These findings inevitably evoke the question of whether it is not a specific culture-bound phenomenon.[55]

For centuries, it was noticed that certain behavioural disorders were closely linked with a particular country or culture. With the scientific evolution of psychiatry in the nineteenth century this aspect gradually came to the fore, although it would be well into the twentieth century before 'transcultural psychiatry' developed into a distinct specialism. Initially the interest was in 'exotic' psychiatric pictures, which are never or only seldom observed in Western countries. From this arose the idea of culture-bound syndromes, which has acquired a central place in transcultural psychiatry, especially in the last decade.[49] Simultaneously it was gradually realized that the Western world also had its own psychosocial disorders. A *culture-bound syndrome* is a coherent entity of behaviours and signs ('symptoms') which are considered uncommon or disturbed. The notion of (ab)normality is, as far as psychological phenomena are concerned, particularly dependent upon the culture where the behavioural pattern in question is observed. The notion 'culture-bound', however, denotes more: it points out that a syndrome (dysfunction or illness) does not occur universally in the population, but remains confined to a specific culture. This implies that the syndrome is only meaningful and comprehensible (diagnosis, explanation, therapy) within the psychosocial sphere of a specific cultural context.

As we underlined above, anorexia nervosa is not only fairly exceptional to non-existent in non-Western(ized) countries, in Western cultures it occurs almost epidemically. Small wonder that anorexia nervosa was increasingly characterized as a typical example of a Western, culture-bound syndrome.[53] This view has important implications for the theoretical explanation and therapeutic practice. In addition, it points to the relativity of medical diagnostics. Strikingly, the 'typical' Western culture-bound syndromes (hysteria, agoraphobia, anorexia nervosa) occur predominantly in women. This cannot be explained merely by biological arguments, since males are also liable to fall prey to these disorders. Traditional medicine does not offer an adequate explanation for the paradox of self-starvation amidst abundance. Consequently the concept of 'mental disorder' as an individual phenomenon needs serious reconsideration. Based on clinical experience many clinicians have hazarded a sociocultural analysis of anorexia nervosa. Conclusions about concrete prevention, however, are scarce.[55] It is not our purpose here to criticize society or to provide practical suggestions for treatment or prevention. In the next section we will outline our psychological historiography. Against this background we will throw light on the culture-bound aspects of anorexia nervosa from a historical perspective.

At the outset we hoped to answer the question of why anorexia nervosa was only discovered at the end of the nineteenth century and whether it occurred in disguised form in more remote times. We soon noticed that these questions were too narrow as well as misleading, for they imply the risk of exploring the past with our own current psychiatric and psychological lenses searching for potential 'patients' to retrospectively label them as anorexics. Even for present-day phenomena psycho-pathological diagnostics is often a questionable undertaking. Any kind of 'psychiatrization' would be *a fortiori* misplaced in the enquiry of a past where such a medical view was almost completely lacking. For this reason we decided to approach the past in as detached fashion as possible with the question: what historical forms and meanings of fasting or self-starvation were known in Western civilization? The following chapters present a chronological account of the history of self-starvation around three consecutive themes: religious wonder, spectacle, and medical disorder. Our chronicle is deliberately descriptive in character. Interpretations will remain in abeyance. Finally, we do hazard an explanation which is connected to the starting-point: a psychological historiography of a culture-bound syndrome.

Psychological history and historical psychology

The writer of a book on the history of a modern disorder has to confess his love for Clio, one of the nine daughters of Zeus and the muse of historiography. Her admirers may be classified in three groups: the dilettante flirts with her, the connoisseur is married to her and the amateur is her platonic lover. We aspire to belong to the latter group, the lovers or 'would-be historians' taking their passion seriously. The following chapters should be read, therefore, as a journalistic chronicle, a collection of accounts from the past, a report about forgotten vicissitudes. It is an essay about the historical roots of a current interest. This cannot be accomplished without bias, however, for – as we soon realized during the preparation of this book – a selection of facts inevitably reflects the favourite colours of the prism through which we are trying to illuminate the distant past and current reality. We would therefore like to make our own perceptual 'filters' clear. Perhaps in this way not only will the 'picture' resulting from our perception become clearer, but the reader may also be offered a better insight into the different 'lenses' we have used during our wondering wandering into the past. In the tradition of the empirical psychology we are personally familiar with – empiricism refers to experience as well as to testing – we will now outline the time- and culture-bound framework from which our study has proceeded.

It was fascination for a 'modern' phenomenon which aroused our curiosity about the past. Our knowledge of this intriguing phenomenon, anorexia nervosa, has been derived from our training in psychology and psychiatry. They were of use as our first guides during the unfinished journey through archives, libraries and antiquarian bookshops. But our great hunger for knowledge and curiosity led us to other paths and tempted us to pursue other branches of knowledge. We hope the reader will forgive our errors during this journey. It is not only hazardous to tread outside your own field of study, it can also be an arrogant example of self-conceit. How pretentious it can seem when non-historians analyze the past from today's viewpoint! Notwithstanding the question about the correctness of our selection, the use of 'modern' hypotheses in enquiring into 'old' phenomena may be rejected as anachronistic: one cannot repeat Columbus' expedition with a radar-guided ship. But could we use any other compass than a handful of present-day hypotheses? We, as 'would-be historians', have chanced it with the advice of many and with our limited luggage of today.

In their work psychologists and psychiatrists are continuously engaged in some form of history, mostly the history of the individual. Historians however discovered only lately that history is the work of man.[38] From this double but often still repressed notion that we are *human* scientists – notwithstanding our training or title – a perception arose from which this book as a 'child of its time' could proceed. This characteristic already betrays a view which attempts to analyze the past in the same way as the present. Such an approach – and even more the other way around: from past to present – contains, however, great risks of deformation, especially the pitfalls of anachronism and self-fulfilling prophecies (*Hineininterpretierung*). Nevertheless we hope to present some critical knowledge about historical timeliness or timely history. This historical orientation as well as the subject of this study reflect a *Zeitgeist* and are undeniably products of our own Western culture.

More than half a century ago it had been predicted that in the future psychology and history would cooperate more intensively. The French journal *Annales* flourished to become the mouthpiece of a new group of historians for whom historiography was neither a collection of striking facts, nor a reconstruction of major events, nor a stringing of names and data. The human being in everyday life – his thoughts, feelings and behaviour in relation to his environment – had to be the subject of history. Only a better insight into the daily life of the former individual might really revive the past and free it from the dust of stuffy archives and dead-alive museums. The new history was labelled in several ways according to the emphases and ingredients from which a particular historiography originated: social history, cultural history, history of mentality, psychological history . . .

The historian passes over the events and searches for structures. It is not the events themselves that make up the matrix of history, but their explanation in mutual relation to each other and embedded in the stream of experience of a particular *Zeitgeist*. The course of this stream from the past until today, however, is not easy to chart, since it previously flowed in a different course from the one it takes today. History does not move continuously in a straight line, but makes sudden turns. This discontinuous evolution renders the reconstruction of the past at once difficult and fascinating; it intrigues psychologists and psychiatrists, for they are familiar with history's unexpected discontinuities in their attempts to fathom the capricious course of their patients' lives and, if necessary, turn them in another direction.

What is at stake in uniting the various historical viewpoints is, on the one hand, the notion of time (course of life, development) – more precisely the phased passing away of lifetime from an individual, social as well as historical perspective – and, on the other, primarily a cultural history or a reconstruction of the civilizing process, as described in such a masterly fashion by Norbert Elias.[40] Historians of all sorts and conditions analyze attitudes, rules, precepts and norms in the Western world, regardless of whether they deal with adolescents and women, for example (the latter example has not been chosen accidentally; it will be elaborated on in Chapter 10). Beyond this, historical research into adolescence strikingly resembles women's history: both attracted the attention of historians in a period during which these target groups were in the limelight of society; both analyses proceeded from the notion that the so-called 'nature' of the adolescent and woman turned out to be the product of cultural definitions and not an artefact of biological programming. The latter thesis will be a major guide in our exploration and explanation of anorexia nervosa as a cultural–historical phenomenon (Chapters 10 and 11). The discontinuity of history and the mutability of the individual are mirrored in the changes – of content as well as form – which self-starvation underwent throughout history.

The invention of syndromes

An analysis of the social and historical relations, under which people live, shows the mutability of psychic phenomena with the change of these relations. A history of the illnesses is conceivable as a history within the framework of the social and mental history. It is showing how the pictures of scientifically identical illnesses change, especially how neuroses have their 'Zeitstil', prospering in particular situations, becoming invisible in others

wrote the well-known German psychiatrist and philosopher Karl Jaspers.[45] The term *Zeitstil* cannot be translated adequately – the style or hallmark of a particular period – and resembles the concept of *Zeitgeist*, the general trend of thought and feeling of an era. If a particular Zeitgeist exists, there should also be time-bound mental disorders. Is the eighteenth century the era of melancholy, the nineteenth one of hysteria, and our twentieth the era of fear? With as much conviction we could turn round the sequence or assert that these phenomena are of all periods. Identifying the emotional climate of a particular period with a striking phenomenon is already a glaring simplification. By choosing a 'sick' extreme as a label for this, it is reduced to a caricature of medicalization. And medical language is as time-bound as the concepts of health and illness, which medicine has tried to establish for centuries within the sphere of influence it is granted by a particular society or culture. Medical language does not arise in a scientific vacuum and nor is science itself an intellectual creation from thin air in tenuity. Scientific reasoning, medical views and clinical pictures are each only comprehensible if one is acquainted with the language of the time.

Since human behaviour changes in history, the object of behavioural sciences – and not just the view of that object – changes likewise. This historicity of behaviour should also be retrieved for so-called 'deviant', 'disturbed' or 'sick' behaviour. Mental and psychosomatic disorders are marked by specific characteristics inherent in a particular man–world relation-ship.[43] These features, just like their causal explanations or their therapeutic changeability, are only comprehensible against the background of a common expectation of patients and surround-ings sharing a collective experience and definition of reality. Symptoms or signs speak then a language which enables the social environment to orientate itself to the problem and deal with it. People who in the days of demonism presented striking behavioural disorders 'knew' that behaving according to the rules of the demonological model might attract attention and perhaps also bring about a solution for their problem. That is what happened to the 'mentally ill' from the previous century and those of today. Without the recognizable language of 'nerv-ousness', 'nervous breakdown' or 'stress' – as common body of thought of physician, patient and society – the concept of neuroses would soon give up the ghost.[54]

Taking up a handbook of psychiatry from the previous cen-tury one seems to turn over the pages of a yellowed catalogue of a museum of curiosities. Psychiatrists who are able to regurgitate memories from their consulting-room or asylum from half a century ago describe clinical pictures which appear completely alien to the young listener. A significant part of these changes in psychiatric pictures cannot be attributed merely to new treat-ments like psychopharmaceutics; the changes are too diverse and multiform. The changing 'style' of psychopathology in general and neuroses in particular, which Jaspers pointed out, has received more attention in the last decades.[43] A characteristic example is the 'disappearance' of spectacular forms of hysteria, a phenomenon not confined to Western psychiatry. Some other psychiatric disorders would no longer occur either, although this may be attributed to a change in diagnostic terminology due to a specific scientific interest. For example, there may be a link between the diagnosis of 'multiple personality' and interest in hypnosis:[41] at the end of the nineteenth century they both received a lot of attention, which disappeared after 1910 to reemerge in recent years. The shift in psychiatric pictures has not been confined to the neuroses. The content of delusions and hallucinations is also subject to change: religious themes ('an order of God'), for instance, have been replaced by technological contents ('influenced by space beams').

Closely related to the historical changeability of deviant behaviour is the idea that mental disorders are increasing in frequency. This idea is not new; in the previous century this issue was already giving physicians cause for concern. Strikingly, in the past as well as today, some observe an increase, sometimes of almost epidemic proportions, for which the 'nervousness of modern life' is blamed. In this sense we can hardly see any difference between what nowadays are called 'disorders of stress' and what a century ago were defined as 'diseases of civilization'.[44] In both, mental disorders have been taken as a starting point for some cultural pessimism, which blames 'modern civilization' and betrays nostalgia for the 'healthy times' of earlier days. This might be described as *the myth of the lost paradise*. Even if an epidemiological study pointed to an increase in a particular mental disorder, it would still be doubtful whether it was the disorder or merely its perception that had been quantified. Psychiatric epidemiology may yield historically interesting data, but it remains itself subject to historicity.

Currently, the relativity and periodicity of new views on health and disease may be illustrated best by theoretical and therapeutic fashions in psychiatry. As a formal medical specialism, psychosomatic medicine developed only shortly before the Second World War. When we define the psychosomatic view broadly as the recognition of possible psychological causes of illness, its history is age-old. Yet only in the nineteenth century was it widely acknowledged that emotions may act as pathogenic factors. The dispute over whether these factors exert their morbid influence peripherally (directly on an organ) or centrally (via the brain functions) took a decisive turn in favour of the central theory at the end of the previous century.[32] Parallel to this evolution an increasing interest in psychological methods of therapy was noticed: reeducation by 'moral treatment' at the outset of the previous century was transformed at the end into changes in personality by 'psychotherapy'.[41] This was the age in which hypnosis was immensely popular and, via the work of Sigmund Freud, lay at the roots of a continuing stream of 'new' psychotherapeutic techniques. But the 'novelty' is time-bound, and so is its success. Therapies which have been applied in psychiatry since 1800 show a striking cyclic pattern: initially people are enthusiastic because of the fantastic results of the therapy, then a period of reservation sets in about the effect and utility of the method, which is finally replaced by a 'new' one. Chapter 9 will point out that anorexia nervosa has been floating for more than a century on such an ebb and flow of theories and therapies.

We may use the changeability of psychiatric syndromes to question the very existence of mental disorders. In the 1960s, the antipsychiatric movement in particular defended the view that the phenomenon of 'mental illness' was merely the result of societal discrimination: what is labelled as 'mental illness' should be considered a symptom of a 'sick' society. This notion evoked a still unresolved conflict between the medical and sociological model in psychiatry. From this ideological dispute we can distinguish two elements which appear to us essential for our further account. The first concerns the existence of 'culture-bound syndromes', a notion which we clarified earlier. The second issue deals with the societal and historical genesis of medical conceptualization, i.e. the process of medicalization through which problematic phenomena or relations in a society are translated into medical categories.[36]

Physicians in the nineteenth century have diligently described and catalogued numerous syndromes or clinical pictures. The decade 1860–70, when the 'discoverers' of anorexia nervosa also came to the fore, had been a prolific period for 'new' clinical entities. But were they discoveries or inventions? When we refer to an 'invented' illness, we do not imply that it had been made up, a kind of medical creation from nowhere. Labelling a particular phenomenon in medical terms is more than the outcome of a cool scientific observation. The phenomenon is judged on the dimension illness – health (an 'aberration'), it becomes a reality as a strange or ego-alien object (you 'have' an illness), and it places the afflicted in a social role (becoming a 'patient'). That is why the creation of illnesses is a sociocultural process which acquires its meaning in the dialectics between medical language and society.[33] After medicalization has been accomplished, illness becomes a metaphor, a figurative concept which arouses the imagination: it may be romanticized as a bogey or cultivated as a myth. Illness becomes synonymous with inexplicable mystery or inevitable mischief. The essayist Susan Sontag is fiercely opposed to this mystification.[52] As examples of such metaphoric usage of concepts of illness she mentions tuberculosis in the previous century and cancer today. In particular the romanticization of 'consumption' (tuberculosis) in the nineteenth century may have been a fertile soil for the new picture of mysterious inanition: the pining anorexic patient.

Popularization of medical language occurs in our culture of information and mass media perhaps even more conspicuously via the process of *proto-professionalization*. This notion refers to the proclivity of people to label their everyday troubles with technical jargon or professional terminology: the common language of lay people derives from and popularizes certain concepts from a respected circle of professionals. The psy-professionals (psychologists, psychiatrists, psychotherapists) have acquired such prestige, that they have taught people to translate 'difficulties' into 'psychological problems'. The Dutch sociologist Abram de Swaan has addressed this idea and applied it, among others, to another 'psychiatric construction' from the nineteenth century, agoraphobia.[39] His view of the 'sociogenesis' of psychopathological phenomena is closely linked to the idea that many psychiatric disorders are culture-bound syndromes, anorexia nervosa being a prime example. This idea became the pivotal point around which our book is constructed. The way anorexia nervosa was medicalized in the nineteenth century will be discussed in Chapters 8 and 9. The preceding centuries display other forms and meanings of self-starvation. That it all began in a religious context will be no 'wonder' . . .

2
Holy Fasts

I am mourning on my high throne for the vast misfortune, because
the Nile flood in my time has not come for seven years! Light is the
grain; there is lack of crops and all kinds of food. Each man has
become a thief to his neighbour. They desire to hasten and cannot
walk. The child cries, the youth creeps along, and the old man; their
souls are bowed down, their legs are bent together and drag along
the ground, and their hands rest in their bosoms. The counsel of the
great ones in the court is but emptiness. Torn open are the chests of
provisions, but instead of content there is air. Everything is exhausted.[289]

This description was engraved on a granite tomb in Egypt in
187 BC. It gives a dramatic account of the drastically debilitating
effect of starvation on people. Throughout history such scenes
have manifested themselves too often. The principal causes were
wars, but more often the loss of harvest because of exceptional
drought, rainfall or frost. But outside these periods of extreme
famine all societies knew people who continuously teetered on
the verge of starvation. In spite of these occasionally dreadful
experiences, or perhaps in response to them, people have learned
to make a virtue of necessity. Quite early in history people
became aware of the uses to which going without food could be
put. Voluntary fasting cures rapidly became one of the most
popular remedies for various diseases (see Chapter 6). But as a
form of punishment or a means of exerting pressure self-starvation also has a venerable history. In almost all communities,
however, fasting played an important role within the magico-
religious practice. Christianity was no exception to this rule.

In ancient Western cultures fasting rituals formed part of
religious practices several times a year. They involved complete
or partial abstinence from food. In the latter form there were
restrictions either as to the quantity or to the choice of what
people were allowed to eat. Fasting as part of magico-religious
practices did not originate from one particular civilization or

religion and then spread to the rest of the world. It arose in widely divergent cultures and religions, which of course will have influenced each other. Fasting manifesting itself in its magico-religious form cannot be traced back to a single motive. In Christianity alone, we find numerous motives in the works of the Church Fathers for instance. According to some of them, fasting was not only a form of mortification, but also a means of uniting Christians. Moreover, what was not eaten could be used to feed the poor. Fasting represented a reconciliation with scarcity, so that God might provide fertility, abundance and redemption. Another motive for fasting was to express grief about Christ's suffering and actually to take part of this on behalf of other people's sins. According to some other Church Fathers fasting was the appropriate way back to paradise. For had not Adam and Eve been expelled from thence for breaking a fasting rule? The Church Father Tertullian mentioned a very peculiar motive indeed: 'An emaciated body will more readily pass the narrow gate (of paradise), a light body will resurrect more rapidly, and in the grave a wasted body will be preserved best.'[105] In spite of the variety of motives for fasting, some of them are found to recur in different communities.

Supernatural power

From the outset many peoples shared the opinion that food is susceptible to demonic forces which might intrude on the body via food intake to exert their harmful influences. By fasting and especially by avoiding food (such as meat) which pre-eminently might contain demons, people tried to ward off danger. Fasting as a protection against evil powers became an integral part of the mourning rituals of various peoples.[98] After a Pharaoh's death, for instance, many Egyptians abstained from meat, wheaten bread and wine. In Old Testament times people fasted when the death of Saul, Jonathan and Abner had been announced. In ancient Greece Priamos fasted after the death of his son Hector, and so did the goddess Demeter after losing her daughter Persephone. Later on, many of these mourning rituals served primarily to prevent the soul of the deceased from entering the bodies of the next of kin via intake of food. Food abstinence could be a safeguard against disturbing demonic influences and was employed to attain a certain level of purity. This purging effect rendered fasts a highly suitable preparation for holy or ritual activities. That is why the ancient Egyptians abstained from food before entering the holy temple, and why their Pharaohs fasted for several days prior to important decisions and religious celebrations. As appears from the New Testament, fasts were held at the election or inauguration of incumbents. In early Christianity fasts have been prescribed to those taking part in baptism or Holy Communion. Through the inner purity brought about by fasting favourable conditions were set up for receiving Divinity. Fasting was regarded in various cultures as an obvious means of receiving dreams, visions and revelations of higher powers. Those who were to be initiated into the mysteries of Isis, Osiris and Eleusis had to spend between seven and forty days without food. The same procedure applied to candidates for the Roman cult of Attis and Cybele in Asia Minor, and to the Babylonian cult of Astarte and Dummuz. Before consulting their oracles the ancient Greeks usually fasted, and in the Old Testament prophets practised fasting in preparation for religious experiences or divine revelations, i.e. a meeting with God. The prophet Eliah, for example, spent forty days without food and drink, after which he received the revelation of God on the mountain of Horeb. In later Christianity fasting as a means of inducing religious visions or divine revelations was of less importance; at least it was hardly ever the sole objective.[86]

The supposed supernatural powers of fasting were also applied to support or strengthen holy or religious activities. The magical act of the wizard might be more successful if his body had been purified by fasting. Sometimes partial abstinence from food was deemed effective for that purpose. To increase the supernatural effect of a magic spell a magician in ancient Egypt had only to abstain from goat's meat and fish. In ancient Israel and later Christianity, fasts served, among other things, to intensify prayer.[60] If you wanted to ask God a favour, you resorted to fasting and prayer. According to age-old Christian customs fasting and prayer were also important expedients for fighting diabolic forces. Christ himself turns out to be the one who recommends fasting and prayer as a means of curing people possessed by the devil. Centuries later both were common exorcistic rituals. By means of fasting and prayer, among others, the exorcist could resist the power of Satan, who held the demoniac firmly in his grasp. Both were part of the requirements the exorcist and the demoniac had to meet, according to the *Rituale Romanum* from 1614. In this work exorcistic rituals were codified by the Roman Catholic Church. It has remained officially valid up until now.[126]

Penance and asceticism

Apart from the above-mentioned motives, in later times fasting developed a more ethical flavour. It was a form of penance, a sign of remorse over sin, committed by the faster or others. It is apparent from their penitential psalms that the Babylonians were already acquainted with this form of food abstinence. In Old Testament times fasting was also known as part of penitential practices. Initially it was intended as a kind of self-humiliation and self-castigation to excite Divine compassion. When Jonah, for instance, came to announce the perishing of Nineveh, its citizens ordered a public fast in the hope that God would repent and turn away from his anger.

The New Testament frequently pays attention to the penance, its necessity and its detrimental effects after renunciation. However, the way this penance should be practised is hardly elaborated. Nevertheless, the Early Christian world provided fertile soil for penitential practices. Pious Christians were deeply imbued with the notion that man is a sinner and unworthy to enjoy the benefits of the Lord. In this period penitents are already to be found who responded to Christ's summon: 'If anyone wishes to be a follower of mine, he must leave self behind; he must take up his cross and come with me.' Fasting was considered to be one of the ways to follow Him. Several writings from this period contain instructions about fasting for penitents. Such fasting, often abstinence from meat and wine or just taking bread and water, played a major role in mediaeval rituals.

Above all, within the Christian tradition fasting grew into the most prominent form of asceticism.[91] Originally the word *askesis* (exercise) refers to the training of Greek athletes, who aimed at improving their physical condition by a rigorous diet and repeated physical practice. Later on, the concept is more related to the pursuit of spiritual and virtuous aims, often precisely to the detriment of the body. In antiquity, fasting was employed by several philosophical sects as an ascetic means. It was regarded as a method of realizing a comprehensive life-aim. According to the views of the sect, its foundation was ethic-rational or religious–mystical in character. Yet they were an exception. In the ancient Western cultures asceticism, which neglected the body almost entirely, did not occur frequently. The mainly positive attitudes towards the body and its functions impeded the spread of ascetic practices in our areas.[89]

Christians took another stand. According to their doctrine bodily, earthly desires were vicious and had to be curbed in favour of the sublime, pure soul. This Christian form of asceticism is rooted in the theories of Plato. The Greek philosopher considered the soul to be trapped in the body. Only by disentangling from the world of the senses may the religious spirit liberate itself to realize its divine potential. The Neoplatonians from the third century elaborated this doctrine.[101] According to them the body would render the soul earthly and alienate it from its actual destination: fusion with and equalling Divinity. Consequently the spiritual life-aim of the neoplatonic philosopher is to detach the soul from the chains of the world of the senses and – just like the Gods – to be totally independent from all physical needs. Fasting is to be recommended because food only benefits the body and harms the soul.

A similar view on the relationship between Divinity, body and soul is recognizable in the Christian doctrine of fasting as part of an ascetic way of life. Asceticism refers to a pursuit of perfection of spiritual life.[108] It was a form of self-discipline and self-castigation with the ideal of complete independence from all physical needs. To attain that aim hardly any means were shunned. As well as fasting, austere asceticism was accompanied by sexual abstinence, sleep deprivation, self-flagellation, burning oneself and other forms of self-torture. By these rigorous practices the 'sinful' flesh was weakened while the 'perfect' soul was strengthened and more ennobled. In this manner the way was smoothed for a virtuous life and Christian perfection, aimed at restoring the image of God. By giving oneself up to fasting, the soul was enlightened and became more equal to the Divine, and if the soul of the ascetic did not equal Divinity, at least the level of the angels might be attained.[105] In the New Testament the prime example of asceticism is John the Baptist. He preached in the desert, wore clothes of camel's hair and is alleged to have fed himself with locusts and wild honey. To the early followers of Christ from the second and third century fasting – especially abstinence from meat and wine – was the most typical form of Christian asceticism. The rigorous asceticism attended by extreme fasts was to be found particularly in the fourth century among the desert fathers and in the late mediaeval period among the fasting saints.

Church's rules on fasting

In the early days of Christianity, when Christians formed a tiny, persecuted community within the Roman Empire, they spurned the worldly attitude of their contemporaries. Every effort was made to mark a sharp distinction between the behaviour of Church members and that of the pagans who menaced them. Life on earth was regarded as a period of trial and only those who persisted steadfastly in their faith could hope for a reward at the return of the Messiah.[90] Adhering to the word of the Lord was highly esteemed. Not only at some important occasions and not only by leaders, but frequently and in all branches of the early Christian society people engaged themselves in fasting. Regulating measures of the Church were lacking: the intensity of the fast was completely left to the piety of the faithful themselves. Jesus had given only the principles for fasting and left the Church to make rules for carrying them out. Initially the necessity of these rules was lacking because of the deep faith of the Early Christians.

Once Christianity had been proclaimed the official religion, a great number of people were converted. Consequently, contemporary Christian morality faded and the former, self-evident evangelical fervour slackened progressively. To cope with this problem, from the third century on, the Church began to increasingly submit the fasts to certain rules. In the early days partial abstinence from food twice a week was instituted. Following the examples of Moses, Eliah and Jesus, Christians in the fourth century were encouraged to observe a forty days' fast prior to Easter.[86] Later the Church ordained forty days' fasts before Christmas and after Pentecost. Several fast-days were also ordered to be kept, like those before Ascension Day and the beginning of every season. The number of fast days increased to such an extent that in the mediaeval period fasts had been appointed for no less than a third of the year. The clerical authorities took great pains to emphasize that the faithful should follow the rules. Popes frequently promulgated decrees to incite the Christian community to stick rigidly to the rules. Moreover, in some regions severe punishments were imposed on those who flagrantly violated the fasting rules: apart from exclusion from the Easter celebration or the knocking out of their teeth, obstinate recidivists sometimes even met the sentence of death. However, such measures could not prevent the practice of fasting from becoming progressively meaningless.[118]

When large numbers of people had been converted, it was evident that the rigid rules about fasting required too much of the faithful. In order to prevent them from losing their hold on the public, Church officials were obliged to make concessions. The initially proclaimed total fast on fixed days was transformed in the fifth century into a partial abstinence from animal products; and to replace meat, somewhat later, the consumption of fish was permitted. Furthermore, in the Middle Ages, extended periods of fasting at Christmas and Pentecost disappeared. Patients, children and the elderly were excluded from the fasts anyway, but from the fourth century others also had the opportunity to withdraw from fasting. The wealthy part of society could afford indulgences and exemptions, which permitted them to consume forbidden food during fast-days. This opportunity was frequently seized by laity, but also by preachers and confessors.

Additionally, at times, other Christians showed remarkable inventiveness to avoid the rules on fasting. The thirteenth-century preacher James of Vitry illustrated this with a story of some monks who were not allowed to eat any meat except game that had been hunted. A bright monk smuggled in some hounds to chase the cloister pigs raised on the monastery farm, and so, at a stroke, transform them into game whose consumption was allowed.[90] After the Reformation, the Roman Catholic practice of fasting was publicly criticized. Beside fasting itself, sixteenth-century reformers were opposed to its compulsory, imposed character. In their opinion fasting – with rules about time and duration, admitted and prohibited food – had developed into a system equal to the formalistic laws of the Pharisees. It was precisely from this that Christ had liberated man, and, as the radical Swiss reformer Ulrich Zwingli (1484–1531) pointed out, He had purified all food; and the Church was not authorized to detract anything from this freedom.[119] Despite this criticism the Roman Catholic Church upheld even into the twentieth century some fast-days. But it could not prevent fasting from degenerating into a ritual with hardly any religious significance. Today only few remain who uphold the original ascetic, body tormenting character. To most contemporary Christians fasting is at best a temporary, slight change of daily meal.

The asceticism of the desert fathers

In the early fourth century the persecution of Christians – and by that martyrdom – came to an end and Christianity was proclaimed the offical religion in the Roman Empire. During this period a number of pious believers turned away from the 'mundane' Church. They looked for poverty and loneliness and retired into the deserts of Egypt and Palestine to dedicate themselves to the Lord in rigorous asceticism. These 'desert fathers' regarded asceticism as a replacement for martyrdom and tormented the body to urge it towards virtuous actions.[106] Some only abstained from wine and meat or confined themselves to dry or raw food, whereas others did not consume anything at all for a particular period of time, sometimes with the exception of the Holy Communion.

Amazing examples of fasting by desert fathers have been passed down to us. In the Middle Ages these biographies were copied frequently and – as appears from the many translations – enjoyed a great popularity. A well-known biography from the fourth century is the *Vita Antonii* by Athanasius. According to this writing, Antony retired at an early age into the Egyptian desert. His desire for further solitude led him to another place in the desert, where he lived for twenty years 'filled with the Divine Spirit' on bread, salt and water.[62] Even on ordinary days, Antony ate but once a day after sunset. Sometimes he would go without eating for two or three days, occasionally when just before a meal a vision reminded him of his sinful life. Despite these years of austerity, we are told that he had not been extremely emaciated. After some time of being the spiritual director of a number of ascetics, who had come out to the desert to imitate his way of life, Antony sought the solitude again. 'At a great age', in the year 356 or 357, he died in the company of two ascetics who used to take care of him.

Another example is a writing from the fifth century, where numerous Eastern hermits are mentioned to abstain from food for substantial periods of time, like the hermit Hero, who only took food once every three months, or Macarius of Alexandria whose rigorous fasting was guided by the ascetic achievements of others.[70] When he heard of a monk who was surpassing him by living merely on one pound of bread a day, he restricted himself to only as much as he could pull out of a narrow-mouthed jar. Eventually, when he heard of the severe fasting of the hermits in the Thebaid, he decided to eat only a few cabbage leaves on Sundays. The above-mentioned writing relates another startling instance of extreme ascetic fasting, which makes clear that it did not only concern desert 'fathers'. Once some travellers heard in the desert the groan of a sick person. They discovered a cave, where a 'certain holy virgin' lay on the ground. She said: 'Behold, I have passed eight and thirty years in this cave and I have satisfied my wants with grass, for I labour with Christ . . . ' Having said that, she died on the spot.[70]

Several other sources also mention the rigorous ascetic fasting of the desert ascetics. Saint Jerome remembered a monk who subsisted for thirty years on bannock and water alone, whereas another stayed alive on five figs a day. Protracted fasts had wasted the body of Adolius of Tarsus to such an extent, that he must have looked like a ghost. The hermit Battheus of Edessa, however, capped everything. He was said to have 'fasted so long that maggots began to crawl from his teeth'.[61] In Western Europe some pious Christians imitated these excessive practices of fasting. In particular Irish monks, with their austere ascetic fasts, equalled their Eastern counterparts. Several early mediaeval severe religious abstainers are known from other parts of Europe.[118] According to a legend in the late fifth century Saint Genovefa gave herself up to extreme fasts between her fifteenth and her fiftieth birthdays. For years she took some bannock and cooked beans only every Thursday and Sunday. Another example is Odo, the abbot of Cluny in the tenth century, who since his youth had lived only on half a pound of bread, a handful of beans and a draught of wine. Finally we mention the eleventh-century hermit Symeon, who travelled through Italy, France and England by donkey. Every year during Lent he satisfied himself with an extremely sparse diet and on Good Friday he drank, in honour of Christ's suffering, the sourest vinegar that was to be found. The two days before Easter he passed the time awake without taking anything. A second flourishing time of extreme fasting only emerged in the late Middle Ages.

Late mediaeval ascetics and mystics

From the twelfth century on not only more women took part in spiritual life, but also the number of female saints increased markedly.[116] Often prolonged fasting became an essential part of their pattern of piety. Partly because of these excessive practices late mediaeval theologians argued for spiritual instead of physical abstinence: people should not so much refrain from food as from sins. Some gave themselves up to extreme fasting, however, precisely because of this tendency to moderation. Just like the desert fathers, who inspired some late mediaeval saints to their ascetic way of life, extended fasts had been partly a reaction to the 'worldly' Church with its relaxed doctrine. In their desire to curb or punish the body with its vicious influences, and also to share Christ's suffering on the cross, nothing was too much trouble for them. As well as excessive fasting several saints exposed themselves to other extreme ascetic practices like flagellation for hours, wearing shoes with pointed nails, piercing their tongues, cheeks or other parts of the body with iron pins, and sleeping on a bed of thorns or iron points.[73]

Some holy women occasionally allowed themselves at least some food. Take for instance the thirteenth-century Saint Hedwig of Silesia, who allowed herself every week for three days some milk and fish; for two days she only took water and bread, and the remaining two some vegetables or dry fare.[63] Others even found such a frugal way of life to testify to overindulgence in bodily needs. They terminated their rigorous fasts only to receive the Eucharist. This symbolized their life-aim, the *Imitatio Christi*: taking part in the suffering of Christ. Stigmata – Christ's wounds which many fasting saints displayed – were a natural part of it. These deeply religious women passionately hungered for the Holy Communion. No wonder, as it was an important source of strength to endure the vexations of the fasts and enabled them to achieve impressive feats.

Numerous examples of this particular female spirituality are to be found in several parts of late mediaeval Europe. Thomas Netter, for instance, in a treatise against the Lollards, referred to a devout Christian girl from Norfolk. She was called 'in the vulgar tongue Joan the Meatless, because it was proven that she had not tasted or drunk for fifteen years, but only fed with the greatest joy every Sunday on the sacrament of the Lord's body'.[73] Many of these religiously inspired fasters did not only refuse all kinds of food, but also appeared totally incapable of swallowing anything but the consecrated Host. One of the many examples is the pious Belgian beguine Mary of Oignies. This thirteenth-century saint loathed all food to such an extent that she could not even endure the smell of it. However, she craved for the reception of the Host. James of Vitry, who knew her intimately, observed:

> On one occasion she went for as long as thirty-five days without any sort of food, passing all the time in a tranquil and happy silence (. . .). She would say nothing for many days but 'Give me the Body of our Lord Jesus Christ' and as soon as her request was granted she returned to her former silent converse with her Saviour.[111]

In the last two months before her death Mary of Oignies did not take anything except for the Host.

Surprising though these accounts may be, hagiographers related still more amazing examples. Late mediaeval sources even reported saints practising unbroken, ascetic fasts not only for a few weeks, but even for years, often in conjunction with sleeplessness and hyperactivity. Saint Angela of Foligno is said to have ingested nothing but the consecrated Host for twelve years. Other saints like Elisabeth of Reute, Nicholas of Flue, Domenica dal Paradiso and Lidwina of Schiedam supposedly fasted for fifteen, nineteen, twenty and twenty-eight years respectively. Numerous similar examples might be added.[64]

The saints who waged war against their own body so relentlessly were treated by many of their credulous contemporaries
with reverence and awe. In the eyes of many their extended fasts
did not originate from self-interest; they were a form of expia-
tion of the sins of all, for just like Christ they took the sins of
mankind upon themselves. The stay of the deceased in purgatory
could be shortened or even terminated. Moreover the fasting
saints were God's chosen ones, with whom He communicated,
to whom He expressed His will by means of visions and to
whom He entrusted supernatural powers and signs. The miracu-
lously prolonged, holy fasts were signs of His attendance in their
midst. Beyond this, they incited imagination, precisely because
they abstained from that which most people craved: a full belly
and good health. In a society in which hunger and even starvation were not uncommon and many suffered from chronic
illnesses, those men and women who willingly pursued still
greater physical deprivation must have aroused respect and awe.
Although many of these extreme fasters lived anonymously,
some of them attracted the attention of the public and became
well known. In spite of the inadequate news service, the fame of
the fifteenth-century Swiss saint Nicholas of Flue, for instance,
would have spread far beyond his region. A contemporary
pointed out that nobody could be found in Germany who had
not heard about Nicholas' miraculous fast.[102]

Nevertheless, in the late mediaeval period most extended
fasters did not easily acquire reverence and awe. The majority,
especially women, had not only to employ a good deal of
perseverance and charisma but also influential connections to
overcome scepticism in some of their contemporaries. Those
who practised fasting more severely than had been proclaimed –
thus moving beyond the Church's rules on fasting – were often
confronted with opposition from the clerical authorities. Laity,
and also monks, should not exaggerate fasting to the detriment
of mental and physical well-being. Catherine of Siena, for
example, urged by a clergyman to pray to God that she might
eat, replied in a letter from 1373 or 1374:

> And I say to you, my Father, and I say it to you in the sight of God,
> that in every possible way I could I always forced myself once or
> twice a day to take food; and I prayed continually and I pray to God

and will pray, that he will grace me in this matter of eating so that I may live like other creatures, if this is his will . . .[64]

How may this attitude of the clergy be explained? Why was rigorous fasting not always applauded as the most superb form of self-denial?

Firstly, extravagant fasting was rejected on theological grounds.[86] Everything God created is well and has been provided to enjoy. For that reason extended fasts implied a denial of the essential perfection of God's creation and thus the doctrines of the heretical sects were dangerously approached. Jesus himself had pointed out to his disciples: eat and drink that which is placed before you. He explicitly denied the contaminating power of food or of eating with 'unclean' hands, saying that what enters the mouth goes to the belly and exits into the privy, leaving the heart untouched. If all foods are clean according to Jesus, what induced ordinary mortals to abstain from food outside the proclaimed fast-days? Excessive fasting was also in contradiction to the utter discretion Christ advocated. In sharp contrast to the theatrical food abstinence of the Pharisees, fasting should be observed inconspicuously and in secret. To fulfil the duty of fasting Jesus expected self-denial instead of a 'public show'. Hence protracted fasting was readily interpreted by Church officials as a form of misplaced self-exaltation: a truly pious Christian did not seek to be singled out for attention of others, but humbly complied with the current rules and rites.

Apart from these moral–theological objections, there were other, more earthly reasons for the rejection of excessive fasts by the Church.[61] Several monastic orders opposed these fasts because they made the fasters a burden on the community. They led to exhaustion and thus left the fasters unable to do a full share of the manual labour required around the convent. In other cases the opposition of the Church originated from scepticism over the question of whether the protracted abstention from food merely proceeded from divine inspiration. Particularly if the faster aroused great attention and reverence, cheating or false motives were suspected. In the early modern period many took up the position that such a way of life might arise from demonic deception. Demoniacs would not be able to eat or would pretend not to eat, while they were surreptitiously fed by the devil. Fighting against this implied combating evil.

Although some regarded merely staying alive without food as a sign of holiness, others acknowledged that such a way of life might proceed from illness or incapacity. The latter did not involve self-denial, for it was no voluntary abstention. Sometimes the saint herself was quite aware of this. Catherine of Siena, for example, stated that her rigorous fasting was an infirmity and not a voluntary religious practice at all. According to a witness, the thirteenth-century ascetic John the Good of Mantua occasionally ate in the presence of all 'more than any other brother and more quickly' in order to prove that his abstinence was under control.[73] In addition, Church officials seriously took into account the fact that the saint might surreptitiously take food. In 1225 Hugh, Bishop of Lincoln, having heard that a nun at Leicester had been for seven years sustained only by Holy Communion, refused to believe it, and immediately deputed not one, but fifteen ecclesiastics to watch her for a fortnight. It was only after this severe trial that he declared himself convinced. Nevertheless, numerous others who pretended to practise excessive fasting in order to be venerated as saints were exposed. In 1577 the prominent Dutch physician Johan Wier (or Weyer; 1515–88) published a treatise on this topic under the pregnant title of *De Commentitiis Jejuniis* (On Alleged Fasting).[218] He refers to the 'maid of Kent', Elizabeth Barton, who was reputed to live on a Host descending from heaven. She was venerated by the faithful, but distrusted by the king. He ordered her to be locked up in a room in a convent to be closely watched. The girl could not stand three days without food. Furthermore it appeared she had accessories who let down the Host by means of women's hair! People did not think lightly of such exposures: together with her accomplices Elizabeth Barton was executed in 1534. Another example mentioned by Wier concerns a girl from Venice who was confined voluntarily with only two bibles. This apparently austere ascetic practice turned out to be nothing but pure swindle, admittedly of an ingenious kind: one of the bibles was hollow and filled with all sorts of food.

A certain Anna Lamenittia from Augsburg in Germany asserted in 1516 to have fasted for sixteen years and to be fed by the Spirit of God.[301] She was alleged to communicate with God who revealed to her special matters, which was why many took her for a saint. But due to Chunigunda, widow of the duke of Bavaria, she had to own up. Presumably on her initiative this 'witch' was left alone intentionally and secretly spied on. Soon it was discovered that she had hidden two bags under her bed: the one filled with all sorts of cakes, the other with apples and pears. After this exposure the tide turned for Anna. By order of the Emperor Maximilian she was put away in a convent, where she was shortly expelled because of her 'wicked way of life'. In 1518 she was drowned in Freiburg for adultery.

Another example of cheating is featured in a work of the Franciscan monk Brognoli.[143] In the mid-seventeenth century one Catharine from Veltlin acquired a considerable reputation as a saint because of visions, ecstasies and a twelve-year long food abstinence (except for the Holy Communion). Several towns invited her to take up residence, as they expected prosperity and fortune under her protection. Brognoli was sent by his superiors to this putative saint to deliver a Lenten sermon. He stayed for a few days in Catherine's house and soon he suspected her of cheating. When the local priest, at Brognoli's advice, refused her the Holy Communion for a couple of days, she secretly took an unconsecrated host to the church. During the Communion she put this piece of bread in her mouth, showed it to her neighbour and asserted that an angel had given it to her. The Inquisition immediately made close inquiry into the matter and concluded that she was quite an ordinary impostor only pretending sanctity. She was sentenced to ten years in gaol and several penitential practices during that period.

Apart from theological objections and from suspicion strengthened by such cases of deceit, there were also political–religious reasons for the Church's opposition to excessive fasting: the clergy's fear of undermining of its authority. The Roman Catholic Church regarded itself as the mediator between God and the faithful. Extravagant fasters, however, pointed out that their life was patterned after a personal, exclusive relationship with God. They bypassed certain forms of clerical control by claiming to have access to Him and to live according to His will. Anxious to defend their powers, clerical authorities could hardly reconcile themselves to such an individualistic form of faith.[64;73] Considering also the threatening danger of imitation by others, there was indeed hardly any reason for the Roman Catholic Church to encourage relentless, ascetic fasting.

Modern fasting saints

We have elaborated predominantly on (late) mediaeval saints. However, centuries later, there were still some women whose lives bore great resemblance to those of their mediaeval predecessors. Even in the nineteenth century women like Maria Domenica Lazzari from Tirol and the Belgian Louise Lateau practised extreme religiously inspired fasting. Often in combination with stigmata and the exclusive ingestion of the consecrated Host, these pious fasting women are to be found even in the twentieth century.[109;111] In Portugal, for example, Alessandrina Maria da Costa allegedly lived for thirteen years without food. In 1924 the 20-year-old girl jumped out of a window, in order to escape from an intrusive man. From that moment on she had to keep to bed until her death in 1955. After a few years she displayed Christ's wounds and a little later she subsisted for thirteen years (from 1942 until 1955) on the Holy Communion alone. According to the rules of Pope Benedict XIV (see further on) she had been watched continuously for forty days, without appearing to demonstrate any deceit. Numerous people paid this wonder a visit.[104]

A similar but far more famous twentieth-century example is Theresa Neumann, from the small village of Konnersreuth in Bavaria. From Christmas 1922 this peasant daughter refrained from solid food and from 30 September 1927 she refused even the small amount of water she had previously taken. Just like many of her illustrious, canonized predecessors she was only able to ingest the consecrated Host. But even of this heavenly bread she only succeeded in swallowing a small part. The entire Holy Sacrament could only be administered in ecstasy. She persevered for thirty-five years until her death in 1962. She attracted the attention of many not only by her startling prolonged fast, but also by other phenomena like visions, stigmata and sleeplessness combined with overactivity. But as in previous centuries the attitude of the Roman Catholic Church towards this 'miracle' was quite critical and reserved. Planned visits of scientists, priests and pilgrims were strictly regulated by the clerical authorities. For a long time nobody was admitted without the bishop's authorization, which was far from easy to obtain. On the initiative of Church authorities she was several times put through an intensive test under the supervision of physicians. Although no deceit could be established, the Church has still made no definite statement on her sanctity.[84]

In our days such cases of modern 'fasting saints' occur only occasionally. After the late mediaeval peak the number of extremely fasting pious Christians gradually decreased. Religious inspiration, in the self-experience of the abstainer as well as in the interpretation of the phenomenon by others, progressively played a minor role. This evolution was brought about by several factors. The first significant factor was the increased opposition of the Roman Catholic Church. In comparison to rising Protestantism the cult of saints remained important within Catholicism, but there was no need of reverence of new heroes. The Catholic Church was aiming at restricting the number of saints and the threat of imitation by others. This is evident from several efforts by subsequent Popes to reduce canonical proceedings to strict rules. In order to subject local initiatives on canonization to the central popish authority, official procedures for canonization were drafted and the requirements of potential saints specified.

Important in this evolution is the initiative of the prominent eighteenth-century scholar and canonist, Prospero Lambertini, the later Pope Benedict XIV. He compiled an extensive work, entitled *De Servorum Dei beatificatione et beatorum canonizatione*, in which he laid down some very stringent rules to prove the authenticity of prolonged fasts.[97] As we will outline in Chapter 4, in the sixteenth and seventeenth centuries physicians had exposed a number of famous fasting girls, which did not increase faith in such cases. On the other hand in some other cases no deceit could be established and such fasts might therefore be miraculous. Benedict wanted to separate the corn from the chaff and to establish a number of rational criteria defining which forms belonged to the intranatural realm and which possibly to the supernatural. Benedict not only studied several important medical works on the topic, but also requested the Academy of Sciences at Bologna to give him a judgement on this matter. The research committee concluded that in many cases of prolonged abstinence deceit, credulity and inadequate observations were the rule. Yet extravagant fasts might be possible, although they should be attributed not so much to supernatural as to natural causes, such as nutritive particles in the air and body fat functioning as an energy reserve.[434]

Partially in view of this report, Benedict concluded that sanctity should not be concluded from the fasts, but that on the contrary the sanctity of the faster determined the holiness of the fast. Hence Pope Benedict advised that prolonged abstainers be subjected to a severe clerical as well as medical investigation. It had to be considered carefully whether the fast originated from an illness and, supposing it did not, whether the person remained in good health during the fast. Furthermore it should be asked whether the person was not prevented by the fast from performing 'other good works to which he was obliged'. Finally, the character and virtues of the person had to be taken into account. 'If all the foresaid considerations are favourable, the fast must be judged miraculous', according to Pope Benedict XIV.

The restriction of canonization was one of the factors which decreased the number of (potential) fasting saints. The path to saintliness through protracted fasting had lost a great deal of its appeal. Besides, a change in the ideal of female piety may explain the gradual decrease of fasting saints.[64] From the seventeenth century on for many religiously inspired women excessive fasting (and self-castigation in general) had lost its significance, as it was gradually superseded by tireless charity, teaching and care. Parallel to this evolution it is clear that from the early modern period on food abstinence did not occur any longer predominantly within a religious context. In the fifteenth and sixteenth centuries bewitchment and demonic possession became a popular interpretation of self-starvation. From the sixteenth century onwards, however, fasting became increasingly alienated from its traditionally religious background. Self-starvation became part of a rather pedestrian circuit where it gradually developed into a commercial spectacle. Particularly in the nineteenth century some exploited the admiration and astonishment which extended fasts still aroused, and made the 'hunger art' into a source of income. This no longer took place in cloisters or cells, but at fairs. Simultaneously self-induced starvation was annexed by the emerging medical sciences and labelled as pathological. Eventually this medical interpretation superseded extended fasting as a religious phenomenon and a spectacle. Self-starvation as a sign of (mental) illness would soon become the predominating viewpoint, as it still is today, with the exception of political hunger strikes.

3

Possession and Witchcraft

In every period and almost everywhere all kinds of mischief have been attributed to the influences of evil spirits. For ages Satan has been the personification of evil and the cause of much tribulation in Christian Western Europe. Although in the first millennium the Roman Catholic Church argued that the powers of the devil should not be exaggerated, the effect of evil was acknowledged. In cases of rare or suddenly emerging illnesses, people readily assumed them to be the consequence of diabolic spirits invading the body. Numerous symptoms, like fits, insensitivity towards pain or complete paralysis have been regarded as signs of demonic possession. Protracted fasts were one of the phenomena which could be assigned to the devil's pernicious influences.

Fasting and temptation by the devil

The relationship between food abstinence and demonic possession is fairly old; it is already suggested in a Babylonian cuneiform text.[137] In our part of the world an anonymous writing from the fifth century presents an early example of prolonged fasting explained by diabolic possession.[134] In a chapter entitled 'De signis Antichristi', the author quotes a few Scripture texts, which among others refer to the Antichrist. Then he addresses a 'demonic and unnatural omen' occurring during the government of Consul Asper of Carthage.

It concerns a young Arabic girl of Christian faith who was confronted with an 'obscene' image while taking a bath. From that moment on she refrained from eating and drinking for seventy days and nights. Strikingly, despite this prolonged fasting she did not waste away, but even looked healthy. The girl confessed that the devil in the form of a bird fed her at night. Her worried parents brought her to a convent, where she was carefully watched but imposture was not uncovered. She persisted in her refusal to eat and drink. However, on the fifteenth day of her stay in the convent the story took a favourable turn, when it was decided to use the exorcising effect of the consecrated host. Early in the morning in the presence of numerous people, she was persuaded by a priest to take some pieces of this heavenly bread in her mouth. But even after half an hour of chewing the girl was unable to swallow them. To explain what happened then the author quotes the following passages from the Bible: 'Can Christ agree with Belial, or a believer join hands with an unbeliever' and 'You cannot drink the cup of the Lord and the cup of demons. You cannot partake of the Lord's table and the table of demons.' The priest lifted the girl's head in order to prevent her from throwing up the host. Then he put the holy chalice to her mouth. After eighty-five days the devil was forced to leave the girl's body 'by God Almighty'.

A second, similar description has been passed down to us from the early mediaeval period. Again it concerns a girl, possessed by an evil spirit, who renounced all food and was finally cured by means of an exorcistic ritual. The incident is featured in a writing from the late eighth century by Bishop Arbeo from Freising in Bavaria.[141] The major part of the text is devoted to a biography of saint Emmeram (or Haimhramn), who probably lived in the seventh century. In honour of this saint the bishop added some events, occurring during his time. One of those took place under Arbeo's predecessor, Bishop Joseph (around 750), and deals with a protracted food abstinence in a girl.

The account begins as follows:

> One day a young girl in the neighbourhood of our diocese set out to herd the cattle of her father. In doing so she was overpowered by some unclean spirit and refused to take either solid or liquid food, and this persisted for many days. Thereafter numerous relatives came to her, who by pleading and hard words tried to compel her to resume eating. However, she refused persistently all food and asserted that her body can live without it and that she is not hungry.

Forced feeding failed: when the relatives violently poured water mixed with milk into her, she vomited out the liquids immediately. At last it was decided to ask Bishop Joseph for advice. He tried to convince her by arguments, but the girl maintained that the necessity of eating did mean nothing to her and that she was not hungry. Strikingly, despite the fact that she had subsisted without food for a whole year, only her pale complexion betrayed this lack of nourishment. Finally the idea occurred to someone to bring her to the tomb of the martyred St Emmeram in Helfendorf. On entering the church the miracle took place. Lying on the ground she prayed, immediately felt hungry and urged for a piece of bread. When people gave it to her, she at once heartily took some food and was henceforth well.

Further cases from the early mediaeval period in which food abstinence is attributed to demonic influences are scarce. From the late mediaeval period we find more cases. In that era emerged an unwavering faith in the power of Satan, who was blamed more than ever for all mischief that could not be understood (natural disasters) or was unwanted (heresy).[131] The ascetic fasting of saints, which usually the clergy did not appreciate, was related to the devil's influences. Satan instead of God might have been the real inspirer.

The afore-mentioned fasting saint Catherine of Siena, for example, was accused of being like a witch in league with the devil and supposedly fed by demons at night. Such accusations from which these holy women could hardly escape might endanger their life. Thus, in order to prevent or refute charges of diabolic practices and in this way to ward off the risk of persecution, several fasting saints made an attempt to overcome their disgust of food and compelled themselves to eat.[64;73] Take for instance saint Alpais of Cudot near Sens in France: she fasted rigorously from 1170 until her death in 1211, but ate just enough to avert accusations of possession. For the same reason Catharine of Siena took pains to eat something every day. Possibly some of these fasting saints were testing themselves, for in a period in which fear of demonic powers was widely diffused throughout the population, many a saint doubted whether or not Satan was tricking them. The fifteenth-century saint Columba of Rieti, for instance, supposed that she had been possessed. Her vomiting, she said, relieved her of evil spirits, just as she had seen in pictorial representations of exorcism. Catharine of Siena and Angela of Foligno have been vexed by similar doubts.

Particularly from the end of the Middle Ages on, several

fasting saints underwent formal trials from the Inquisition on charges of witchcraft. The above-mentioned Columba of Rieti, who was a conscious imitator of Catherine of Siena, was suspected several times of this kind of practice. Evidence of her contacts with the devil were, apart from her prolonged fasting, a collection of bones under her bed and a basket full of hosts she had vomited. Several clergymen not only watched her carefully, but also tried to lure her into a trap. A visiting provincial inquisitor from the Sorbonne concluded that she might be *areptitia*, meaning 'out of her mind' or at least 'in error', quite a dangerous conclusion from the mouth of an inquisitor. Other investigations followed, always with the same result: not guilty, but not quite innocent either. Even after her death Columba was not left in peace. In order to answer the question of whether she had been possessed or not, an autopsy was performed. This post mortem clearly showed that she had starved herself to death: 'Not only did she not have the breasts of a woman, but truly only little trace of a human body. One could count all her bones as if they were covered only by a clear veil.'[64] Her faecal matter was minimal whereas urine seemed normal. Although the medical examiner claimed no special expertise in such matters, he found no reason to doubt an earlier observation of the prioress that Columba had never menstruated. Nevertheless, this medical enquiry could not allay scepticism about her prolonged fasting.

But the relationship between fasting saints and Satan is more complex. Apart from the growing belief that rigorous ascetic fasting was the work of the devil, people also assumed that Satan's role might be totally different in character. According to some hagiographies, the representative of evil may try to persuade the fasting saint to give up piety and stop the rigorous fasting.[64] In the thirteenth century the devil reasoned with Margaret of Cortona that it would be sufficient for her to follow the general rules on fasting observed by all Franciscans. No doubt the latter are also destined to go to heaven, are they not? A little later, when Margaret was dying and she herself deemed the time appropriate to render her purified body to Christ, a ferocious devil told her: 'God will never forgive you or show the mercy you expect because with your fasting you have committed suicide.' Satan did not only try to persuade a fasting saint to start eating again; at times he acted more vigorously. This was experienced by the holy faster Maria Magdalen de Pazzi, who lived at the end of the sixteenth century. As she was walking by the dispensary, demons opened up cabinets displaying before her their culinary treasures and thus seducing her to interrupt her diet of bread and water.[64]

The devil was indeed a torment to religious fasters, but sometimes faith in the power of the devil was quite useful. During their protracted fasting some saints now and then gave themselves up to binge eating. Of course this fact would not contribute at all to the faith in the sanctity of the person in question and normally would better remain undisclosed. But an explanation might help as well. When, around 1400, meat and salt were found under the bed of the fasting saint Elisabeth of Reute, it was readily assumed that it had been hidden there by the devil to put her in an unfavourable light.[66] Another example is saint Veronica Giuliani who, in about 1700, was practising extreme ascetic fasting. On numerous occasions sisters saw her sneak into the kitchen and gorge down food. A contemporary, Sister Hyacinthe, reported this and attributed the incidents to the work of the devil. In her view Satan wanted the sisters to assume that Veronica was really an impostor.[64]

Worn out and bewitched

In the period between the fifteenth and seventeenth centuries, when demonological views were widely spread, less religiously inspired fasters as well as fasting saints were suspected of possession. An account, published in 1584, relates the story of Jeanne Fery from France, who several times was prevented by demons from eating and drinking for at least three days.[123] One Catharine Somnoata was even averted by no less than seven demons from taking anything for seven days. Another demoniac, who had been brought to the church of saint Benedict in Orleans, was not allowed to eat bread. Incidentally he took some water, but exorcised water was only ingested by violation amid fierce opposition.[143]

In these cases the initiative originated from the devil. At this time, however, demons were supposed to have confederates on earth, the witches. Growing fear of the devil was a fertile soil for

the deluded belief in witches. In the same period in which
scientists were increasingly questioning traditional theories, belief
in witches was popular. Whereas formerly this faith had generally been deemed heretical, scepticism about it was now interpreted as heresy. It was commonly assumed that witches –
predominantly women – were part of an international Satanic
movement, aiming at blasphemy and the undermining of the
Roman Catholic Church. They were accused of being in voluntary league with Satan and by that token being able to cause
mischief to others. By means of demons they caused bad harvests
and storms, hate and love, miscarriages and impotence. Beyond
this, they were supposed to be able to cause several diseases:
hundreds of witches were indicted for wasting people.[127] Furthermore, in the imagination of many, witches themselves were real
lightweights. To be able to fly, it was told, they necessarily had
to weigh less than ordinary people. According to the *Malleus
Maleficarum*, the notorious handbook for inquisitors from 1486
by Heinrich Kramer and Jacob Sprenger, witches together with
the devil and his imps aimed at ending the world.[132] That is
why Mother Earth was not able to have intercourse with them
and pushed them off. In this way witches were enabled to travel
through the air.[125]

This fact lay at the roots of a peculiar method to prove
bewitchment: the 'weighing test'. The design of this test was of
staggering simplicity. If a woman's body weight on the scale
turned out to be less than reasonably might be expected considering her stature, this was evidence of bewitchment. Presumably
in reality only a few women were involved, as the inquisitors
frequently felt compelled to deceive: they not only made the
weighing scale indicate less, but were sometimes so fraudulent
that the accused seemed to weigh nothing at all. In Holland, for
many women the weighing test implied salvation. For, from the
mid-seventeenth century on, putative witches could resort to the
Heksenwaag (the 'witch-scale') in the Dutch town of Oudewater.
At that place the accused or those afraid of being charged were
carefully weighed without any cheating. The Dutch, who hardly
took the faith in witches seriously any more, made sure that
weight always corresponded with the stature of the woman
concerned. Then, on behalf of the town council, a certificate
was drafted of the proceedings, which enabled the accused to

return home quietly. This official document was accepted as proof of innocence far beyond the boundaries of Holland.[122]

We previously noted that for a long time protracted food abstinence was indicative of demonic possession. When the faith in witches was restored by the Roman Catholic Church itself, it was thought that prolonged fasting as a form of demonic possession could be caused by their supernatural ally, the devil. In seventeenth-century New England several 'bewitched' adolescent girls displayed – aside from symptoms like sensations of pricking and burning and periods of extreme immobility or exactly the opposite – an inability to eat to varying degrees.[124]

Another example is figured in a pamphlet from 1669 entitled *The Hartfordshire Wonder or Strange News from Ware* (written by one M.J.).[136] The 'wonder' in this title refers to the 20-year-old Jane Stretton, a maid of Ware in Hertfordshire. The story began somewhere at the end of the 1660s, when Jane's father lost a highly prized bible. Ultimately he consulted one of his neighbours, 'who was such a one as the Country people term a Cunning Man, a Wizard or Fortune teller'. When this neighbour told him that he knew who had his bible, Stretton then bluntly concluded that he must be either a witch or a devil as he could neither read nor write. These words struck home and the neighbour's heart was 'inflamed with the fire of revenge'.

A month later the wife of the Cunning Man afflicted Stretton's daughter Jane with dreadful 'raging fits'. About a week later the fits were aggravated when Jane gave the woman a pin she wanted from her. Jane recovered in part, but in six months she neither ate anything nor voided any excrements. Soon the report of this strange wonder drew 'a great concourse of people' to her house. She was watched continuously, both night and day, by attendants, who 'now at last began to distrust that her sickness proceeds from more than an ordinary cause.' At last there proceeded from her mouth

> two flames in resemblance of fire, the one of red colour and other blew, and soon after in some short distance of time eleven pins, in several crooked forms and shapes, some bowed one way, some another.

Of course, such a wonder could not be confined: 'people came in multitudes to see her, some out of pitty, to help and comfort her, others out of curiosity, to be ascertained of the truth of these relations.' Nevertheless, the story does not seem to have spread to any extent beyond the immediate neighbourhood of Ware.

Jane continuously complained of an extreme pain in her back, as if being slashed with a knife. To the surprise of everyone, somewhat later a knife was found in her bed. As a whole range of remedies were of no avail to Jane, it was apparent that her distemper 'proceeded from the malice of the Devil's instruments on whose body God had permitted them to exercise their envy.' People could see that it was done by witchcraft as she was haunted with the Devil or his Imps, sometimes in the shape of frogs, mice, toads and the like.

Ultimately, when the witch was brought to the sufferer's house, the spell was broken and Jane began to mend. She had abstained from all food 'for about nine months, save only some few liquid Meats, impossible in human reason to have preserved life'. However, she had not been cured completely, as she took nothing but 'surrups and such like liquid ingredients' at the end of the story. For the truth of the narrative the writer might have inserted the names of several 'Eminent persons' who freely offered to assert the 'Strange News from Ware'. However, he considered it 'a vain thing to go to prove that which we suppose none will deny.'[136]

Exorcism as treatment

In the case of Jane Stretton, it was not immediately evident to her environment that Jane was possessed by a witch. Apparently people considered a natural cause more plausible and only in the course of time came to another conclusion. This illustrates the problem diagnosticians at the time were confronted with: in order to choose the right therapy, they had to distinguish between natural illnesses, possession caused by the devil, and that caused by the intervention of a witch. In the first case a medical treatment was indicated whereas for the other two exorcism was required. From the fifteenth century on these three possible explanations together with their remedies were widely acknowledged. Clergy, laity and a majority of prominent physicians alike accepted demons as one of the causes of illnesses.[131]

Many physicians were convinced that the lack of an obviously natural cause of an illness as well as the failure of otherwise efficacious medication betrayed demonic influences. In cases of putative demoniacs often physicians had to establish whether the symptoms were naturally caused or not. This was far from an easy task, as a supernatural cause did not necessarily exclude symptoms of a natural origin, for the devil was said to be able to pretend a 'natural' illness in order to hide his involvement. In addition, as Johan Wier has remarked, Satan usually chose as his victims especially those suffering from melancholic or hysteric delusions. We already noted in the case of Jane Stretton that people initially suspected a natural cause for her sufferings, whereas it later appeared to be the work of the devil. But the reverse might occur as well.

Sometimes people had been prematurely diagnosed as demoniacs, as is illustrated in a seventeenth-century case history. The above-mentioned Franciscan monk Brognoli reported on a girl suffering from violent head- and stomach ache.[143] She had the feeling of a ball rising up and down in her body. Her appetite had completely disappeared; she had great difficulty in eating and each day she became weaker, more emaciated and melancholic. Brognoli, apparently assuming that this was a case of possession, decided to call the name of Jesus Christ over her and make the sign of the cross. Through that procedure she recovered: her stomach ache disappeared and she became more cheerful. But the next day the problems returned and violent, persistent fever set in. Brognoli concluded that she was more in need of a doctor than a priest, who indeed succeeded in curing her by the right remedies and blood-letting. It is striking that Brognoli did not presume to deal with a stubborn demon. Considering his referral to a physician, he apparently suspected a natural cause for the girl's afflictions.

Several behavioural patterns and experiences of this girl might have been undoubtedly interpreted as possession. This appears from the *Enchiridium*, a famous eighteenth-century handbook for the practice of exorcism, written by Vincentius von Berg.[138] In this work the author gives a list of 'indications, by which it could be ascertained if anyone were bewitched into possession'. Apart from signs like frequent and sudden pains, the bewitched are unable to retain and digest their food and are irked by continual vomiting. Others experience a heavy weight in the stomach, as if a sort of ball had ascended from the stomach into the gullet and which they tried to vomit in vain. Some feel a gnawing in the lower belly. In others, the body is weakened and extraordinarily emaciated. A number may feel something like the coldest wind or a fiery flame run through their stomach, causing violent contractions in their entrails and sudden swelling of the stomach. Many bewitched are oppressed by a melancholy disposition and may be sometimes so weakened that they do not wish to speak to people. The body, and especially the face, is most completely suffused by a yellow or ashen color. Finally, one can be sure of bewitchment, according to the *Enchiridium*, if skilled physicians are unable to diagnose the affliction with any certainty or if the prescribed medication does not offer any relief and even aggravates the sickness. Von Berg published his work in 1743. At that time the belief in witchcraft and demonic possession was already waning. The author is a late representative of a trend, which was dominant for three centuries, but gradually met increasing opposition.

From possession to patienthood

In the world of medicine, from the seventeenth century on, demonological explanations of illnesses were increasingly disputed. An early expression of this evolution is a medical treatise from 1603 by the English physician Edward Jorden (1569–1632).[144] In this work he discusses the natural causes which may underlie demonic possession. Although he does not deny that there may be genuine cases of possession, he expresses the view that 'strange actions and passions of the body of man which were imputed to the Devil were in fact natural manifestations of a disease then called suffocation of the mother.' Jorden is listing symptoms, commonly supposed to indicate possession, that are typical of hysteria and epilepsy like insensibility, regular recurrence of fits and difficulty in eating and drinking. He suggests that the curing of these symptoms by fasting and prayer may also be natural, since a spare diet will reduce the exuberance of the humours and the prayer will increase the patient's confidence.

In a work published in 1612 by a Northampton physician

John Cotta (1575?–1650?), the devil even played a minor role in the explanation of illnesses. Cotta wisely stated that 'everie thing whereof everie man cannot give a reason is not therefore a miracle'.[127] By the later seventeenth century this new scientific attitude manifested itself more clearly: increasingly physicians gave priority to more naturalistic explanations of illnesses. What had been attributed in former days to demonic powers was now explained ever more by empirical medical theories. Physicians collected detailed case histories of demoniacs and began to speak of physiology and pathology in connection with these.

A growing number of physicians no longer accepted Satan as the ultimate explanation of prolonged food abstinence.[139] The latter was considered a symptom of a number of illnesses, of which the explanation had nothing to do with the devil. When a physician, examining the German fasting girl Maria Jehnfels in 1728, tried to establish whether demons were involved, he was watched with scepticism by his colleagues. The physician put a burning vessel between Maria's legs and sprinkled some obscure powder, being strongly convinced that if the girl was unable to stand the penetrating smoke, demonic powers had been evidenced. The ritual turned out to be totally ineffective and only made those present laugh. The German physician Christian Joachim Lossau (1693–1753), describing this scene to us, qualifies it as a wash-out and 'superstitious Satanic medicine'.[181] But in the eighteenth century the physicians' increased scepticism did not totally eradicate demonological interpretations of protracted food abstinence. Just like the voluntary starvation of holy women, alleged fasting demoniacs kept emerging now and then well into our modern times.

In the beginning of the nineteenth century, the German physician and romantic poet Justinus Kerner (1786–1862) was asked to examine a woman for whom regular medical treatment had appeared to be of no avail.[130] The patient, a 34-year-old farmer's wife from a religious family, without any obvious cause had begun to suffer in August 1830 from violent convulsive fits, during which a demon spoke to her. As soon as this voice manifested itself, her own personality dissolved away and another entity ruled her. The demon was terribly vituperative. God in particular and 'everything holy' was the target of her curses. Pregnancy and taking medicines for five months did not bring

about any relief. Only continuously praying, to which she had
to compel herself with might and main as the evil spirit opposed
it fiercely, kept the demon quiet for some time. Once she was
even possessed by two demons cursing and swearing every
moment she was praying. When the woman regained consciousness for a while and was confronted with the stories of those
present and the injuries she had inflicted upon herself, she burst
into tears.

After some time people succeeded in exorcising one of the
demons by means of a 'magic-magnetic' (a kind of hypnotic)
treatment, but the remaining demon now became even more
vituperative than ever. When the woman tried to pray, he
distorted her face and compelled her to a demonic laughter and
spitting. She was not allowed by the devil to take anything but
watery soup made from wholemeal bread. As soon as she
wanted to take other food, the demon presented himself in her
and cried: 'You bastard shall not eat anything good.' Suiting the
action to the word he turned her spoon around. The woman
often went for two or three days without food and drink, and
during those periods the demon was most quiet. Finally the
woman was extremely wasted by sorrow, pain and fasting: 'Her
suffering was often day and night so great, that it is indescribable
and we were frequently driven to the utmost despair with her,'
Kerner relates.

Anorexia nervosa and exorcism

Far into the twentieth century, albeit particularly in orthodox
religious settings, the belief in a devil invading the body or
causing illness still existed. In those circles a disorder like anorexia
nervosa could still lead to suspicion of demonic possession.
Moreover, some anorexics experience their self-starvation in a
way which closely resembles the possession of earlier days.
Several clinicians report that a few of their anorexic patients
firmly believed they were in the grip of some evil spirit which
tormented them whenever they attempted to eat. One patient
referred to a small, red devil inside her, who explicitly prohibited
her to give in to her hunger. His order was short and sweet:
'Don't eat anything'. The patient spoke about her devil as a real
opponent, whose orders she could not possibly disregard.[133]

A notorious case, in which self-starvation was interpreted as demonic possession by the abstainer as well as by her environment, is the one of the student Anneliese Michel from Bavarian Klingenberg. In the summer of 1976, during an extended ritual of exorcism, she died of starvation.[128;133] Anneliese was a pious, conscientious and delicate child from a solidly Catholic German middle-class family. In 1969, about the time of her sixteenth birthday, she was struck by attacks which completely paralysed her. In the years thereafter the attacks returned. Physicians considered her to be suffering from epilepsy and recommended anticonvulsant medication. From 1970 onwards Anneliese saw *Fratzen*, ghastly distorted faces. She started smelling a horrid stench not perceived by others and was plagued by depressions. She herself was convinced of being possessed by the devil. She consulted a number of psychiatrists without being offered any relief for her troubles. Anneliese derived more benefit from her sessions with Father Alt, one of the priests she had consulted previously. Whenever she prayed with this priest, her troubles disappeared like snow in the sun. Nevertheless, not even he could prevent her condition from finally worsening. Her parents, with Anneliese's consent, desperately begged Father Alt to see that she was exorcised.

Meanwhile Father Alt and his colleague Renz were also convinced of her possession. In their view all signs undeniably indicated that Satan had invaded her and that demonic forces were using her body. Although the Bishop of Würzburg took a reserved position towards the affair, he finally relented and gave permission for both priests to say the exorcism over Anneliese. For nine months she was exorcised almost seventy times for two to six hours. During this period she injured herself and at times screamed raucously, howled and bellowed. Besides, frequently she did not take anything for a couple of days; she wanted to but 'was not allowed to'. If she tried it anyway, she was either unable to open her mouth or could not swallow anything. This alternated with times when she gobbled a surprising amount of food, particularly bananas, fruit juices and milk. If she was forced to eat, she spat the food out, pressed her lips very firmly together and moved her head violently from side to side. According to a theological advisor prolonged food abstinence might be an indication of possession. Her enormous restlessness and the impressive bodily efforts to which she subjected herself only strengthened this assumption. Her becoming abusive at the exorcist and using obscene language was interpreted as further irrefutable evidence of demonic possession.

On the first of July 1976 her sufferings came to an end: that night she died in her sleep. A post mortem established that starvation had caused her death. A judicial inquiry was held into the matter. Anneliese's parents and the exorcists involved were sentenced to six months imprisonment, suspended for three years. According to the court, from May 1976 at the latest, Anneliese no longer had any ability to freely decide her own fate. The exorcism and the influence of her environment aggravated her illness. By not calling in a physician all four defendants were considered guilty of negligent homicide. Had Anneliese been taken to a hospital and treated properly, she would have survived, according to the court.

Four hundred years ago, most probably Anneliese would have been viewed as being possessed. Her attacks, stench and hyperactivity, the injuries she inflicted on herself, her depressions and food abstinence, her behaviour during the exorcism and the physician's failure to cure her would all have led to almost no doubt that it was Satan's work. Nobody would have objected if a clergyman rather than a physician had taken on the treatment. In the twentieth century a wholly different standard is applied. Outside orthodox religious circles, supernatural explanations are considered out of the question: Anneliese is now seen as suffering from epilepsy, psychogenic psychosis and anorexia nervosa, which require medical treatment. Within this view no room is left for exorcism. The latter treatment is not only rejected, but even leads, in fatal cases, to judicial prosecution. The supernatural event has become a medical matter!

4
Miraculous Maidens

Although religiously inspired fasters closely resembling their mediaeval counterparts manifested themselves up into the twentieth century, their number had markedly decreased from the seventeenth century on. Due to the meanwhile formalized reservations of the Roman Catholic Church towards prolonged fasting, the practice had lost a good deal of its appeal for many pious Christians. Nor did Protestantism cater for such phenomena. Protestants emphasized the possibility of a direct relationship with God, without intermediaries like priests or saints. In the true Church there was no room for wonders: what papists called a miracle, was in their view nothing but devil's work, delusion or deceit.[110]

Simultaneously a process of secularization had developed, which made it decreasingly self-evident that uncomprehended phenomena like self-starvation should be attributed to supernatural causes. In this process the emerging medical profession played a major part. When the connection between fasting and religion became more and more loose, physicians succeeded in transforming food abstinence into a medical problem. They, in particular, increasingly expressed their doubts about the miraculous and supernatural veil that had surrounded prolonged fasting from time immemorial. Instead, physicians stressed more and more strongly that it was a sign of morbidity, which could be explained by means of empirical-medical theories. This view did not immediately find wide acceptance, not even in medical circles.

The transformation of fasting saints and demoniacs committed to the clergy into patients in need of medical care came about only gradually. The process started in the sixteenth century and was completed in the nineteenth century. Characteristically for this transitional period, food abstinence still occurred in close relationship to Christian religion and could give rise to either devout veneration or suspicions of possession; on the other hand physicians began to study the phenomenon more intensively, and an increasing number of people regarded it as a symptom of disease. However, not until the end of the nineteenth century was it widely accepted that self-starvation was a pathological state requiring medical treatment. Against this background emerged the phenomenon of fasting girls or miraculous maidens and later on of hunger artists and living skeletons. They are the connecting link in the transition from rigid mediaeval fasting within a religious context to the clinical picture of anorexia nervosa within a medical setting.

Self-starvation as a spectacle

From the sixteenth century on, protracted food abstinence was the sensational news of the time in various parts of Europe. Like giant babies, sea monsters and other monstrosities it was a curiosity that appealed to everyone's imagination. Until well into the nineteenth century fasting girls or 'miraculous maidens' achieved local and even national notoriety, because they ate very little or even nothing at all and nevertheless stayed alive, sometimes even in excellent health! Just like their illustrious mediaeval predecessors these 'natural wonders' lived for months or even years.

Numerous examples of these miraculous maidens can be found in the literature of those days. At Over-Haddon 19-year-old Martha Taylor, 'The Famed Derbyshire Damosell', carried on an extreme fast from 1667 on for more than thirteen months. Occasionally she wetted her dry lips with a feather dipped in water and now and then she drank 'a few drops of Syrup of Stew'd prunes, Water and Sugar, or the juice of a roasted Raisin'.[192] By the end of the seventeenth century Mary Vaughton from Wigginton (Staffordshire) had supposedly taken for years only once a day a spoonful of water or milk and a piece 'not above the size of half-a-crown in bread and butter; or if meat, not above the quantity of a pidgeon's leg at most'.[193] And in Bavarian Frasdorf one Marie Furtner lived for forty years on water from the nearby brook. Until her death in 1884 she was said to have subsisted on nothing else.[215] But several sources mentioned cases of prolonged fasting that even surpassed all this. Some miraculous maidens even claimed tenaciously not to have taken anything at all for years and years. Jeanne Balam from Confolens (near Poitiers) was alleged from 1599 on to have lived without food for three years.[158] And in Gall (near Bern) Apollonia Schreier started to eat again in 1611 after ten years of complete food abstinence . . . [186;187]

These cases of extremely prolonged fasts may appear unusual and astonishing to us; attitudes were no different in earlier days. During a period of time in which food shortage was not exceptional, people were well aware of the necessity of eating to stay alive. No wonder prolonged fasters provoked amazement, curiosity or admiration. As the Swiss physician Jacob Zwinger (1569–1610) pointed out:[235] if daily food is so essential that we can easily succumb to a lack of it, and if this has been considered of old the severest punishment, is it not a miracle that some live for days and months without food and drink? Extreme food abstinence did not appear impossible to many, but it was certainly regarded as a peculiar phenomenon. Although early on some physicians aimed at explaining it with naturalistic theories, it continued – just as in the mediaeval period – to arouse metaphysical speculations.

When the first signs of food abstinence appeared, people usually consulted a local quack or doctor. If their treatment was not efficacious, all kinds of rumours started to spread rapidly. Instead of being sick, the fasting girl might well be a miracle. In 1587 the German miraculous maiden Catharina Binder, for instance, was venerated by some as a saint, because she 'hath thus continued without eating, drinking, or, sleeping, the space of nine whole yeeres compleat, and yet miraculouslie liveth through the singular, pure and incomprehensible grace of almighty God'.[178] The fact that Martha Taylor stayed alive after months of fasting was attributed in 1668 to 'God's love from heaven to the sinners on earth'.[206] Maria Jehnfels from the German village of Steinbeck near Hamburg, allegedly having fasted for years, was looked upon in 1728 as an extraordinary 'Wonder of God': God supposedly kept her alive by His miraculous powers in order to demonstrate that miracles were still occurring.[181] Due to such speculations a prolonged fast sometimes became a more or less 'acknowledged' miracle of great fame.

Although several prolonged fasters died anonymously, the fame of the fasting girls usually spread beyond their own village or region, especially after the invention of printing. Physicians, among them prominent doctors, exchanged extensive correspondence and published learned treatises on the subject. But probably in much wider circulation and for a larger audience, the news about miraculous maidens was spread by pamphlets. These bulletins or booklets – forerunners of the newspaper – were frequently reprinted and translated. From the seventeenth century on, when regular newspapers increasingly reported on the latest events, miraculous maidens also frequently figured in this medium. Due to the improved means of communication and the widespread fascination with the miraculous, many a fasting girl became a spectacle attracting crowds of visitors. They came from far and wide to the often remote villages to gaze at the miracle. The visitors were able to convince themselves of the miracle by having a chat with the girl or by being shown how impossible it was for her to take sustenance. A typical example is the Dutch fasting girl Engeltje van der Vlies from the village of Pijnacker near Delft. In the summer of 1826 more than one thousand people paid a visit to her and she even appeared as an attraction in an English traveller's guide.[210]

Dignitaries were often among those interested; nobility and even kings visited or summoned them. At the beginning of the seventeenth century one of the few 'fasting boys', Jean Godeau of Vauprofonde near Sens, attracted the attention of a number of dignitaries because of his abstinence extending well over four years. He was summoned by some dukes and also to Fontainebleau by Queen Mother Marie de Medici and her little son, Louis XIII.[190] The German fasting girls Margaretha Weiss and Eva Vliegen also attracted royal attention. Margaretha was summoned by emperor Ferdinand I in 1542 and Eva was even twice favoured with a visit by the Dutch prince Maurice at the beginning of the seventeenth century. It goes without saying that such royal visits markedly increased the credibility and appeal of the miracle.

The fasting girls often exploited these visits. In honour of the miracle or simply in gratitude for the spectacle, people offered them money and goods (we will mention several examples of this below). Apart from the fasting girls, their social environment also benefited from the attention. In 1869 the local youth profited from the prolonged fasting of the 'Welsh Fasting Girl'

Sarah Jacob (whom we will describe below). In the neighbourhood of the nearest railway station, little boys offered their
services as guides by bearing placards with the words 'Fasting
Girl' and 'This is the shortest way to Llethernoryadd-ucha'.[111]
That the phenomenon did not arouse merely surprise and curiosity may be apparent from the rest of this chapter.

The miracle put to the test

At first sight food abstinence by miraculous maidens hardly
differs from that of the mediaeval saints. They were both
renowned and generally regarded as supernatural phenomena
attesting to God's miraculous works. Nevertheless we have
enough reason to make a clear distinction between the two. First
of all, compared to their mediaeval predecessors, miraculous
maidens were less religiously inspired. Although many fasting
girls showed some religious fervour, they no longer referred so
explicitly to divine inspiration as explanation of their food
abstinence. Penance or mortification of the body in pursuit of
becoming united with Christ, which induced many saints to
food abstinence, was alien to fasting girls. But the context in
which the phenomenon occurred was also markedly different –
and ever more so in the course of centuries – from that of
mediaeval fasting saints. In comparison with fasting saints, opposition against prolonged fasters seems to have intensified and
spread since the sixteenth century. Even as late as the nineteenth
century some physicians still gave credence to extensive 'prodigious abstinence' and suggested that the fasters were living
literally on air. Yet at the same time a growing number of
doctors expressed their doubts about the phenomenon. Ever
since the sixteenth century both camps had fiercely disputed the
question of whether human beings (just like some animal species)
were able to live without food for an extended period of time.

In an era in which scientists began to attach great value to
empiricism – that which can be established by observation,
measurement and experiment – physicians agreed that the assertions of fasting girls ought to be verified. An extensive investigation would end all speculations and reveal the naked truth, all
parties agreed. Everyone hoped to take advantage of the results:
those who gave credence to the miracle were looking for more

acknowledgement after the investigation; those who suspected deceit expected the girl to be exposed. Although many treatises on food abstinence as a medical problem were published in the same period in which fasting girls created a furore, the question of whether a disease might account for the miraculous fasts did not concern physicians too much. Primarily most physicians considered it their task to settle the question of whether the fast was a miracle or a fraud. Such a priority is not incomprehensible. Indeed, everybody was familiar with the prolonged fasting of Moses, Eliah, Jesus, numerous ascetics and some well-attested cases of fasting girls. Yet the accounts of fraudulent fasting saints and miraculous maidens were a serious warning to credulity. From this bitter experience, people at the time began to realize that food refusal might originate from motives of financial gain or craving for attention.

Consequently physicians were on their guard and in most cases advised the making of inquiries. As the length of the fast, the fame of the faster or the number of visitors increased, an extensive investigation became more likely. For the fasting girl there was no escape: refusal to cooperate would soon be interpreted as fear of detection. From the sixteenth century on the proceedings of these investigations were more or less fixed. In agreement with the basic principles of the experimental method, food intake was controlled by isolating the fasting girl from the outside world and watching her continuously for several days. Usually a cross-examination of those who were involved and a medical examination of the fasting girl preceded the observation. Once the observation had started, women guards closely watched the girl's health as well as anything else that took place. The results of these watches were quite divergent, varying from a happy end to deep sorrow.

In a number of cases the observations confirmed the prolonged fasting, as in the case of the previously mentioned Catharina Binder from Schmidtweiler. At the beginning of the year 1585, allegedly having lived without food for seven years, Count Palatine Johann Casimir requested some respectable men to make further inquiries into the case. This commission of inquiry began by gathering information about this prodigious fasting from Catharina herself, her parents and some neighbours. After this preliminary inquiry the commission was still unable to assess whether Catharina stayed alive by the 'special providence of God Almighty' or by deceit. Partly 'to avoid rumours and idolatry' it was decided to observe her for several days. Four reliable women guards were appointed to watch her carefully day and night. After a fortnight the observation was terminated and the guards testified that Catharina had not taken any food or drink from the start.[178]

Around 1600 the French king Henry IV ordered his best and most prominent physicians to make inquiries into the prolonged fasting of Jeanne Balam, who had been fasting for years. But in spite of the fact that some physicians kept her in isolation for weeks or even months, none of them was able to catch her at any deceit.[158] The observation of the prolonged fasting Martha Taylor around 1668 yielded a similar result. At the request of the Earl of Devonshire she had been observed for at least a fortnight by physicians and surgeons.[192] A final and more recent example is Zélie Bourriou, a 45-year-old peasant woman from Bourdeilles (a village of Périgord) who was said to have lived without food for nine years. In 1896 she was brought to the hospital, where she remained under strict observation for no less than 125 days in all. Slices of fresh bread and other comestibles, continually renewed, were left in a drawer in her room, but she never touched them.[111]

Inquiries with such results considerably increased the reputation of the miraculous faster. For now it was a fact verified by learned gentlemen. Besides, some jumped at these results to substantiate the existence of prodigious abstinence. It could be referred to as undeniable evidence of the supposed ability of some to live without food for a long time; hence their survival was attributed to some extraordinary capacity but without the interference of supernatural powers. However, in view of the alleged length of many fasts and the rigorous methods of observation, it does not come as a surprise that not every case ended as happily. In a considerable number of cases it became crystal clear that the fasting girl, sometimes with the aid of accomplices, had thrown dust in everyone's eyes. One of them was Margaretha Ulmer from Esslingen (near Württemberg). She supposedly went for a long period of time without eating and had a swollen stomach from which she could pull out worms and snakes. Particularly after imperial court physicians and some distinguished men had been unable to establish any deceit, rumours about her spread throughout Germany. For four years many paid her a visit and smothered her with presents. At last the magistrate intervened. In 1546 he ordered some physicians and a midwife to liberate the animals from the woman's body by a caesarian section. But it did not come to that, because the investigators soon discovered that Margaretha had taken food on the sly for all those years and the swollen stomach was nothing but an air cushion. Mother and daughter confessed that they had given themselves up to these practices 'at the instigation of the devil' and from motives of gain.[174;218]

At the beginning of the nineteenth century several treatises on the miraculous fast of Ann Moore from Tutbury (Staffordshire) spread her fame throughout England and America. A 'likeness in wax' was even exhibited at the Columbian Museum in Boston. In 1807 Ann announced publicly that she lived without food. A watch in 1808, which could not establish any deceit, increased her notoriety considerably and multitudes of visitors came from all parts of the country.[152] According to a contemporary, Ann Moore turned the exhibition of her person to such account, that she was able to save the sum of £400. Visitors even had to pay an admittance fee. By 1813, after five years of fame and fortune, doubts had arisen again. Several physicians bluntly stated in medical journals that she was an impostor. A second watch in 1813 had to be terminated prematurely, because Ann fell gravely ill. However, shortly afterwards her long deceit was uncovered by accident. Her daughter had contrived, when washing her face, to feed her every morning, by using towels made wet with gravy, milk or strong arrowroot. She had also conveyed food from mouth to mouth while kissing her mother. Ann Moore was able to escape from judicial prosecution by a written confession. After a few months she left Tutbury early in the morning. According to an eye-witness account, she was seated in an open cart amidst several articles of furniture and was taunted by the crowd. Later on she was reported to be in gaol for 'robbing her lodgings'.[7;193;216]

As we will describe below some miraculous maidens who appeared to be impostors, we will confine ourselves now to just one other example. It concerns the notorious 'Welsh Fasting Girl' Sarah Jacob from Llethernoryadd-ucha (South

Wales).[159;166] In her case deceit was discovered in a very harsh way. She started her extended abstinence when only 10 years old. Because of the disbelief her prolonged fasting encountered, particularly on the part of physicians, a local vicar pressed for an investigation of the 'wonderful little girl'. Shortly thereafter a public meeting was called and a committee was appointed to watch her constantly for a fortnight. When this committee came to the conclusion that there was no question of any deceit, her notoriety became still greater and she acquired the reputation of 'miraculous faster'. However, renewed discussion was provoked by Dr Robert Fowler, vice-president of the Hunterian Society; in *The Times* of 7 September 1869 he called her case one of 'simulative hysteria'. Many, by contrast, considered her miraculous fast a matter of Welsh national honour and something that had to be defended against criticism of 'local credulity and foolishness'. Therefore, after a few months a second public meeting was called to make arrangements for another, closer vigil. This time four nurses from London's Guy's Hospital were appointed to watch her carefully for fourteen days. However, Sarah did not persist that long. After a few days she grew noticeably weak and her parents were counselled to call off the watch. They refused, saying there was no need, as she had often been like that and that it was not from want of food, etc. Unfortunately they were wrong. On 17 December 1869, at 3.30 pm, the Welsh fasting girl passed away. On the basis of the watch and the results of the post mortem it was concluded that she must have regularly eaten surreptitiously.

People did not think lightly of such exposures and often responded furiously. Of course those who had given credence to the 'miracle' felt themselves seriously deceived and ridiculed. Beyond that, both faster and accomplices were accused not only of faking a miracle, but also of swindle from a reprehensible craving for attention and motives of gain. This kind of affair was viewed as a deliberate deception of the public that had to be brought before the court. Severe punishments were imposed upon the girl and her accomplices. In the case of Sarah Jacob her death incited a storm of indignation. A coroner's inquest was held and the parents were found guilty of criminal negligence of their daughter. They were given prison sentences of hard labour: a year for the father and six months for the mother. We know nothing of what happened to the six other children in the family, although their home was lost and the farm sold. Since it could not be established that the physicians involved in the watch had done anything else but give advice to the four nurses, they were acquitted . . . [159]

Also in other cases of deceit the persons involved were severely punished. For instance Anna Maria Eeltiens from Tilburg in Holland, who had pretended to live without food for years, had to pay for it. In the year 1736 she was put in Antwerp on a knacker's cart barefoot and dressed in a white chemise. Accompanied by some police officers and in the presence of a large crowd she was led to the major churches of Antwerp, holding a burning candle. She was forced to kneel in front of the doors, begging in a loud voice for God and the law to forgive her. Hereafter she was returned to prison, where she had to subsist every Wednesday and Friday on water and bread.[174] And in another case from around 1800 a second extensive watch ascertained that the alleged two-year fast and stigmatics of Anna Maria Kienker in Borgloh in Germany were nothing but deceit. Her 8-year-old brother had provided her regularly with some food and water, and removed excrement. She was sentenced to one hour at the pillory in front of the local church, wearing the inscription 'Public Impostor', and to a further six months in a house of correction. Her brother, father and mother were also sentenced for aiding and abetting.[28;95] All this, however, was mere child's play compared to what happened to Margaretha Ulmer after her exposure in 1546. Because of complicity her mother was tortured, garotted and burnt. Margaretha herself escaped with life and limb. Her face was 'only' pierced with a red-hot piece of iron, after which she was incarcerated for life . . . [174]

However, people did not always respond to exposures in such a furious way. Sometimes the case was simply covered up, as will be apparent from some cases discussed below. These examples will illustrate the phenomenon of miraculous maidens in more detail than we have done so far. We will now discuss Margaretha Weiss, Barbara Kremers and Eva Vliegen.

Margaretha Weiss, the miraculous maiden from Roed

In the sixteenth century one of the sensations of the time was a girl who refused to eat and drink from her tenth year on. Her fame must have been widespread. Several pamphlets and treatises by leading physicians concerning her miraculous fast were published during her lifetime.[169;191] A poet and several artists chose her as a topic, and even the German king summoned her.[161] On the basis of a report from 1542, written by the personal physician of King Ferdinand I, Gerardus Bucoldianus, we will reconstruct the vicissitudes of this miraculous fasting girl.[155]

In 1529 Margaretha Weiss was born in the village of Roed near Speyer. At the age of 10, she was plagued during Christmas by stomach ache and headache. At the same time her food intake as well as the quantity of faecal matter decreased. After Christmas she stopped eating altogether and she did no longer evacuate her bowels. The pains persisted, and round about Lent her hands and feet began to stiffen. Finally, the worried father consulted an old wife from a neighbouring village, who was reputed because of her medical qualities. She advised boiling certain spices to prepare a bath twice a day for Margaretha. But for the duration of eighteen days this treatment was of no avail. For this reason her parents consulted another woman who peddled all kinds of medicines. She recommended using another spice for the baths. After four weeks Margaretha's stiffened hands and feet recovered. After Easter she also refused to drink despite the dry hot summer of 1540.

As appears from the various efforts of the local authorities to put her to a test, her prodigious fasting did not merely incite reverence and awe. On the instigation of the bishop of Speyer, Margaretha had been observed continuously for ten days without any deceit being established. After a few months the guardian of the castle of Kiseleck summoned her in order to be investigated carefully. But when she refused all food and drink for five days, he sent her home again. Finally, efforts of the bishop of Speyer, who apparently supposed her fasting to be the devil's work, to cure her by exorcism in October 1541 were in vain.[161]

In February 1542 the Reichstag – an important political meeting – was held in Speyer; King Ferdinand I was present. He soon heard the news of the miraculous maiden from Roed and had the girl and her father summoned. As the king was astonished by their account, he ordered his personal physician Bucoldianus to make further investigations into the case. Margaretha took up her residence in the physician's house. Probably to exclude any deceit, her clothing was replaced by new, granted by the king. Then she was continuously observed by the royal valet Hans Grave from Vienna. According to Bucoldianus' description Margaretha was of a fine build with a height conforming to her age. She had big eyes in a simple, childish face, liked to sit in a heated room and slept quietly and naturally. Her stomach was somewhat fallen in, but her milt and liver were healthy. Her mouth was dry and she never vomited. When she was incited to drink, she kept the wine or water in the front of her mouth and had to spit it out after a while.

During his observation Bucoldianus made several attempts to induce the girl to take food. But despite the fact that the physician used food 'by which a girl of that age is easily to be seduced' he did not succeed in persuading her. After twelve days the watch was terminated. Still she needed no food and drink and had neither urinated nor defecated. Her physical condition was invariably good and her behaviour was qualified as normal: 'She walks, cries, laughs and does everything children of that age used to do in such circumstances.' After King Ferdinand I had granted her some presents, he sent her home 'not without surprise'.

What happened then to Margaretha is obscure: available historical sources are contradictory in this respect. According to a contemporary of Margaretha, the Italian philosopher Simone Portio (Porzio or Porta; 1497–1554), she started – albeit in scanty measure – to eat again after Bucoldianus' watch.[145;189] She would have persisted in this way of life up to the moment he was writing down his observations (around 1550). Also several sixteenth- and seventeenth-century sources mention that Margaretha did not totally abstain from food beyond the age of 13.[158;218] However, drawings of the German painter Hans Baldung Grien (1484/85–1545) have passed down to us.[177;183] On these drawings is mentioned in a seventeenth-century handwriting that the girl had not eaten for ten years. Assuming that Grien had indeed drawn Margaretha and that we may trust the added handwriting, the miraculous maiden would have lived until the age of 21 without food.

The seventeenth-century physician Stalpart van der Wiel from The Hague has rejected both possibilities: in his view Margaretha was nothing but a fraudulent faster. In an extensive treatise of prolonged food abstinence, he provides a concise description of 'Margareta van Spiers'.[301] The account closely corresponds with Bucoldianus' report, but unlike the latter, Stalpart makes mention of deceit and includes the Margaretha case among the 'false histories'. In his view it took some time before it was discovered that she had sewn some gingerbread into the hem of her dress. We have not been able to find Stalpart's report confirmed in other writings, but years after her death Margaretha remained a celebrity. Although the public soon found some other subjects to be amazed at, until well into the seventeenth century learned physicians referred to the prodigious fasting of Margaretha, the *Puella Spyrensis*. None of them mentioned any deceit.

The alleged fasting of Barbara Kremers from Unna

Apart from Margaretha Weiss the prolonged fasting of a 10-year-old girl from the German village of Unna was at least as sensational in the seventeenth century. We are extensively informed about this fasting girl by Johan Wier, the famous sixteenth-century physician we have already mentioned. Wier, who is remembered chiefly as the debunker of the popular belief in witchcraft and as a founder of modern psychiatry, opposed the credulity and craving for miracles of many of his contemporaries.[393] In his treatise *De Commentitiis Jejuniis* (On alleged fasting) from 1577 he expressed his doubts about the numerous stories on 'fasting miracles'.[218] He gave credence to the examples of extended fasts in the bible, of desert fathers and saints, but he was suspicious that such supernatural phenomena could occur among simple, natural people. He found support for this attitude by the fact that on closer examination several of such 'miracles' appeared to be nothing but deceit. This scepticism induced Wier to make personal investigations into the case of the miraculous maiden from Unna. We will closely follow his vivid and keen description.

In 1573 Wier accompanied a German duke to Königsberg as his personal physician. One of the subjects of particularly frequent dinner-table conversations among the dukes and the counts at that time was a girl in Unna who never ate and yet was perfectly well. Wier would not believe this and upon his return from his trip with the duke at the end of 1873 he went to Unna. He found Barbara Kremers living together with her mother, stepfather and her 12-year-old sister Elsa. Barbara was only 10 years old, but physically developed beyond her age. Her mother said that the miracle of not eating had followed a severe illness of six weeks' duration. Throughout the illness she only took some wine, beer and milk and did not speak for about half a year. Since her recovery, according to her mother, she had taken neither food nor drink, nor likewise moved bowel or bladder. Her mother praised her daughter because of her piety and pointed out that Barbara had been examined by all kinds of noblemen and magistrates, all of whom attested to the fact that the girl's story was in no way fraudulent. Then Wier himself examined her. He observed that the girl looked well (*colore vivido*), though her belly seemed to be quite drawn-in (*ventre collapso*). According to her mother, the girl's umbilicus had been from birth stuck to her spine from the inside. However, when Wier tried to palpate that area, the girl wriggled away from his hands amidst much whining and crying.

Barbara created a furore at the time. According to Wier many people streamed in to see the child and donated a great deal of money. In a special certificate the city council of Unna declared that after a watch for nine days the miracle appeared to be authentic. None the less, Wier told everyone that the whole affair was of lies and deceit. He was particularly astonished by the fact that the girl looked so well despite her extended fasting. Human beings, he said, were kept alive by warmth and if they did not take food to replace burnt matter, life necessarily had to be extinguished.

In April 1574, Barbara along with her parents and sister went to the court of the duke in Cleves. They requested the dignitaries to issue a certificate testifying to the fact that Barbara had neither eaten nor drunk, urinated nor defecated for thirteen months. Wier took advantage of the occasion and asked the duke for permission to have Barbara brought to his house. To convince her of his good intentions and good will, he offered her some toys and agreed with the request of the worried parents to have the girl accompanied by her sister Elsa. To prevent the parents from stuffing Barbara with food that would enable her to hold out during a fast of a few days, Wier saw to it that the girls were with him the very next day.

Wier gave Barbara and Elsa free rein to wander anywhere in and out of the house as well as the garden. His servants were instructed to pretend they noticed nothing at all. That very day they were caught. After supper, his wife Henrica sat as if half asleep from exhaustion at the kitchen table, her face covered with a thin veil, through which she could easily see whatever the girls were up to. Barbara, assuming Wier's wife to be asleep, laid hold of a huge goblet filled with beer and immediately downed a very liberal portion. Shortly afterwards the servants observed Elsa slip a separate portion of an apple to Barbara and caught sight of her urinating a tremendous volume and passing a large stool. The second day she was observed once again drinking huge draughts of beer. The third day she ate part of a loaf of rye-bread, hid another part underneath her dress and took a fair amount of beer. When Henrica told her what had been discovered over the three-day period, Barbara denied everything. Wier did not want to push matters to extremes and decided to hide food under lock and key. The following day 'she was now so drawn in the face and so dry of tongue, that she came into the garden to say she felt sick. This day, which happened to be the last of April, was the one day truly consecrated to fasting.'[218] When she was pressed hard again, Barbara confessed and within a week she began taking regular meals.

The next problem for Wier was to protect the girls and their parents from the wrath of the duke in whose eyes the girl was a criminal swindler; her parents were even more guilty. The duke was ultimately persuaded and he sent the girls back to Unna, supplied with a ducal letter for the magistrate, reproaching him for having been so credulous and urging him to be more intelligent in the future. The duke advised bringing up the two children more carefully and teaching them to fear God. As to the various certificates and testimonials about Barbara's alleged fasting, they should be gathered carefully and burnt in the market place. Wier concludes the story with the remark 'This was the cheerful catastrophe of this comedy.' Barbara passed the events off. When she had returned to Unna, she broadcast that she really had fasted for months, but that doctor Wier had composed a potion through which her appetite returned with God's mercy and she could eat once again.[379;393]

Eva Vliegen, the mendacious maiden from Meurs

Around 1600 the alleged prodigious fast of Eva Vliegen from North Rhine Westphalia (close to the Dutch border) created a furore in Western Europe. She did not fall into oblivion until a long time after her death. Until well into the nineteenth century she was one of the attractions of a kind of waxwork show, that foreshadowed Madame Tussaud's. William Brereton has described in his *Travels in Holland*, that he went in 1634 'to a house called Dole-hoose' in Amsterdam, where Eva was presented to the audience as follows: 'Here also the picture in wax of the Maiden of Meurs, who is reported to have lived fifteen years without meat.'[198] Causing hilarity in the audience, one arm of the wax figure made a movement to wipe breadcrumbs off her mouth. Who was this woman who served for ages as an impostor to entertain the audience?

At the end of the sixteenth century it was rumoured that there lived in the town of Meurs a woman who neither ate nor drank. According to an English pamphlet from 1611 the parents of this Eva Vliegen, nicknamed Bessie of Meurs, were very poor

> so that in her yonger dayes (they being not able to maintaine her) she was compelled to keepe swine for the country people, enduring (by that hard course of life) the bitternesse of much hunger, as she her selfe confesseth. Living in this extremity of misery, she often (so well as she could, seeing no other wayes nor hope of comfort) made earnest prayers to God, that he would take pitty of her wretchednes, and relieve her, from that daily hunger, by which her body was tormented & consumed: her prayers were heard, according to her request.[150]

In 1594 at the age of 19 she began to lose her appetite. After three years she stopped taking any food and drink.[146;147]

Shortly afterwards the countess of Meurs managed in persuading her to take one cherry

> and had no sooner eaten it downe, but that the Lady with her servants were in feare shee would there presently have dyed, shee fell into so sodaine and violent passion of an extreme sickenesse: in the which she continued a long time . . .

Just like the Astoni described by Pliny, Eva was said to live on the scent of flowers.[185] She was a pious woman and asserted that every second day an exceeding cleere light shineth round about her body; the common light or brightnes of the day, being nothing comparable to it: which light when she beholdeth and (as she saith) feeleth shining upon her, she hath likewise a feeling on her tongue of a strange and extraordinary delicate sweetnes, the moisture of which strengthens her (to her seeming) for her eies can behold no other thing but only that perfect and unusuall light.[150]

Partially because her Protestant co-religionists widely broadcast this marvellous wonder, Eva acquired great notoriety. People from all regions paid her a visit and made gifts to her. Among the visitors were numerous noble people such as the Dutch prince Maurice, the countess of Meurs and Palsgravine Elisabeth. But like almost all her counterparts Eva did not merely encounter devout admirers. Some people called her a witch or believed her to be possessed by the devil.[179] Still others, assuming that she indeed fasted for a substantial period of time, refrained from a judgement as to whether a good or a bad spirit was involved. The local preacher Coenraad Velthuizen also had his doubts about the case. For this reason

he tooke the said Eve (being come to heare the evening Sermon) home with him to his owne house (. . .) and (at the end of 13 daies and nights) being demanded whether she where then either hungry or thirsty, she answered no: so that the Preacher now having by the experience of his owne eyes, found out that which he could not before beleeve, is now inforced with admiration to acknowledge to be true.[150]

The wonder also attracted the attention of the famous German surgeon Guilhelmus Fabricius Hildanus (or Wilhelm Fabry von Hilden; 1560–1634). This physician showed a particular interest in such prodigious fasts and with a view to a future publication he visited her in 1612. According to his observation she was a pious woman of moderate stature, with a pale complexion and a depressed expression in her eyes. She had been strikingly emaciated: her stomach almost touched her spine. She had neither urinated nor defecated and even menstruation had been absent. She cried a lot and Hildanus established that she was in no way compromised and had continuously lived with pious, God-fearing people.[235]

Two years later a Dutch pamphlet extensively described Eva's death.[151] After a visit of the Palsgravine she had been sick for ten to twelve weeks. She called the neighbours, who perceived in her room 'a great light' and immediately sent for the preacher. Once again 'a great brightness' appeared, which frightened those present so much that they fainted. Then Eva asserted that an angel had appeared and ordered her that God could no longer endure the sins of the world and that He would punish mankind (unless people were converted hurriedly) by 'great mortality'. To those who doubted her account, Eva said: 'Believe me then by the signs God will reveal to you.' From that moment on she would not have spoken any more and on 1 March 1614 she 'has rested in the Lord'.

Had this been the dramatic end of an once famous fasting girl? By contrast, her story ended totally differently, albeit no less dramatically. The first indication that the pamphlet provided misleading information is to be found in Hildanus' work. He added a letter from 1625 by the son of Gottschalk Monheim, apothecary in Düsseldorf, who asserts that 'the Daughter in Meurs, is still living without Food and Drink'.[235] Later sources not only confirm that she was still alive, but also mention the outcome of the story. Having convincingly alleged for thirty years that she abstained from food and drink, she had been ultimately unmasked. The way this happened was reported by the Dutch poet and physician Nicolaes van Wassenaer (1571/72–1629). It all began when visitors smelled the stench of faeces. The local authorities immediately sent a few women to watch Eva carefully. Soon she asked for some buttermilk, which she appeared to have already taken for two years. Everyone was astonished and it was decided to search her room. When butter, cheese, honey and other edible ware were found, Eva asserted that they were meant for the poor. It was also discovered that she had defecated for many years. Thereupon she was arrested.[213]

A Dutch journal from 28 June 1628 reported:

In Moers has been arrested a daughter, named Eva Vlieghe, who pretended for 30 years to the public that she had not eaten, and though she had been carefully watched by the Countess as well as Preachers and other People, they could not establish any deceit; then due to the death of a Woman who secretly helped her, it was revealed, that she has cheated many thousands of people.[160]

Judges condemned Eva to public flagellations. But since she was a simple old woman, Prince Maurice not only pardoned her, but even granted her five pennies a day during her lifetime. Eva Vliegen must have benefited from this donation for at least a couple of years, in view of the following passage in a church-book of Meurs: '10 June 1637, Eva Vliegen, who cheated the whole world by scandalous lies and blasphemy, has been buried.'

From miraculous maiden to hysterical patient

In the second part of the nineteenth century some girls still aroused astonishment and attracted attention by protracted fasting. At that time even some physicians continued to consider prolonged food abstinence as an incomprehensible, though not impossible, phenomenon and tried to establish whether the abstainer was cheating. Take for instance the 'living miracle' Betsy Hays from the American town of Horicon. In 1859 this 28-year-old mother of two children alleged to have abstained from food and drink for two years. Notwithstanding the fact that at their annual meeting, the State Medical Society disposed of the case as a 'successful fraud and deception', the physician L.E. Whiting decided to examine the woman. After his visit he was convinced that any motive for deception was lacking. Having met this 'wonderful woman', one 'will be strongly inclined to call it no fraud', Whiting concluded.[217]

Even after the concept of anorexia nervosa had been intro-duced and food abstinence was transformed into an acknowl-edged clinical syndrome (as described in Chapters 8 and 9), the phenomenon of miraculous maidens did not disappear com-pletely. Although many parts of their behaviour might fit the description of the new syndrome, in medical literature several reports on fasting girls were published without any reference to anorexia nervosa or any other syndrome. The physician James Dougal, for example, reports in two articles about the 14-year-old Christina Marshall from the village of Chapelton, who subsisted for months on hardly any food until her death in 1882. Dougal does not hazard any diagnosis, let alone call her a case of anorexia nervosa. Yet he feels obliged to emphasize that he believes 'the honesty and integrity of their characters to be above the faintest tint of suspicion'. He never heard 'even the gentlest murmur of gossip pointing in the direction of latent channels of food-supply'.[163;164] In the case of the late nineteenth-century American 'Brooklyn Enigma', Mollie Fancher, who supposedly abstained from food for fourteen years, her medical attendant told a journalist: 'The case knocks the bottom out of all existing medical theses, and is, in a word, miraculous.'[172]

Nevertheless the climate for fasting girls had worsened markedly during the nineteenth century. In the meantime most physicians were convinced of the impossibility of protracted fasts. By now theories about the existence of so-called prolonged fasters who supposedly lived, for instance, by the mercy of God or – more earthly – on air, were considered untenable. For the majority of physicians prodigious fasting had been non-existent. They discredited the accounts about this putative miracle. It was simply at complete variance with contemporary scientific knowledge and therefore impossible. Logically, the strict watches of miraculous maidens belonged to the past for ever. Not only was necessity lacking (it was just impossible), but additionally any cooperation with such watches might give the impression that physicians still attached credence to the assertions of fasting girls.

Yet in 1869 some physicians still deemed it necessary to institute a careful watch on account of the 12-year-old Sarah Jacob, who alleged to have fasted for two years. More sceptical physicians ridiculed such a watch, but sanctioned it none the less as it would undoubtedly provide the irrefutable evidence of swindle to the credulous public with their unremitting craving for sensation. The traditionally approved method in such cases, strict surveillance, was the only means available to end all speculation. Yet it was a thankless task, for if against expectation the physician should not be able to establish deceit, he would be ridiculed by his colleagues. However, should he reveal the opposite, he only confirmed what everyone knew in the eyes of many physicians. Consequently, the watch of Sarah Jacob was an exceptional – and dramatic – occurrence in the second half of the previous century. Instead of the question of whether a person had really abstained from food for so long, physicians had gradually focused on the clinical signs of the phenomenon and its most effective therapy. Numerous publications on prolonged fasts as a pathological phenomenon appeared. Parallel to this evolution the behavioural pattern of fasting girls was designated by most physicians as pathological. Yet physicians had to admit that some of them were able to live on extremely small amounts of food. Such a way of life, combined with the need to pretend prolonged fasting, was regarded from now on as morbid behaviour.

Sarah Jacob has been mentioned several times before. In 1867, at the age of 10, she began a two-year fast. She acquired national notoriety when in spring 1869 a watch, suggested by the local vicar in a newspaper, could not discover any deceit. Discussion flared up after a physician had called her a case of 'simulative hysteria'. A second watch in December 1869 was dramatically ended by Sarah's death. Her parents were found guilty and condemned to prison sentences of hard labour. We will illustrate the reactions of physicians regarding the occurrences in South Wales by the editorials of *The Lancet*, one of the most prominent British medical journals.

In *The Lancet* of 27 February 1869 the above-mentioned vicar's letter is described in a somewhat condescending manner:

> We occasionally meet with credulous people; and a most remarkable specimen of the class is a Welsh parson, the Vicar of Llanfihangel-ar-Arth – wherever that may be. The Vicar writes to the Welshman newspaper, calling the attention of its readers to 'a most extraordinary case' (of credulity on his part, we think).

Then some passages of the vicar's letter follow. A month later, when the first watch was going on, *The Lancet* criticizes the watch and is of the opinion that

> these good people have taken a very indirect, expensive, and unsatisfactory way of investigating it. (. . .) Obviously the best and most economical plan would be to take her away altogether from the place, forward her to the nearest county infirmary, dismiss all her friends, prevent the access of all visitors . . .

On 1 May 1869 an editorial is devoted again to the 'Welsh Fasting Girl'. It is apparent that the earlier-mentioned vicar was offended by the response to his inserted article. He had sent another letter to a local newspaper to express his displeasure about this. Therein he describes the responsible editor of *The*

Lancet as the 'Pope-editor' and medical science as 'universally acknowledged to be the most uncertain and immature of all sciences'. *The Lancet* viciously retorted

> how it is that he, in common with all Protestants, pooh-poohs the idea of miracles as related by the Romish Church in past ages? As far as human testimony is concerned, they rest upon a basis as irrefragable as the case he narrates, and yet he would probably put them aside without a thought, or listen to them with a shrug of incredulity.

Referring to results of 'stronger branches of physical science – chemistry, for example' and the fasting girl at Tutbury (Ann Moore), the medical journal points out that staying alive without food is 'contradictory of an immense body of facts of various kinds'. Once again it is argued that for a reliable scientific investigation, Sarah could have been better sent to an infirmary to have her watched by physicians. The investigation which ended almost a month ago and could not discover deceit goes totally unmentioned . . .

A few months later, on 18 September 1869, the editorial board of *The Lancet* refers with approval to Dr Fowler's letter in *The Times*, in which he called Sarah a case of 'simulative hysteria'. It is pointed out that 'perversions of volition' are by no means uncommon among children. For the third time the right method is rehearsed: infirmary, separate room, medical care. In this way, within a week there would have been an end to the mystery and

> she would soon be cured sufficiently to eat Welsh mutton with a relish. The question now arises whether the stupidity or selfishness of parents, as in this case, ought to be allowed to bar the way to their child's return to health and happiness.

When the second watch was in its second day, *The Lancet* writes on 11 December 1869: 'We may at last hope that the statements which have been made respecting this case will be properly tested, and their truth or otherwise ascertained.' Without in any way wishing to anticipate the result, according to the journal, it is pointed out rather tendentiously that several similar cases are on record 'but none of them rest on evidence which, scientifically speaking, would be deemed satisfactory'.

After nine days of observation Sarah Jacob dies on 17 December 1869. But ironically enough, this news did not reach *The Lancet* in time and the journal remarks one day after her death: 'Of course, every precaution has been taken in the event of the girl showing symptoms of exhaustion, and the nurses have special instructions to administer stimulants and food subject to the advice of the daily medical attendant'. A week later the earlier firmly expressed trust in the importance of the watch has totally disappeared. The conclusion is put above the article: 'Starved to death' and Sarah is called

the miserable victim of her own delusions and of the superstition, ignorance and fraud of some of those about her. We confess to a feeling of indignation, and a sense of shame, as we read the account of this cruel demonstration of that which needed no proof.

To *The Lancet* it is beyond all argument that Sarah died of starvation and it is described as monstrous that such an occurrence should have taken place in the nineteenth century.

The girl was no doubt the victim of a diseased volition, and an hysterical aversion to food on her part was so fostered by everything that took place around her that it even dominated the stronger natural instincts.

That she commonly took some food must have been clear to everyone:

From the first moment that we heard of this so-called miracle, we did not hesitate to characterise it as a gross imposition. Every scientific man knew that it was a palpable absurdity, and in contravention of all known laws and experience, to suppose that the temperature and the development of tissue could have been maintained without any waste or change of substance. The only medical aspect of the case of any interest ought to have been the cure of the child, and this would have been mainly induced by moral means easily accomplished in the wards of an hospital, whither she ought to have been removed long ago.

The Lancet has every confidence that the affair will meet with a searching investigation, for there can be no doubt that Sarah had been surreptitiously supplied with food. The editorial concludes with the following words:

The practical lesson is clear – the medical profession should have nothing to do, directly or indirectly, with the investigation of any of the absurd stories arising from time to time out of ignorance, deceit or superstition. The sacrifice of this child ought to be enough in all conscience to make any future attempts at similar impostures penal.

No doubt the character of this editorial has been partially determined by the fierce commotion after Sarah's death. The physicians involved as well as the parents were considered to be responsible. Probably *The Lancet* therefore (and because of the editorial blunder shortly after her death) tended to keep its distance from the affair. Now the journal is qualifying the investigation as a 'cruel demonstration of that which needed no proof' and disapproves of the involvement of physicians, whereas before it did not oppose such an investigation! Although its opinion about the Jacob case, in the light of its ending, appears to be somewhat more peremptory than before, it has to be acknowledged that from the outset *The Lancet* had been sceptical about the news from Wales. The length of the fasts was considered to be in contravention of contemporary scientific knowledge, those who gave credence to them were qualified as credulous, and the only adequate method put forward was to place Sarah in an infirmary under the care of physicians.

It is striking that during her life *The Lancet* had hardly related Sarah's behaviour to a certain clinical picture. Apparently, everyone was still too preoccupied with the question of how deceit could be established. Only after her death did the editorial board speak in plain terms of 'diseased volition' and a hysterical aversion to food. For a reflection on the clinical aspects of the case another medical journal should be consulted: *The Medical Times and Gazette*, in whose editorial comments from 25 December 1869 indignation about the events again prevails. 'Silly people' had been misled by sensational reports and formed a committee to investigate the case. 'The whole thing is as great a national disgrace as it would be to try a woman for witchcraft by the ordeal of drowning.' The 'poor hysterical child' is not the first person to blame, but it is evident that she must have taken food in preceding years. That she denied the fact is only a common symptom of hysterical disease:

and that she found persons in her father's house to humour her and assist her in the deceit is not surprising when it is remembered that she attracted sightseers who paid or made her presents. Those who are most to blame are the educated gentry and Professional persons in the neighbourhood, who, instead of scouting the idea of anything but hysteria and fraud in the case, lent their aid, by talking and writing in a half-credulous fashion, in spreading the girl's reputation as a living wonder.

To the editors of *The Medical Times and Gazette* the case is relatively simple:

> If a Physician had in the first instance told the parents that simulating fasting was a well-known phase of hysteria, and that the proper treatment was to introduce a tube into the stomach or rectum, and to feed her thereby, and had insisted on seeing his prescription carried into effect, or, in case of opposition, had appealed for power to a magistrate, the poor girl's life might have been saved.

The view that Sarah Jacob suffered from a form of hysteria – a widely used concept at the end of the nineteenth century – was generally accepted in medical circles. In 1890, for instance, Sarah is described in the *British Medical Journal*, with reference to the well-known French neurologist Charcot, as a case of 'hysteria major' or 'hystero-epilepsy'. In 1894 W.J. Collins expressed the view that anorexia nervosa (according to some at the time a form of hysteria) may have been Sarah's 'morbid mental basis'.[404] He refers to 'other notorious cases of quasi-religious sort', for the other fasting girls did not escape from the physicians' efforts to annex the phenomenon. This is also apparent from a reaction in *The Medical Times and Gazette* of 20 March 1869, in which a physician, with reference to his findings of Sarah Jacob, asks whether the readers are familiar with similar cases and whether human beings are able to stay alive so long. A schoolmasterish editorial responds that the letter writer should realize that several instances are known of hysterical girls pretending to live without food, but that careful observation solved the mystery time and again.

In the *British Medical Journal* of 1876 Dr R. Sephton gives a short account of the 'Fasting girl in Lancashire', Ellen Sudworth, who from 1871 on

> has not partaken any solid food, but has been supported with soups and milk-puddings; therefore, this case might not be called one of fasting (. . .) I have always considered this extra-

ordinary case to be one of hysteria, only requiring moral treatment and discipline.

In a short comment the journal underlines that 'Dr. Sephton is evidently correct in treating this as a case of early and pro- nounced hysteria, to which class nearly all similar cases have been found to belong.'[204]

The 'Market Harborough Fasting girl', Martha White, who took no food from April 1874 until her death in December 1877, is designated (together with Sarah Jacob) as a case of 'hysterical insanity' by J.A. Campbell: 'No one can be considered sane who, without cause, starves so as to endanger health and life', stating that in these cases 'the necessary physical as well as moral force should be used'. Campbell – at the time medical superintendent at Garlands Asylum in Carlisle – is clearly con- vinced of the efficacy of his approach:

> In this asylum, it is and has been the practice that, in all cases of refusal of food for two full days, it should be administered artificially (. . .) Considerable numbers of girls in the hysteric state, who had refused food at home, when they were brought here, and the means and manner of giving it were explained to them, have at once given in and taken their food. I always make a point of taking such patients to see another fed with the pump, if one is being fed in the house at the time . . . [156]

In 1879 the prominent American neurologist William A. Ham- mond (1828–1900) elaborated the 'real nature' of the fasting girls.[172] In his conviction, cases like those of Sarah Jacob and Mollie Fancher were nothing but hysteria. Hysterical women do exhibit a marked ability to go without both food and drink, but mostly the length of time is strongly exaggerated. In Hammond's view the latter is precisely an essential characteristic of hysteria: 'A proclivity to simulation and deception is just as much a symptom of hysteria as pain is of pleurisy.' Just like in other diseases, the hysteric cannot be blamed for this kind of behaviour. His conclusion, for instance, that Mollie Fancher deceived every- one through her long-continued abstinence, should not be inter- preted as an imputation on her honesty: 'Other women naturally as moral as she, have under the influence of hysteria perpetrated the grossest deceptions.' After Hammond followed many who retrospectively expressed a similar view on the miraculous maidens. In 1888 the London professor of clinical medicine W.R. Gowers, for instance, commented: Such hysterical anorexia has given rise to the extraordinary cases of 'fasting girls' which, in all ages, have excited popular wonder. In many of these, however, there has been unquestionable fraud.[424]

What formerly had been called mere criminal swindle is now designated as a pathological phenomenon with deceptive behaviour as one of the symptoms. In the latter part of the nineteenth century people realized that the assertions of the fasting girls should hardly be taken seriously. Their cheating was no longer interpreted as deliberate fraud, but the consequence of a disease. Eating on the sly, in the past the undeniable evidence of fraud, was now viewed as a symptom, a sick form of behaviour, which fitted the clinical picture of hysteria and for which the patient cannot possibly be held responsible. Initially with the exposure of miraculous maidens and later with the clinical reinterpretation of the phenomenon, the era of the 'medicalization' of the miraculous maidens was heralded. Ever since it had been established that deceptive assertions of fasting for years originated from a pathological aberration; the medical profession rather than the legal authorities have had to deal with them.

It will be apparent that due to this 'medicalization' the conditions for manifesting oneself a 'miraculous maiden' had progressively deteriorated. The credulous section of the public, who craved for miracles, declined more and more, and instead the views of the medical profession became more widely spread. The successful annexation of prodigious abstinence into the medical field heralded the decline of the phenomenon. A miracle appeals to everyone's imagination, whereas a sick girl is far from exceptional. Instead of amazement, the latter arouses at best pity. Just as two centuries earlier in cases of demoniacs physicians transformed the possessed into sick people, prodigious abstinence became a disease. By the beginning of our century observations and judicial prosecution had been altogether supplanted by medical diagnoses and treatment.

5
Hunger Artists and Living Skeletons

With the decline of the miraculous maidens as a result of their medicalization, self-inflicted starvation as a spectacle did not completely disappear. Several forms still survived on the public scene. First of all, at the end of the nineteenth century the phenomenon of the hunger strike emerged. Although some people, including authorities and physicians, sometimes consider this behaviour to be 'sick', it is not really an illness. The hunger striker's deteriorating physical condition is caused by a conscious and deliberate act for which he or she is totally responsible. Often it is the last weapon in a struggle for power of someone who feels desperate or powerless. By abstaining from food people hope to enforce negotiations or at least attract attention to a weak position or problematic situation. Here, self-starvation is a form of public protest or overt defiance towards situations viewed as illegal or unfair, like conditions in camps or prisons, decisions or sanctions of authorities, legal proceedings and many other things.[264]

Hunger strikes are an especially twentieth-century phenomenon. Yet, earlier in history similar forms of protest can be found. Tertullian mentioned one Lycurgus who starved himself, because people tried to change his laws. In the late mediaeval period the fasts of Clara of Assisi and Cicely de Rygeway (or Ridgway) originated from opposition against authorities. The former threatened that she would not eat if the pope refused to allow her to preach. The latter was indicted for the death of her husband, 'justices appointed to deliver Notyngham gaol, because she kept mute was adjudged to her penalty, in which she remained alive for forty days in a narrow prison without food or drink by a miracle.' The king pardoned her.[198]

A curious case occurred in the late eighteenth century. In 1773 the 33-year-old Marie-Joseph Dahl, from the French Disonguin, fell in love with the son of a farmer for whom she worked. The farmer opposed the match, as the girl was poor. One day during harvest he said to her in a jest: 'Mary, if in three days, you will reap this field of wheat without the assistance of any one, I will give you my son.' The girl laboured day and night, and finished her task. When she realized that the farmer had been joking, she remained in a crouched posture for eleven years and refused any food whatever. Like many modern hunger strikers, she could not escape from forcible feeding: since she kept her teeth shut tight, they poured watered honey through a gap that was made by breaking off three of her teeth.[232]

However, hunger strike for societal or political goals is the most common form. An early form of mass political protest by self-starvation was the 1774 fast of the Massachusetts and Virginia colonists to express their dissatisfaction with England. One of the first more recent hunger strikers was the Russian woman Vera Figner, who in 1889 protested against the conduct of a prison-governor by fasting. In the first decades of our century, hunger strikes had become a particular weapon of antimilitarists opposing their sentence of imprisonment as criminals. In this period, the suffragettes – the advocates of women's liberation – frequently resorted to hunger strikes. In England especially it became front-page news, when authorities tried to end these hunger strikes by forcible feeding under physical coercion.[599]

For their political aspirations two hunger strikers acquired a great reputation. In 1920 Terence MacSwiney, the Irish liberator and Lord Mayor of Cork, starved himself to death in Brixton prison after 74 days.[243] The most famous example is Mahatma Gandhi, who in the 1930s rebelled against British domination in India by means of long hunger strikes.[259] Yet, these prominent figures are merely the vanguard of a large number of people all over the world, who have carried out hunger strikes as an ultimate means of pressure, though many never received any publicity. During the most recent decades, the phenomenon has become so widespread that almost every week some hunger striker is mentioned in the mass media, although they are now only incidentally front-page news.

Apart from hunger strikes, two rather bizarre forms of entertainment managed to withdraw emaciation and food abstinence from the physicians' direct sphere of influence. In the late nineteenth century, so-called 'living skeletons' and 'hunger artists' ('fasting artists') have exploited their extreme emaciation and extraordinary food abstinence. Initially at fairs and later in circuses and amusement parks they were on view for payment. Of these two forms of entertainment, the hunger artist is obviously a modern variant of the former fasting girls, for both created a furore by unequalled fasting and used it as a source of income. Besides, hunger artists and miraculous maidens alike have been confronted with scepticism, which in both cases often appeared to be well founded and led to prosecution.

Besides the striking fact that hunger artists were almost without exception males, there are other reasons to distinguish them from fasting girls. In the latter case the motive or cause of the prolonged fast was surrounded by secrecy, whereas the former made no secret at all of their lucrative intentions. In order to gain maximum profit they employed an impresario or a manager, and unlike fasting girls who hardly ever left the intimacy of their living-rooms, the hunger artists preferably showed themselves at public places where they could be sure of attention. Prodigious abstainers pretended to fast for years, while hunger artists had adapted to the meanwhile increased scepticism towards the phenomenon and therefore restricted the length of their performances to some weeks. Both were accorded a different reaction by the audience. Apart from a great deal of curiosity, the visitors of the fasting girls came to wonder at the unbelievable phenomenon, whereas among the spectators of the hunger artists admiration prevailed for a special stunt. The fast of the former was a wonder of God, the latter's an extraordinary achievement.

Well into the twentieth century these secularized and commercialized epigones of the miraculous maidens displayed their art of fasting or extreme emaciation to the audience. After 1930 they almost completely disappeared from the scene. They lost out increasingly to other forms of entertainment (film, television) and the improved social security system prevented them from having to earn their living as freaks. In addition, they were widely regarded as human beings with psychological disorders and defects, whose public exhibition was no longer deemed ethically justified. Though both forms of entertainment disappeared during this century, we will describe their heyday in more detail now.

Thinness as entertainment

Artists parading as 'living skeletons' mostly did not abstain from food. Unlike the hunger artists they exclusively derived their appeal from their extreme thinness. Only the body wasted to the bone was presented as a horrible attraction. The craving for sensation and the need to shudder tempted the public to visit.

An early example is to be found described in a pamphlet from Tirol, published in 1620.[220] The extremely emaciated 50-year-old Wolffgang Gschaidter was exhibited in a local church in Innsbruck. A picture shows a wasted man lying somewhat crookedly on a bed beside a crucifix. The pamphlet characterizes the man as a symbol of the town and urges the reader to visit him and give him alms. In the seventeenth century, thinness was also found in the more secular entourage of fairs. A poem of the Dutch Constantijn Huijgens (1596–1687) describes what fairs had to offer in this respect. Besides a girl without arms who was able to sew with her toes, a dwarf and a monster with an oversized head, he mentions an extremely wasted, bearded servant, who was often very thirsty.[242]

However, it was not until the nineteenth century that the exhibition of extremely lean persons acquired some popularity. In that period they were part of a motley crew of attractions at fairs (later circuses and amusement parks). As forms of spectacle in the category 'living natural wonders' they were exhibited amidst acrobats, illusionists, ventriloquists, fire-eaters, clowns, quacks and fortune-tellers. Apart from freaks of nature – giants, dwarfs, Siamese twins, extremely fat people, women with two faces, men with three hands, etc. – young and old came to gaze at emaciated people.

One of the most famous living skeletons in history was undoubtedly the Frenchman Claude Ambroise Seurat [229;251]. This *Homme Anatomique* was born in 1797 in Troyes in France. Initially, he was no different from his peers, but at a somewhat advanced age he progressively developed an ever more emaciated state. He was exhibited in many European countries. In 1825 he visited several towns in Great Britain and was even presented to the royal family. A contemporary, who attended his exhibition, described him as follows:

On his entrance to the room, his bent posture and fleshless arms and legs, sunken eyes and skeletel face, etc. gave spectators the impression that he had just returned from a long sickbed or rather, that place from where no-one returns.[221]

When Seurat spoke or sang, his heart-beat could be clearly seen and, according to some physicians, in darkness his belly was even translucent when a candle was put behind his back! Allegedly weighing only 72 pounds and 5 ft 7 inches tall, he was none the less a healthy person.

An examination of Seurat's skull by Dr Wood, apparently a phrenologist, revealed that various organs were fully developed and functioning. In a positive sense particularly 'the organ of sexual desire' and 'courage' distinguished themselves; there was no question of a lack of 'intellectual faculties'. Seurat ate seven or eight ounces of food a day, preferring nourishment which required the least effort from his masticatory muscles. His muscular strength had decreased to such an extent that he had to feed himself by bringing his head to his plate. His stepmother had to help him to drink. He sipped water-diluted wine and porter: one big draught might possibly have suffocated him. During the exhibition of 'this inconceivable, indescribable, incomparable creature', he only wore a loin-cloth, which was taken away at the request of the public. Questions from the audience were answered without any reservation and in a lively way. When people's curiosity had been satisfied and the shock of the first confrontation overcome, many were struck with pity 'for this poor creature is almost completely excluded from all enjoyments of life, and doomed to a condition of living death'.[221]

Five years later Seurat was on view in Amsterdam. Upon payment, varying from 15 cents for the cheapest to 50 cents for the most expensive seats, he was shown in a booth from 10 am until 11 pm. To arouse curiosity instead of aversion, an advertisement announced: 'His skeleton is completely devoid of all flesh, notwithstanding nothing horrible, one may fearlessly look at his person, even the ladies.' A visitor endorsed this canvassing text: 'I had imagined a monster, but I found him white and his face has nothing terrifying; on the contrary, his colour is flushing and he speaks in the presence of spectators.' In 1833 at the age of

35 his curious life came to an end. Autopsy revealed a tape-worm of 16 feet . . . [246]

Meanwhile in America the living skeleton Calvin Edson created a furore. He weighed only 60 pounds, which he attributed, according to an old handbill, to his having slept on the damp ground the night after the battle of Plattsburgh in 1812. Seurat and Edson were widely imitated.[233] By the second half of the nineteenth century the American Isaac Sprague, often referred to as the 'The Original Thin Man', attracted attention. This ex-shoemaker and grocer was born in 1841 and at about the age of 12 began to lose weight at an alarming rate due to an unknown cause. Eventually he weighed only 52 pounds. Later on, being part of P.T. Barnum's famous amusement enterprise, like many of his colleagues he was invited by numerous physicians for further examination. The diagnosis that Sprague suffered from 'excessive progressive muscular atrophy' was unanimously confirmed. This did not prevent him from devouring an amount of food enough to feed a giant, as a stupefied contemporary observed.

Another famous living skeleton of American origin was James W. Coffey, who for years travelled with many circuses around America and Europe. Because of his elegant appearance – morning coat, wing collar, bow tie and high hat – Coffey was billed as 'The Skeleton Dude'. He had a good appetite and must have been perfectly healthy.[233] In contrast to the exhibited heavy-weights, most thin people put on view were male. One of the few female living skeletons was the American Emma Schiller from a small town in Lousiana. A booklet, published in 1890 and sold to line the artist's purse, describes her amazing life.[223] After a healthy youth at the age of 20 she weighed 133 pounds. Shortly thereafter extreme wasting set in until her attested weight was 48 pounds (height 5 ft 5 inches). Numerous and even prominent physicians examined her, but their treatments were of no avail. The 'wonderful little woman' decided to study medicine, consulted a number of recognized works and decided to pursue a course of strict dieting. However, despite the farinaceous food she took, she was growing worse all the time. At present, the booklet relates, 'Miss Schiller feels that this disease called atrophy is now being controlled by a will power.' Nevertheless, as a devout Christian young woman she still has hope that in a short time the wasting of her body will entirely cease and that in time she may, by the mercy of God, gradually regain her lost form, so that in the future she may present herself to the public as 'the fleshy old lady'.

Yet she fulfilled an engagement at the Doris' Museum in New York, where thousands were gazing upon 'the greatest of all living skeletons'.

In Europe several extremely thin persons followed in the footsteps of Seurat and Edson. At a mid-nineteenth-century fair in Amsterdam 'the winged man or living skeleton' Pierre Joseph Lefebvre was on view together with an extremely fat Dutch girl.[246] In 1873 *The Lancet* published the report of a medical examination of Robert T., the 32-year-old 'Skeleton Man', who 'travelling the country with an itinerant showman, is exhibited to the vulgar gaze at twopence a head'.[258] Another example, which illustrates the usually tragic life of this kind of artists, is the Frenchman Dominique Castagna, nicknamed the 'mummy-man'. As early as the age of two his extraordinary thinness had become manifest and ten years later his growth had arrested. As an adult he was 6 feet tall and weighed 46 pounds. In addition to his tiny bodily proportion, he was handicapped by an ugly, bird-like face. In 1896 Castagna was exhibited on payment in Marseille for the first time. However, he was very unhappy with his repulsive appearance and when his friend and manager let him down, he committed suicide in a Belgian hotel in 1905.[233;260]

Although the number of living skeletons had markedly decreased at the beginning of this century, some of them still continued to be exhibited. Apart from the American Harry Lewis with the illustrious nickname 'Shadow Harry', in the 1920s the living skeleton Pete Robinson was a commercial success at New York's Coney Island. This man, weighing 58 pounds, was married to the fat lady Bunny Smith, officially weighing 467 pounds. Such marriages between skinny men and fat ladies were frequent. Although many of these marriages were arranged for business reasons, the contrary was the case with Mr and Mrs Robinson. Yet apart from fond love they were tied by commercial interests: the couple did a dancing act that was a great hit for many seasons. In 1932 Pete, together with a number of other 'natural wonders', appeared in the American movie *Freaks* by Tod Browning.[233;260]

This is not to suggest that the living skeletons benefited from this young medium and found therein a new stage. By contrast, from the turn of the century on, 'freak shows' lost out increasingly to the emerging film industry: the show spectacle moved more and more away from fairs and circuses to the cinema. In Europe rising National Socialism, abhorring these *Untermenschen*, was another serious threat. In the 1930s public exhibition in Germany was prohibited without a medical attestation of mental and physical health. After World War II a few living skeletons, who had survived the horrors of the war, still tried to revive some of their past glory. One of them was the American Glenn Pulley, who earned his bread at the Ringling Circus at the beginning of the 1950s.[260] However, he belonged to the last representatives of a meanwhile forgotten group of artists, who tried to live from their wasted bodies.

Fasting for a living

Although the art of fasting enjoyed great popularity particularly at the end of the previous century, there are indications from earlier periods that people earned their bread through fasting on stage. At the end of the sixteenth century several sources report a case of 'prodigious abstinence' near Cologne: this 14-year-old *Puella Coloniensis*, Veitken Johans, was said to have abstained from food for three years. An English pamphlet from 1597 points out that she is 'of a very good complection, and to all mens seeming of perfit health.' It is supposed that 'God inwardly nourisheth her withall.'[148] According to the prominent German surgeon Fabricius Hildanus (whom we have already mentioned in the discussion of the fasting girl Eva Vliegen), her loathing of food was so intense, that she fainted after someone secretly put some sugar in her mouth.[235] In Hildanus' view the most astonishing was that Veitken 'walked, jumped and played as if she had not been deprived from anything'. So far this case does not differ from the miraculous maidens we have described in Chapter 4. However, an important element of the story of Hildanus' statement is that 'she had been on view in the Inn of the "White Horse"'. There she would have been gazed at by many with astonishment, after which she travelled elsewhere and the surgeon lost her from sight. Considering that it was not uncommon for touring artists (among whom also 'living natural wonders') to have themselves on view in inns, it is conceivable that the *Puella Coloniensis* was one of the first to exploit her food abstinence in a place of public resort.

Should this case be unconvincing, a woman who undoubtedly exhibited her food abstinence on stage, was Maria van Dijk, from the small Dutch village of Vleuten near Utrecht. An unknown Dutch physician Pieter Nielen, discussing her case in his book on protracted food abstinence, pointed out that Maria was widely known in Holland.[255] The prolonged fasting, from which she derived her reputation, dated back to the year 1767 when she was 47 years old. In that year her sister died and since then she had almost totally abstained from food, a fact her family attributed to 'a curse'. Apart from the intake of tea, sugar, sugar-plums and gin, she could bear the Holy Communion without any problem just like so many fasting saints in earlier days. She had twice been closely watched, though deceit was not discovered. Nevertheless, after her death in 1774 autopsy revealed 'excrements and especially of the plum-stones'.

This result gave Nielen no cause to qualify Maria posthumously as an impostor. For she had several times been carefully watched, and additionally a motive for cheating was lacking:

> for she did not try in this way to benefit herself by receiving any gain from it; she had not been on view for payment, apart from the last year of her life, and as far as I am aware, only at the fairs of Utrecht and Amsterdam.

Perhaps she expected to die soon and wanted to do a good stroke of business, for in the same year she was exhibited at an inn near Amsterdam. In the *Amsterdamsche Courant* of 23 August 1774 the following advertisement is to be found:

> At Matthys Dennewalt, Innkeeper in Nieuw Roosendaal at the Houtwaalder Weg, outside of the Muiderpoort, has arrived a Woman, named Maria van Dyk, Wife of Jan de Groot, of Vleuten, who since the year 1767 completely lost the Appetite, and presently takes nothing but some Tea with Sugar:-.

Here the advertisement abruptly breaks off. A contemporary,

assuming that Maria was there on view for payment, adds the following:

> The mentioned Innkeeper invites all curious devotees to order to him at their own costs somany Bottles of Wine, Breakfasts, Suppers, Meals, separate Rooms and Apartments as they like, to see this Woman, to talk to her, to interrogate her, or investigate everything about her, what people considered to be able and to have to know on account of her condition.[188]

Thus the exhibition of prolonged abstainers was not exclusively confined to the late nineteenth century, though it did not, just like that of living skeletons, assume enormous proportions before that period. The heyday of the art of fasting was undoubtedly the last two decades of the nineteenth century. The American physician Henry S. Tanner was the instigator of this unprecedented prosperity.[240;578] In 1880 he came upon the notorious affair of Mollie Fancher, the above-mentioned 'Brooklyn Enigma'. This woman was alleged to fast for years and to have supernatural powers. When the renowned physician William Hammond publicly proposed to investigate these wonderful phenomena, she refused to cooperate 'for decency's sake'. Tanner offered himself as a chivalrous substitute, 'to show the power of the human will, and to prove to materialists that there is something beside oxygen, hydrogen, and carbon in the brain'. He believed that during a long fast he could by force of will 'absorb atmospheric oxygen and electricity'.

In 1848, at the age of 17, Tanner had emigrated from England to the United States. After his graduation in medicine, he and his wife practised as physicians and ran electrothermal baths in Ohio. Tanner believed that people ate too much and that food abstinence was the solution to a number of illnesses. Fully convinced that one's character is modified by what one eats, he took up the habit of week-long fasts. Having become a temperance lecturer and proprietor of a Turkish bath, he undertook a successful forty-day fast under the watchful eyes of two doctors. As Mollie Fancher refused an examination, Tanner wanted to show his art of fasting in New York. However, he was unable to make an agreement with Dr Hammond on the terms for the supervision. Presumably opposition on the part of the medical establishment against Tanner's experiment was too strong. His homeopathic views and his ideas about fasting as a therapeutic method aroused suspicion among regular physicians. Furthermore, if against expectation his fast was unexpectedly successful, this might be used against them.

Without the auspices of some acknowledged scientific institute, the 50-year-old Henry Tanner undertook a fast for forty days in the Clarendon Hall in New York City in 1880. He had assured himself of the constant supervision of a few 'irregular' physicians, who would take his pulse and his temperature, but were particularly determined to procure the experiment at least some credibility. After eleven days regular physicians deigned to observe him, as did hundreds of visitors who now had to pay 25 cents admission to see the haggard Tanner. As the 'Starvation Comedy' – so called by a New York newspaper – went on, Tanner's popularity increased. Each day he received an enormous amount of mail, women serenaded him at the piano and newspapers reported daily on his condition. He even received an offer from a museum to stuff him if he should die.

Apart from a letter from Mollie Fancher, whose contents he would not reveal, he also received a note from Dr Hammond. In an earlier stage of the experiment the latter had expressed his doubts about Tanner's 'unbalanced mind'. This time Hammond granted the integrity of the fast and asked Tanner to stop at once, a request he did not comply with. During the final week at least six thousand people paid to stare at his tired, wasted body, which had lost 35 pounds in the last weeks and weighed only 121 pounds. On 7 August, 1880 – the fortieth day – Tanner broke his fast, though the show had not yet come to an end. In a crowded hall, to the astonishment of the spectators, he ate a quarter of a peach, drank a glass of rice milk and then devoured a Georgia watermelon. Astonishment mounted to the highest pitch, when Tanner additionally consumed half a pound of broiled beefsteak and half a pound of sirloin by supper time.

His experiment not only aroused admiration and astonishment; the medical establishment regarded the performance with complete incredulity. Medical journals qualified it as 'absurd', 'a fool-hardy experiment' and 'humbug'. When it appeared afterwards that Tanner had earned no less than $137.640 his experiment was equated with a show in P.T. Barnum's amusement enterprise. Apart from Tanner's integrity, physicians also doubted the scientific value of his fast. This criticism was concisely put into words by *The Medical Record*:

> One set of his watchers was confessedly in sympathy with him, and wished strongly for his success. The regular physicians were not continuous in their attendance at first, and he was not always under their eye. Dr. Tanner was taken out to drive, went to the photographer's and the barber's, and took occasional strolls about the neigboring square. Finally, his physical condition was considerably different from that which all past experience has shown to follow abstinence from food (. . .) If to this is added the manner in which the experiment was conducted – a manner which had the mixed character of a variety show and a patent-hammock advertisement – we feel sure that the profession will agree that little practical or scientific value can be given to the alleged fast.

The medical journal recommends Tanner to 'return to the simpler joys of his electrical baths and normal diet'.[222]

This sharp criticism did not in any way restrain the aroused interest in fasting as a spectacle. *The Medical Record* was aware of this: 'The widely advertised announcement of the fact that a person had comfortably passed many days without food will lead many other persons to try the same thing, to a greater or lesser extent.'[222] This supposition appeared to be of great predictive value!

Heyday and decline of the art of fasting

Tanner would gradually be forgotten and at the end of the nineteenth century he was even assumed to be dead, whereas he had yet another twenty years to live. Nevertheless, he appears to have been a real trendsetter with his experiment or as *The Lancet* commented: 'one fool begets many imitators'. Only three weeks after Tanner's performance, newspapers reported one Signor Goldschmidt from Naples, betting that he would fast not forty but fifty days. His compatriot Alberto Montazzo even proposed to go without food for six months! Other examples are the Americans John Griscom and John Roth, and the Sicilian painter Stefano Merlatti.[28;230] They all sought publicity with their fasting and tried to exploit the commercial possibilities, created by the fascination of the crowd for long fasts. For in this way fame and fortune seemed to be easily obtainable. However, the practice was notably different.

Like Tanner, potential hunger artists had to accept persistent insinuations about deceit: many expressed doubts about their intellectual faculties or bluntly qualified them as impostors. Moreover, prolonged fasting was hazardous. Those who wanted to be famous hunger artists had to come up to at least the length of Tanner's achievement. Although these record-hunters were permitted (just like Tanner) to drink some water, several of them had to pay for their hunger exploits with their lives. To the sensation-seeking public this macabre side of the fasting art only increased its power of attraction. One part of the medical profession overcame its resistance and seized the opportunity to study the consequences of starvation accurately. Experiments with animals had provided some knowledge in this respect, but comparable data on human beings were scarce (see Chapter 6). For this reason several fasting men were subjected to an extended watch, daily recording not only weight and size of parts of the body, but also breathing, blood and excrement. For its scientific value, but also because many physicians had their doubts about the length of the fasts, they wanted to be sure that the hunger artist did not commit any form of deceit. The American physiologist Francis G. Benedict, for instance, studying the Italian hunger artist Agostino Levanzin, devised a foolproof chamber to prevent cheating.[272]

These severe precautionary measures did not appear to be superfluous. The famous Norwegian fasting man Francisco Cetti had been considered to be honest and authentic after a watch for eleven days in Berlin in 1887 under the supervision of the renowned professor in pathology Rudolf Virchow (1821–1902).[261] Some months later, he owned up in an English watch, where he was subjected to a thirty-day experiment in London's Royal Aquarium. After ten days physicians were surprised at Cetti's increase in weight. Upon closer examination, he appeared to possess foodstuff. Of course with the exception of these cases, fasting men mostly benefited from these medical experiments. When the conditions were severe enough and reputed medical men were involved, it was good publicity for the fasting man and raised his market value considerably. That is why hunger artists very willingly cooperated with these experiments. The more so as there was a 'murderous' competition between the fasting men by the end of the nineteenth century. In some cases the fasting was part of another rather odd behaviour: in 1895, for example, one Schlatter climbed the mountain of the Holy Cross in Colorado and coming down unkempt, unshaven and worn in body, declared that he had spent forty days in fasting up on the mountain so that he was ready now to heal mankind. From all parts of the country people flocked to be touched and healed![267]

Although a minority, some female hunger artists were also in the limelight, especially in the United States. Some of these nineteenth-century cases may also be seen as late examples of miraculous maidens,[7] like for instance the 'Fort Plain Fasting Girl' Kate Smulsey in 1884, who raised a lot of publicity and controversy: was it an illness, a miracle, a stunt or simple fraud? The fasting of Josephine Marie Bedard and Helen Coppague, respectively in Boston (1888) and New York (1897), was clearly lucrative. Marie Davenport in 1904, on the other hand, was considered to be a 'scientific' demonstration that females too could fast for the Testamentary length of forty days. Most clearly showing the 'exhibitionistic' character of hunger artists is Clare de Serval, known as the 'Apostle of Hunger', who around 1910 often fasted in an hermetically sealed glass box for forty days and always regretted having to eat again in the end.[578]

The most famous hunger artist was Giovanni Succi from the Italian Cesenatico. From 1886 on, he had been on view with his fasting performances in almost all the big cities of the Western world.[250] In the first year of his career, after a fortnight's fast in Forli, he showed his art of fasting two months later in Milan and again two months later in Paris, each time for thirty days. In 1890 he declared to have accomplished no fewer than thirty-two fasting performances, varying from twenty to thirty days. Succi was a colourful personality. During his wanderings as a young man in Africa he discovered that he felt better than ever after a few days of food abstinence on account of a disease. He considered this to be a great discovery and supposed himself to be possessed by a spirit, which enabled him to preserve his strength. When people in Europe ignored his ideas, he returned to Africa where he publicly gave himself up to prolonged fasting, often while taking a poisoned draught. Once returned to Europe he was admitted several times into an asylum because of delusions: people abstaining from food and drinking poison inevitably had to die but the fact that he survived should be attributed in his opinion to a spirit. Physicians, however, supposed that his brain was seriously affected by his fasts and vainly trusted that Succi's fate acted as a warning to those who would follow in his footsteps. In June 1886, a month after his second stay in an asylum, Succi started a fortnight's fast under the surveillance of a committee consisting of farmers. A notarial act, signed by several witnesses, had to substantiate the performance. Local newspapers reported that his secret was a mysterious potion he had taken before the hunger exploit. Although Succi, with his psychiatric history, ran the risk of being taken for a madman, a series of performances followed which made him into a celebrity.

Succi was well aware of the commercial importance of hunger exploits being acknowledged by prestigious researchers or institutes. So on his own initiative he was able to arrange scientific investigations in famous institutes which provided the result he desired. Yet in the 1890s it was discovered during a hunger experiment in Vienna that he had taken food with the aid of a member of the research committee.[239] This serious finding did not, however, herald the end of his career. People were just more on the alert during later exploits. One day in the big arena of Verona he had been immured in a small house without windows, while for a hunger stunt in a pub in Florence he was locked up in a cell. Even in 1924, being 71 years old, he still made an attempt to break contemporary fasting records!

Succi's fame, however, dates back to the last two decades of the previous century, precisely the period in which the art of fasting enjoyed great popularity. Afterwards not only Succi's fame, but the art of fasting in general, waned. In the 1920s it passed through a short final heyday. The fasting man Wolly, for instance, created a furore in cities like Geneva and Paris. In the French metropolis, he continuously fasted for twenty-eight days and three hours, until he smashed his glass room into pieces in anger over laughing spectators.[248] Hunger artists must have been particularly popular in the German capital Berlin. In the year 1926, for instance, six hunger artists were performing simultaneously. The peculiar entourage of those performances has been described as follows:

The attraction of the restaurant Zum Goldenen Hahn is the hunger artist, who in the middle of the hall under a sort of glass bell can be gazed at by visitors; a kind of human skeleton in dress-jacket, smoking cigarettes, with a glass of water in front of him on a little marble table. His achievements are announced on a blackboard: the hunger artist had not eaten for 28 days. Around him corpulent gentlemen and fashionably dressed ladies are consuming Wiener Schnitzel with fried potatoes. They are discussing whether the hunger record will be broken this time.[228]

The entourage may have remained unchanged since Tanner's experiment, so had the rigorous character of the art of fasting. Overestimation of their own capabilities or underestimation of the rigorous character of fasting exploits still made great demands on the hunger artists: several record-hunters had to pay for the art of fasting with their lives. Some succeeded in escaping from this sad destiny by prematurely deciding to terminate the exhibition and put up with the scornful laughter.[248] The fasting man Harry Leut from Dresden wanted to save himself the humiliation and decided after thirty-one days of fasting to leave at night on the sly. According to an age-old tradition some fasting men brought all their inventiveness into play to secretly obtain some food. As in the case of miraculous maidens, deceit by a hunger artist would sometimes lead to judicial prosecution. In 1926 Siegfried Herz, alias Jolly, overreached himself. In the Berlin pub Das Krokodil, he had himself locked up in a sealed glass case to fast for forty-four days. At the end the net profit amounted to 130,000 marks from no fewer than 350,000 spectators. After three months he was arrested. His agent had lodged a complaint against him after a quarrel and declared that Jolly had received ten pounds of chocolate during his fasting performance through the wires of his radio. Jolly was initially sentenced to a fine of 1000 marks, but he was acquitted on appeal. A fasting record combined with chocolate was no deceit, the more so as nobody had felt themselves deceived and the spectators had enjoyed themselves, according to the peculiar sentence of the court. Not everyone got off so lightly. In the same year, 1926, the police removed the hunger artist Reinhold Ilmer, nicknamed Harry Nelson, during his forty-five-day fast in Leipzig from his glass case, because he had surreptitiously received food. After a summons 20 out of 60,000 spectators felt themselves deceived; he was sentenced to two and a half months' imprisonment.[248]

The 1920s are the last period in which the art of fasting regained at least something of its lost glory. This was just about the end of this rather bizarre form of entertainment. The phenomenon would recur sporadically until the 1950s. One of the most persevering was Willy Schmitz, whose sobriquet was, significantly enough, Heros. An English handbill, published in 1952, advertised this German hunger artist as follows:

> Come and see the Starvation Artist Heros; World's Champion in 1950 at the Frankfurt Zoo with 56 days of starvation; he will establish a new World Championship, 75 days without taking any food in a sealed glass box; medical care, controlled by the Red Cross Frankfurt-Main; during his time of starvation Heros will have only cigarettes and Hassia Mineral Water . . .

In the following years he even made several attempts to improve his record and it was rumoured that in 1956 he continuously fasted for ninety-three days.[262] But his achievements no longer obtained the response accorded hunger artists at the turn of the century. The heyday of the hunger art was over for good.

The art of fasting in literature

The heyday and decline of the art of fasting, which we outlined above, was described impressively by Franz Kafka. Before detailing his description, we will look at another literary description of this peculiar phenomenon by an almost unknown Dutch author.

In 1927 official and writer J. van Oudshoorn (pseudonym for Jan Koos Feijlbrief; 1876–1951) published the short story *Laatste Dagen* (Final days).[265] Herein he describes among other things a visit of the principal character De Waal to a hunger artist called Arthur. The latter made an effort to fast for forty-four days and had been on view for payment in a glass box in a restaurant. At the entrance to the restaurant a large calendar recorded the number of days he had fasted and his condition. Apparently Arthur was plagued by a headache, stomach ache, sleeplessness, nervous attacks and an eye infection.

Having paid 'the hunger premium', De Waal saw the hunger artist in blue silk, worn out pyjamas lying on a bed and surrounded by a radio-loudspeaker, eau-de-Cologne, reading matter and a large number of cigarettes and bottles of Seltzer water. In one of the corners behind a green curtain a provisional lavatory had been installed to remove the digested Seltzer water discretely. With his swollen, wax-white and stubbly face the hunger artist tried to preserve a certain distinguished loftiness, but his fixed facial expression only betrayed 'unbearable torture'. Confused by the sharp contrast between the 'greedy-smacking eaters' and the solitary torture of the fasting man, De Waal left the restaurant and mused:

> But even (. . .) if the Seltzer water had been sweetened, the cigarettes are full of morphine, in short, if the whole case appears to be a humbug, are the 23 days on this bed in the show-case by themselves not enough torture? Three weeks of whispering with death and insanity in the presence of a cheerful fed-on citizenry.

In just a few pages Van Oudshoorn succeeds in providing a detailed and accurate sketch of the fasting performances; it must have been like that in those days. In all likelihood his realistic description is based on an eye-witness account, for Van Oudshoorn had sufficient occasion to observe this peculiar form of entertainment. He had been a diplomat of the Dutch embassy in Berlin from 1905 to 1932, where he finished his short story in 1926. As we noted above, Berlin had been the centre for hunger artists: in the year when he wrote his *Laatste Dagen*, six of them at the same time were on view in the German capital.[231]

A famous, more elaborate and profound description of the art of fasting was provided by Franz Kafka (1883–1924) in his short story from 1922, entitled *A Fasting-Artist*.[244] In the first part of this story the narrator looks back in nostalgia to the heyday of the hunger artists. Every day people came to see the fasting-artist, 'a pale figure in his black leotard, ribs grotesquely protruding'. He sat in a cage of straw and sometimes even stretched his arms through the bars to have spectators feel how skinny he was. Now and then he took a draught of water to moisten his lips. He was guarded – usually by three butchers – in order to prevent him from eating on the sly. However, according to the narrator, this was a pure formality, introduced to reassure the masses, for the initiates knew well enough that the fasting-artist during the period of his fast would never, under no circumstances, not even under compulsion, have eaten the smallest morsel; the honour of his art forbade it.

Instead of watchmen who were very lax about the watch they kept, the hunger artist preferred guards who sat close up against the bars and kept him in the beams of the electric torches. For him, to fast was the easiest thing he could do and so he said, but no one properly appreciated his achievements. His words were interpreted as modesty, publicity-seeking or fraud.

To his regret, he was never permitted by his impresario, for business reasons, to fast any longer than forty days. Experience had shown that the public's interest could be spurred on for about that period of time and this when he, the champion performer, knew that his capacity to fast was boundless. The forty-day hunger shows were always ended with gala performances. Amidst an excited crowd and to the accompaniment of a military band, firstly two physicians entered the flower-bedecked cage. They carried out the necessary examinations and announced the results through a megaphone to the public. Then two young ladies escorted the exhausted performer to a small table where carefully chosen foods were laid. Supported by both women, who could hardly suppress their disgust for that little bundle of bones, his impresario poured some food in his mouth. After that a toast was proposed to the public, the festivities were concluded by a great fanfare of the band. No one, except the fasting-artist, had any cause to feel dissatisfied with the show.

However, in recent decades, public interest in exhibition fasting had suffered a marked decline and had been abandoned for other spectacles. For one last time his impresario went chasing round through half Europe with him, but everywhere they merely encountered disgust towards public fasting. Being too old and above all too fanatically dedicated to his fasting for a change of job, the heroic faster had to accept a position with the side show of a great circus. People passed his cage in the circus tent only because it was next to the menagerie. His new employers were not interested in the unbelievably high number of fasting days; they even stopped recording them: 'no one, not even the fasting-artist himself, knew how great his achievement was and his heart grew heavy'. Finally, nobody knew why this perfectly good cage with the rotten straw inside was unoccupied.

At last, they poked around in the straw, whereafter the hunger artist asked the overseer forgiveness for his fast. It was nothing to be proud of:

> 'Because I have to fast, I can't help it', said the fasting-artist. (. . .) 'Because I could never find the nourishment I liked. Had I found it, believe me, I would never have caused any stir, and would have eaten my fill just like you and everyone else'. Those were his last words, but in his failing eyes there still remained the firm, if no longer proud conviction that he was fasting on.

Then they buried the hunger artist along with his straw and into the cage they put a young panther, which lacked for nothing and was brought the food that he liked. The story ends with a lyrical description of the new attraction:

> He seemed not even to miss his freedom; that noble body, furnished almost to bursting point with all that it needed, seemed to carry freedom itself around with it too; somewhere in his jaws it seemed to be hidden; and the joy of life glowed so fiercely from the furnace of his throat that the onlookers could scarcely stand up against it. But they mastered their weakness, surrounded the cage, and simply refused to be dragged away.[244]

Kafka's short story has given rise to many interpretations, from sociocultural to psychoanalytic (we will address these reflections, and also the question whether Kafka was an anorexic in Chapter 11). We would do no justice to the richness of Kafka's narrative, if we merely focused on its deeper meaning. Taking the text in its literal sense, a striking and almost historically reliable account of the art of fasting remains. Only the way in which the fasting-artist languishes in the circus appears grotesque. Here, a prominent characteristic of Kafka's work, through which he often succeeds in evoking a mysterious, estranged effect, manifests itself: realism pushed to the extremes, quasi-absurd.[263]

However, the major part of *A Fasting-Artist* is no grotesque distortion of reality at all. The great public attention for the hunger artist, the continuous watches, the role of the impresario and the publicity, the contact with the public, the festivities at the end of the performance, are all elements whose description undoubtedly betrays thorough knowledge. The waning popularity of the art of fasting in favour of other attractions fits with the facts, although at the time when Kafka put his narrative on paper the phenomenon was passing through a renewed heyday, its apogee had been in the late nineteenth century. Only someone who had investigated the matter thoroughly would have been able to provide such an accurate description. Indeed, Kafka was greatly interested in the world of variety. This is not only apparent from numerous passages in his diaries and the choice of certain characters in his narratives (for instance the trapeze-artist in *Erstes Leid*), but also from the fact that he has read at least one specialist journal on the subject.[245] Considering his interest he had probably not missed news reports on the art of fasting. In June 1916 a news item on a fasting-artist was published in the *Prager Tagblatt*, a newspaper in Prague which Kafka read regularly. Curiously enough the hunger artist concerned had been engaged with a circus under circumstances comparable to the fictitious person in his narrative.[226] Kafka may have derived from such publications – and possibly from his own observations – the details of the history and rituals of the art of fasting.

However, *A Fasting-Artist* moves far beyond a matter-of-fact description of the fasting art. As a more than experienced analyst Kafka sketches the hunger artist's motives and inner life. He is depicted as someone who eventually arrived at the tragic insight that his life was built on illusion – a *vie manquée*. The fasts he was attached to and which had been the pride and meaning of his existence, retrospectively appeared to be worthless. His fame was the result of an innate deficiency, for he was unable to eat the food that others liked. The crowds came to admire a hero with an iron will, who was able to accomplish what seemed impossible: conquering man's grimmest enemy, hunger. But in fact people did not gaze at a hero nor an artist, but a sick freak, an incomplete human being. This could hardly be called a merit. Spectators and watchers intuitively felt that something was wrong with the fasting-artist. For this reason he was treated with suspicion, but there was no question of their expecting deceit. The real deception of the hunger artist was totally different in character. He did not deceive the audience by eating on the sly, but by keeping up against his will the myth that only with great pain and difficulty was he curbing his appetite. His actual deceit consisted in 'giving his want out as virtue, his natural urge as achievement'.[241] The fasting-artist was quite aware of this and it gnawed at him, though he was only partially to blame. For he did not conceal the fact that fasting was easy for him. Efforts to reveal this to the public encountered disbelief or were prohibited by his impresario for business reasons.

As will be argued in Chapter 11, Kafka expressed in his narrative a major part of his own art of fasting. Although we guard against uncomplicated 'psychiatrization', his life and work do contain sufficient elements to substantiate the supposition of an anorexic problem. Against the background of Kafka's own life, his choice of a hunger artist as the leading character in his narrative need not surprise us. This character gave him the full opportunity to interweave brilliantly his own anorexic problems in his narrative. He was able to identify with the fasting-artist better than anyone.[254] His striking and gripping description provides the best evidence for this. Kafka drew the art of fasting and anorexia nervosa more closely together: he himself was the connecting link. In our chronicle of self-starvation Kafka stands at the crossing between the decline of the nineteenth-century art of fasting and the twentieth-century emergence of anorexia nervosa. That he ultimately died of pulmonary consumption – that typically nineteenth-century affliction – colours his life with the flavour of a historical tragedy which turns real people into myths.

6

Food Abstinence: Medical Mystery and Therapy

So far we have thrown light upon prolonged fasting from two sides: as a religious phenomenon and as a form of entertainment. This journey among fasting saints, miraculous maidens, living skeletons and hunger artists has made it clear that the currently obvious connection between food abstinence and illness is a time-bound phenomenon. From the early modern period on the medical profession gave the initial impetus to this connection, but only at the beginning of this century – with the decline of fasting as a spectacle – was the process of medicalization almost completely accomplished. However, whereas prolonged fasting was disconnected from the supernatural, food abstinence was applied traditionally by physicians as therapy: diets belong to the oldest medical remedies. In this chapter we will elaborate the specific histories of both facets in medicine.

A miracle of God

The sixteenth century heralded the period of the Scientific Revolution, which by means of the experimental method laid the foundation for an enormous growth of scientific knowledge. Although from that period on an undeniably growing number of physicians relied on the tangible, visible and verifiable, this view was not widely shared from the outset. Not every scientist rejected the old theories about the influence of supernatural powers on earthly existence. In spite of the Scientific Revolution, for a substantial period of time religiously inspired metaphysical presumptions were put forward beside empirical observations and the pursuit of reliable knowledge. That there was no yawning abyss between religion and science is also apparent from the medical treatises of those days.

Like many of their contemporaries, physicians were fascinated by the extreme length of some fasts. Most intriguing for them was the question as to how long a human being could live without food.[271] The sources consulted in the early modern period to answer this question did not offer any definite solution. Scholars, of course, turned to the authorities of the Classics. In the Hippocratic writings the sober conclusion was to be found that a human being cannot live without food any longer than seven days. According to Hippocrates (460–377BC) – later endorsed by Galen (AD129–200) – food abstinence was endured best by the aged but least by adolescents and children.[334;343] These observations were not only contradicted by other Classical sources, but every pious Christian was familiar with the forty-day fasts of Moses, Eliah and Jesus as well as with the extreme ascetic fasting of so many saints.

Available information on fasting girls, reports on the vicissitudes of shipwrecked sailors or trapped miners, observations of patients who were unable to eat because of laryngitis, etc. did not provide a reliable conclusion. Several physicians observed that (particularly young) women were able to endure 'prodigious' fasting for months or even years.[192;383] On the other hand, everyday experience taught that ordinary mortals under comparable conditions only survived for a few weeks at most. In the early modern period efforts were made to investigate prolonged fasts through experimentation.[247] This is exemplified by the Italian physician, natural scientist and poet Francesco Redi (1626–97), who subjected several species of animals to extended fasts.[286] But these experiments did not provide definite answers to the baffling question. Apart from the fact that some species of animals were able to live without food for substantial periods of time, the phenomenon of animals hibernating for months caused still more confusion. People had to be content with these ambiguous results until well into the nineteenth century, when the Genevan experimental physiologist Charles Chossat (1796–1875) became famous because of his experiments with starving animals.[278] The contradictory views on extended fasts made a German physician remark in 1844:

> The variety of opinions, however, is to be explained easily, for where do the sources of clean and reliable natural observations flow more scarcely than here? Undoubtedly, thousands in dungeons,

languishing and pining away, under circumstances where suffocation could not kill them, died of starvation, but who has observed them?[277]

More insight into the processes of starvation in human beings was only acquired from the late nineteenth century onwards. In this period hunger artists, from well-understood self-interest, willingly made their art available to scientists, thus enabling them to investigate starving people under controlled conditions (see Chapter 5). In our century this kind of research has been replaced by starvation experiments with volunteers.[272;289] Such research and data from people in situations of compulsory starvation (famines, concentration camps) have provided a wealth of data.[293] Due to the lack of empirical facts from preceding centuries, however, the belief in extended fasts and their metaphysical explanation was not easily rejected. At the beginning of the early modern period several physicians pointed out that the phenomenon had to be explained by referring to God Almighty. In medical literature the term *inedia prodigiosa* or 'prodigious abstinence' was introduced. The opinion on this phenomenon by many a physician from the sixteenth and seventeenth centuries is exemplified by the Swiss physician Jacob Zwinger (whom we have already mentioned in Chapter 4).

In his treatise from 1611 Zwinger first addresses the authenticity of prolonged fasts.[235] Besides the often quoted examples from the Bible and from Classic sources, Zwinger highlights the lives of fasting saints and miraculous maidens (like Margaretha Weiss from Roed) as well as descriptions of similar cases by a number of 'reliable writers'. On this basis he concludes that human beings 'against the irrefutable laws of Nature' were able to live without food and drink. Having established this, he comes to the kernel of his treatise: the causes of the phenomenon. Following Aristotle he defines hunger as 'a craving of Heat and Drought', which arises from emptiness of the stomach and from the sucking of veins, and is aimed at restoring the original humidity of the body. For in a condition of starvation this humidity has been consumed by the innate warmth of the body. Consumption of food is meant to satisfy one's hunger, to take away the discomfort which attends being hungry, 'to restore the wasted parts of the Body, and to preserve, as long as possible,

Body and Life.' In order that humidity and innate warmth are not harmed, as soon as hunger manifests itself one should not postpone the intake of food. Otherwise death is a real danger. Endorsing Hippocrates' observation that someone who does not take food for seven days necessarily has to die, Zwinger is nevertheless of the opinion that human beings cannot live without food any longer than four or five days.

Zwinger distinguishes a category of prolonged fasters who break their health by fasting and vomit up the ingested food, and 'in this way disappoint the Hope and Prayers of their Friends'. He attributes this kind of prolonged food abstinence to the lack of causes which prompt us to eat, i.e. the stimulation of hunger influencing the human will. But this human will is able to defy hunger; if it does not even listen to nature, health is endangered and death will follow soon. Nevertheless, Zwinger deems it impossible

> to feel no Hunger at all, and yet feeling it, to endure any longer than some hours or days its stimulation without loosing Life; and thus that this Fasting of many Days, Months, Years, moves beyond the limitations of human Nature, and should be regarded a miracle, originating from Divine power.

Then Zwinger addresses some other hypotheses regarding prolonged fasting. If people are even able to become accustomed to the intake of poison, why not to prolonged fasting? According to the Swiss physician such a supposition contains 'more folly than depth'. For the best part of the human body is the original humidity that is exhausted by protracted fasting, through which the innate warmth is extinguished. Denying this fact is, in his view, as absurd as the opinion that a lamp might habitually burn without oil. Other popular hypotheses are also rejected by Zwinger: if an animal passes the winter without food and apparently 'the original humidity is not digested, how more likely is this to occur in man, who is beyond all animals the most excellent'. However, according to Zwinger this comparison between man and animal will not hold water. In contrast to the strong human warmth, animals are afflicted with a weak warmth, digesting thick and tough food only slowly. Besides, nature provided them with food they could hide in their entrails and consume in winter. This is why Zwinger concludes once again, that prolonged fasting does not fit the laws of nature and should be regarded as 'a Miracle of a Divine and Higher cause'.[235] For, if these fasts are natural, why should we consider Christ's fast in the desert as miraculous?

Miracle or natural phenomenon?

In the course of the seventeenth century, metaphysical explanations like Zwinger's were gradually substituted by more earthly, though not far less speculative theories. Zwinger implicated in his considerations natural causes for prolonged fasting, but ultimately conceived it to be a supernatural phenomenon. In the late seventeenth century the influence of the 'Long Finger of powerful Providence' with respect to extended fasting was still acknowledged. In the actual explanation, however, natural causes increasingly came to the fore. Exponents of this transitional period are John Reynolds and Cornelis Stalpart van der Wiel.

In 1669 John Reynolds, a Protestant master at the old grammar school of King's Norton, published *A Discourse upon Prodigious Abstinence* on account of the extended fast of Martha Taylor (see Chapter 4).[192] The subtitle of the treatise clearly states its major purpose: '*Proving that without any miracle, the texture of humane bodies may be so altered, that life may be long continued without the supplies of meat & drink.*' Just like Zwinger, Reynolds first addresses biblical examples and many cases of fasting for months or even years. He takes a nuanced position regarding these cases: 'as it is human fidelity to disbelieve all such reports, because some are false; so it is superstitious charity to believe all, because some are true.' He is careful not to discredit all biblical accounts of fasting. In sharp contrast to the Taylor case, these fasts had a purpose and did not break the health of the abstainer. Reynolds then addresses some possible explanations.

His first assault is directed against the 'miracle mongers' who believe the pretended fasters to be invisibly fed by angels:

> but is it incredible that such a favour should be shewn to persons of no known sanctity, as some of these were: moreover, either this food was visible, or invisible; if visible, it is strange that vigilant observers and jealous suspectors, could neither discover the ingress at

the fore-door, nor the excrementious egress at the back-door; but, if it were invisible, then altogether incongruous to our bodies, and therefore miraculous.

He neither considered it 'of easy credibility, that food should be supplied by demons possessing them', for there were 'no footsteps of such a possession' in the Taylor case and it would be strange 'if the devil should grow so modest as to content himself with a single trophy' (such as Martha Taylor). Rejecting the presumptions that the fasters may be dead or even under the influence of celestial bodies, he leaves all these speculations 'to their retirements, whilst we hunt the more perceptible prints of nature's progress in these anomalous productions'.

Finally, Reynolds thoroughly elaborates his empirical explanation of Martha's prolonged fast. He suggests that particular bodily elements, called 'ferments', independently enriched her supply of recirculating blood without the addition of new chyle produced by eating and digestion. In prolonged fasters the excretion was reduced and the body actually conserved elements already in the blood.[7] Strikingly, he links this particular process to adolescent female development:

> It will much strengthen our hypothesis to observe, that most of these damsels fall to this abstinence between the age of fourteen and twenty years, when the seed hath so fermented the blood, that various distempers will probably ensue, without due evacuations.[192]

A similar careful, rational approach characterizes a treatise by the Dutch physician Cornelis Stalpart van der Wiel, published seventeen years later.[301] In 1643 he had been appointed parish doctor in The Hague and, later in his life, he gained wide reputation because of his great knowledge of injection techniques and mummifying. Only in advanced years did he start to report on his clinical experiences; his collected works have been translated in Latin and French. In the second volume of his *Zeldzame Aanmerkingen* (Rare Observations), originally published in Dutch in 1686, an extensive chapter is devoted to 'very protracted abstinence from food and drink'. Elaborating an explanation of this phenomenon, the physician displays here his erudition and wide reading. He refers to scripture texts, the works of Hippocrates and Galen and numerous sixteenth- and seventeenth-century sources. His efforts were not in vain: for decades his account was referred to by many a scholar.

Stalpart explains his views on prolonged fasting on account of one Aaltje Kuyper, who supposedly fasted for some months. This girl was born in 1667 in the village of Helselaar, in the eastern part of Holland. At the age of 15 she was enlisted as a servant, but suffered shortly afterwards from fevers for seven weeks. She recovered but her appetite had been reduced, except for apples and turnips. After a month she did not move and abstained from food completely, so that everybody expected her to die soon. That she did not excrete was interpreted by Stalpart as evidence of the fact that she really neither ate nor drank. She suffered from stiffness, cold limbs, 'internal oppression', faintings and fits, which finally impeded her from opening her eyelids. She slept only in the evening and also occasionally one or two hours in the afternoon.

Despite the fact that Aaltje hardly took anything, she did not lose her interest in food at all. Stalpart portrays her peculiar behaviour as follows:

> Due to the frequent multitude of fits, her mind seemed to be affected, and though she could not eat, yet she asked for gingerbread, apples, raisins, figs and plums etc., paying attention that nothing was missing, the reason why she counted them repeatedly. After her Father had frequently requested to be allowed to bring his Daughter home again, she was transported eventually on April 13th of the year 1683, with all her supply of gingerbread, apples and so on, to Helselaar, one hour from Diepenheym; where, though being blind, she hit nails in the clay wall, and put thereon small ledges, where she set down her Wares, as she had done in Diepenheym. And this was (beside the consolation of God's Word and prayer) her major pleasure, that she was allowed to count and move these things: She was as sparing with her supply as before, which for that reason putrefied, or grew mouldy.

After a stay of four days in her father's house her eyelids opened again and she drank some wine for the first time without immediately vomiting. Ten days later she started to eat again: first some white bread with honey and the next day a piece of bacon. In spite of a cold Aaltje recovered rapidly. The constipation disappeared, the fits diminished and after some time she could leave her bed. In the beginning of August she was able to visit the church to thank God 'for his great mercy.

It is apparent from his comments that Stalpart considers her case to be authentic. Although he does not want to deny the possible involvement of divine powers, he expresses his doubts whether this case really is a miracle. He points out that the fasts of Eliah and Moses were not natural, but that they were strengthened by the 'power of God'. Neither does Stalpart exclude the influence of Satan: several 'Devil's children' would have been fed by the evil spirit. Moreover, he is aware of the possibility of deceit: there are people, pretending to holiness and pursuing gain and admiration, who deceive 'simple individuals'. As a warning Stalpart adds several cases of fraudulent fasting.

After these conclusions the Hague physician elaborates on, in particular, food abstinence attributable to natural causes. Referring to Galen he points out that people may lose their appetite, because hunger is not felt due to a relaxed or paralysed cardia or because the acid which normally speaking evokes hunger in the stomach has been neutralized by mucous or fat foods. In Aaltje's case her body was filled with 'mucous fluid, and raw juice' from the intake of apples and raw turnips. This raw fruit was not digested properly, so that the fluid mixed with her blood. This gave rise to the secretion of poison, through which the stomach nerves were not stimulated and hence she did not become hungry. To substantiate this view Stalpart refers to hibernating animals surviving on raw, cold, tough and 'sticky' matters in their body. Some kinds of plants would survive without mould and do not wither due to similar juices. Aside from this cause, Stalpart suggests the possibility that Aaltje's pores have been almost totally closed, resulting in reduced evaporation and intake of food.

According to Stalpart, Aaltje's food abstinence has natural causes. In fact, he attributes her non-eating to wrong food, possibly combined with non-dilated pores. But he only came to this conclusion after having acknowledged the involvement of God or Satan.[301] The learned treatises of Zwinger, Reynolds and Stalpart reflect the increasing frictions between religious interpretations and medical explanations of extraordinary behaviour. Neither Zwinger, Reynolds nor Stalpart have rejected the possibility of supernatural causation. Whereas Zwinger, after careful reflection, only accepted supernatural powers, Reynolds and Stalpart emphasized more earthly explanations. The latter two marked the transition to a development in which metaphysical explanations were gradually substituted by often speculative theories.

Living on air

Although as early as the sixteenth century some scholars seriously doubted the ability to live without food for years, many physicians in the eighteenth century still gave credence to 'prodigious abstinence'. Because of the sensational news about the exposure of several fasting girls, suspicion had markedly increased but did not completely undermine belief in the miraculous nature of prolonged fasting. In Italy, for instance, the noted professor of Medicine and Anatomy at Pisa, Giuseppe Zambeccari (1655–1728) described the life of the ascetic and alleged holy woman Maria Caterina Brondi, who after a putative fast of thirteen years died in 1724 at the age of 35.[348] Zambeccari narrated miracle after miracle connected with Maria, with no hint of incredulity or scepticism, and he even gives the impression of welcoming any evidence which might be used to confirm the veracity of this miracle. A post mortem showed that Maria's body was 'well formed, fleshy, and well developed' and that her colon contained 'a few pieces of dry stool'. Yet, even the latter, highly suspected fact was neutralized by Zambeccari as follows:

> At first this was thought to be excrement derived from food, but the mistake was soon detected, because when the stool was taken out of the colon and thrown into water it sank, thus differing from human stool derived from food, which floats.

An unidentified contemporary, however, who critically annotated Zambeccari's account, unequivocally stated that Brondi was a hysteric. With regard to Zambeccari's explanation of the revealed stool, he soberly concluded: 'The author of these notes can testify that he has repeatedly seen his own stools go to the bottom.'

Since the view of extended abstinence from food as a pathological phenomenon was far from widespread, sceptic contemporaries like this commentator were faced with the task of developing an alternative, acceptable explanation.[285] In the treatises of Reynolds and Stalpart a declining inclination to account for prolonged fasting by supernatural causes had already appeared. Yet, others had realized far earlier the importance of natural causes: in the mediaeval period several fasting saints were treated medically or were obliged to show that their food abstinence did not originate from some affliction. People also took into account the possibility of deception. The thirteenth-century Franciscan scholar Roger Bacon (1214?–94) said of a contemporary fasting woman at Norwich that her survival without eating for twenty years was not miraculous

> but rather, a work of nature, for some balance was at that time able to reduce to a state of almost complete equilibrium the elements that were before that in her body; and because their mixture was from their proper nature suitable to a balance not found in other makeups, their alteration happened in her body as it does not in others.[73]

Another explanation was provided by Poggio Bracciolini (1380–1459). In his *Liber Facetiarum* from 1450, this Florentine humanist made mention of one Jacob, who neither ate nor drank for two years. The account may seem, according to Poggio, incredible to the reader, because it is in contravention of nature. Numerous differing opinions were circulating about this case. Some thought he was possessed by the devil, but others were sure that the melancholic character of his body fluids was feeding him.[296] Yet such opinions gained some popularity only from the early modern period on. Gradually a growing number of (sometimes extremely) speculative hypotheses was suggested, in which supernatural powers did not play a role at all. Some physicians suggested that tobacco enabled people to sustain fasting. Stalpart van der Wiel, for instance, pointed out that many shipwrecked sailors survived for some time on tobacco. This would induce a kind of insensibility in the cardia or evoke phlegm in the stomach, through which the body could be fed for some time, according to Stalpart.[301]

Another no less curious explanation for prolonged fasting was suggested by Johann Jacob Ritter (1714–84). In 1737 this physician graduated at the university of Basel with a Latin dissertation *On the Impossibility and Possibility of Prolonged Abstinence of Food and Drink*.[297] This treatise specifically deals with the Swiss miraculous maiden Christina Kratzer, who started to fast at the age of 28 until her exposure in 1728, three years later. Ritter works out for the reader that the body daily loses a certain amount of solid and liquid matter by evaporation and necessarily has to emaciate without the intake of food. Surprisingly, Ritter finally addresses the question as to whether people are able to live without food. On account of numerous cases of protracted food abstinence in animals, he concludes that this possibility should not be excluded in human beings either. In the Kratzer case Ritter refers to her absence of the menses as a possible explanation. Women feed the foetus with their own blood: why would Christina not have been able to feed herself with her retained menstrual blood? The body might absorb from this necessary nutrition. In this way new life was breathed into the thirteenth-century opinion of Roger Bacon.

One of the most favoured explanations for prodigious abstinence, however, was based on the assumption that people could live on nutritive elements in the air. In the early modern period almost every author, addressing the problem of prolonged abstinence, devoted a passage to this theory. The air as food theory is rooted in antiquity. Aristotle had already made mention of someone who neither ate nor slept and only lived on air, and the Roman chronicler Pliny referred to a people on the Ganges, called the Astoni, said to have had no mouth and lived by smell alone.[181] And Democritus was alleged to have become 109 years old and to have fed himself with honey and warm bread. In the early modern period these stories were retold and amplified with personal observations. Returning from exotic countries, voyagers told of people living solely on the smell of fruit and spice. In addition to the observations of hibernating animals that did not eat and 'thus' only lived on air, such tall stories formed the main sources of inspiration for speculations about living on air.

In 1551 the Neapolitan Portio had written a treatise about the two-year fast of an unnamed miraculous maiden, in which he extensively elaborated the question of whether people could live on air alone.[189] Many after him would take this possibility seriously into account. Pieter Nielen, an unknown Dutch physician, wrote in 1775 a comprehensive work on prolonged fasting as exemplified by the seven-year fast of Maria van Dijk (see

Chapter 5). He points out that 'diseased particles' in the air may cause inflammation via the lungs and the copious smelling of spirituous liquors may lead to 'light-headedness' or cheerfulness. Likewise so-called 'nutritive particles', whether or not in the form of vapour or smoke, may be transported through the air, and assimilated into the blood. However, such nutritive particles also may be absorbed from the air via the pores in the skin, for putting one's limbs in brandy one gets drunk . . . [255]

In the same period in which Nielen wrote down his curious views, some revolutionary scientific developments took place. Independently and almost simultaneously the British clergyman and chemist Joseph Priestley (1733–1804) and the Swedish apothecary Carl Scheele (1742–86) discovered a particular kind of gas: oxygen. Building on the results of their discoveries, the French chemist Antoine Lavoisier (1743–74) demonstrated experimentally that the functioning of a living body is based on a combustion process: particles of food are burnt in the body by means of oxygen, through which resulting energy is liberated as warmth. This discovery was a fundamental breakthrough in the theories of digestion, circulation and respiration. The far-reaching insights, however, did not put an end to the notion of air as a nutritive element. The latter view continued to be referred to by some physicians to explain the prolonged fasts of the miraculous maidens.

In about 1800 the German physician Ludwig Schmidtmann (1764–1840) rejected every suspicion of deceit, on account of his extensive investigations made into the two-year fast of Anna Maria Kienker from Osnabrück (see Chapter 5). In his view the miraculous maiden was fed by resorbing elementary particles from the air.[202:203] Somewhat later similar explanations were suggested in the case of Ann Moore from Tutbury (see Chapter 5). Doctors who gave credence to her protracted fast had to face the problem of a rational explanation. One of them was Dr Bourne, who concluded in 1808 that

> the nutrition of the system is evidently introduced by the lungs; it is not our purpose to inquire here by what means it is afterwards assimilated; 'she lives apparently on air alone; to use her own expression 'she loves air', and has the chamber window open. As she almost continually lies in bed, it is not probable that much is furnished by absorption from the general surface of the body.[274]

Bourne's conclusion was shared by Benjamin Granger, who published two articles in 1813 on the notorious 'Fasting Woman from Tutbury'.[281;282]

Such explanations of absorption of food from the air via skin and lungs were not exceptional in the first part of the nineteenth century. In respect of the two-year fast of the Italian Anna Garbero, Dr Osella suggested in the 1820s that she extracted chemicals from other people by way of the air. That would explain why her sister, who slept with her, had lost weight . . . [111]

Similar explanations can even be traced in our century. According to Dr Kröner, the prolonged fasting mystic Theresa Neumann (see Chapter 2) extracted food from people around her by means of a sort of magnetic power.[291] Peculiarly enough, in 1948 the well-known psychiatrist and former pupil of Freud, Carl-Gustav Jung (1875–1961) suggested the possibility that in the case of the late mediaeval fasting saint Nicholas of Flue nourishment might have been effected by the passage of living molecules of albumen from one body to another.[288] Yet, as we noted before, in the nineteenth century a growing number of physicians was convinced that fasting was an ordinary affliction instead of a divine or natural wonder. Although the exact length of time remained to be disputed, it was widely agreed that fasting for years was just impossible and could only be based on a hysterical form of deceit. By the exposure of miraculous maidens and the new scientifically grounded insights of medicine the mystery had been solved and at the end of the nineteenth century the era of prodigious fasting was over for good.

The beneficial effect of food abstinence

Historically, physicians were familiar with food abstinence from quite another perspective: it was frequently applied as a form of therapy. Regulation of food intake is one of the oldest forms of treatment recommended by physicians; in fact the history of diets is as old as medicine itself. In order to prevent us from losing our way in a history with so many byroads across so many centuries, we will confine ourselves to the essentials.[268]

The Hippocratic writings are the basis of the age-old usage of diets in medicine. In his comprehensive oeuvre from the fifth and fourth centuries BC, a rich and systematic treatise is to be found about dietetics aimed at preserving health (prevention) as well as at curing illnesses (therapy). In imitation of Hippocrates, other leading physicians from Graeco-Roman antiquity have also propagated diets as an important therapy. The different medical schools in those days did not totally agree on the principals of dietetics. According to Pliny some physicians even prescribed such rigorous diets that their patients almost starved to death. In contrast to these 'starvers' other physicians overloaded their patients with food as a kind of therapy.

Disputes about the character of the diet would continue for centuries, though the beneficial effect was widely agreed. Echoing the Classics, Sir Francis Bacon (1561–1626), the famous English philosopher and statesman, argued that medicine could cure disease, but that only a sound diet could prolong life. This view received its fullest development in Luigi Cornaro's (1475–1566) influential work, *A Treatise of the Benefits of a Sober Life* being *'the sure and certain method of attaining a long and healthful life'*. This Venetian author subjected himself to an increasingly strict diet until he only ate one egg each day. Due to Cornaro's great age his method gained credence: he wrote his book in 1558 when he was already in his 80s; he died at the age of 91.[578] In the same period the well-known astrologist, prophet and physician Michel Nostradamus (1503–66) recommended regular dieting as a means of purifying the body from poison and refreshing it in this way: 'health and youth are closely linked to dieting', he said.[270] Still well into the eighteenth century prominent physicians like Friedrich Hoffmann (1660–1742), Herman Boerhaave (1668–1738) and William Cullen (1710–90) were advocating adapted forms of Graeco-Roman dietetics.

From the seventeenth century on – parallel with the waning influence of Classical medicine – dieting as a form of therapy lost popularity in favour of pharmaceutical treatments. At the end of the eighteenth century dietetics reached an all-time low. Leading reformers like the Scotchman John Brown (1735–88) and the Frenchman François Joseph Victor Broussais (1772–1838) had to offer nothing but hunger therapies in this domain. In Brown's view illness had predominantly to do with (too much or too little) stimulation of the organism, while Broussais reduced everything to an 'irritated stomach'. Physicians did not pin their faith on a balanced composed diet, but more so on extended, complete food abstinence. More level-headed physicians abhorred such extreme forms of therapy and backslid into Hippocratic dietetics and their revisions.

This period of stagnation came to an end in the second half of the nineteenth century. Major discoveries pertaining to metabolism and dietetics revived the attention for and trust in the beneficial effects of diets and led to their revaluation in the cure and prevention of illnesses. Although traditionally the importance of food for human beings had been acknowledged, it was only in the previous century that people had acquired scientifically grounded knowledge of its composition and effects on the human body. Lavoisier's discovery, that respiration was a process of combustion, enabled scientists to quantify food according to its combustion value (in calories). Instead of the old theories which saw digestion as a mechanical process or a form of putrefaction, in the course of the nineteenth century scholars realized that it was a chemical process. Meanwhile, beyond this, essential knowledge was gathered about basic elements in foods like carbohydrates, fats, proteins, minerals and (at the beginning of this century) vitamins. Of course these developments markedly influenced dietetics: they led to the first scientifically sound diets in history. A hundred years ago, all kinds of special diets for diverse afflictions were popular, as promising discoveries with regard to bacteriology had not yet provided practically useful results.[268]

In the same period in which hunger artists enjoyed great popularity (see Chapter 5) and anorexia nervosa was introduced in medical literature (see Chapter 8), numerous people gave themselves up to prolonged food abstinence in order to cure particular afflictions. At the turn of the century prolonged fasting almost seemed to have become a fad. On the same day that the American physician Henry Tanner began his exhibition, his compatriot Agnes Dehart began a thirty-one day fast to rid herself of stomach ulcers. Still others surpassed the length of her fast and abstained from food – just like the hunger artists – for forty days or even more. Among the fervent propagators of these 'beneficial' hunger cures were the American author Upton B. Sinclair (1878–1968)[300] and Dr Edward Hooker Dewey (1837–1904)[280] from Pennsylvania, whose 'no-breakfast plan' and crusades against 'the slavery of the kitchens' were also endorsed in Europe. Especially in Germany up to the 1950s fasting cures for all kinds of ill-health were propagated and some spas were renowned for it.[287] The explanations of 'the healing power of fasting' and the arguments for its beneficial influence varied greatly. The American physiologist Hereward Carrington (born 1880), for instance, accounted for such a therapy by pointing out that constipation is the cause of all afflictions: illness would be nothing but the fight of the organism to dispose of the retained matter. This natural cleaning process should not be impeded by new impurities intruding the body via the intake of food![276]

Considering such explanations it is not surprising that severe fasting predominantly held sway in the world of the alternative ('natural') medicine. Meanwhile, 'regular' physicians have turned away from this therapy, although mild and selective diets are still prescribed for illnesses, varying from diabetes to psychosomatic afflictions. The age-old hunger cures may have been scornfully rejected within regular medicine, yet people make use of them more than ever. For large numbers of people diets are no longer a specific therapy, but the most important weapon in a relentless pursuit of slenderness. This completes the circle. Medicine not only played an essential role in the medicalization of food abstinence, it also provided for the 'new' illness its most striking element: dieting as one of the driving forces of anorexia nervosa.

7

Food Abstinence and Emaciation as Signs of Illness

For centuries extraordinary food abstinence had been restricted to fasting saints, miraculous maidens and hunger artists, but from the early modern period on it was gradually transformed into a medical problem. However, while medicine only managed to annex this phenomenon in the course of time, less severe forms of fasting belonged to its domain from time immemorial. When the first signs of food abstinence manifested themselves, even in possible cases of fasting saints or miraculous maidens, physicians had been consulted. Only if their efforts appeared to be of no avail and abstinence continued, did people suggest the involvement of supernatural powers. Slightly decreased appetite or intake of food were considered to be naturally caused and needing medical treatment. The better off consulted regular physicians, while the less well-to-do population turned to quacks. In comparison to prodigious abstinence slight eating problems seemed to be more comprehensible, appealed less to people's imagination and thus failed to give rise to metaphysical speculation. If the eating problems were accompanied by complications known from other clinical pictures, a natural cause was self-evident.

From Classical antiquity, eating problems (and emaciation) have been important to physicians because of their referral function, as signs or symptoms of certain illness. For example in the work of Soranus of Ephesus (early second century), which was passed down to us in a Latin translation by Caelius Aurelianus, a distaste for food is to be found as symptom of chronic headache, epilepsy, phthisis and stomach ache among other things.[308] The latter group of afflictions was particularly characterized by this symptom in the work of other authors from those early days.[311] It is beyond the scope of this book to elaborate upon this. We will confine ourselves to those illnesses or clinical pictures in which eating problems and emaciation obviously cannot be attributed to somatic causes: atrophia nervosa, hysteria, melancholia, love-sickness and chlorosis. Before paying attention to these disorders, we firstly dwell on anorexia or lack of appetite. Although physicians considered this primarily a symptom of various afflictions, it has also been presented as a discrete problem with a distinct aetiology. Some historical information about a concept which, despite its misleading denotation, is persistently upheld in the modern terminology of anorexia nervosa, should not be lacking in a book like this.

Anorexia

Traditionally physicians employed a number of concepts to define eating problems, although these were far from consistently differentiated. Particularly in the early modern period numerous terms have been used for food refusal, aversion to food, lack of appetite and so on. One of these concepts was *anorexia* with its Latin equivalent *inappetentia*. Although Hippocrates occasionally mentions food abstinence, anorexia is not to be found in his comprehensive oeuvre.[343] In the more general meaning of a state of insufficient *orexis* i.e. general lassitude, the term was used in a pseudo-platonic treatise composed in the first century AD.[25] Shortly afterwards Galen was one of the prominent medical men of the time who used the term in the more restricted sense of want of appetite. In a commentary on Hippocrates' first book of *Epidemics*, Galen writes:

> Those, who refuse food and do not take anything, are called by the Greeks anorektous or asitous, that means, those who have no appetite and refrain from food. Those however, who after the intake of food distaste or even loath it (they call) apositous.

After a passage on vomiting, he states:

> This is often clearly observed in those who loath food (apositon) and when made to eat, have not the strength to swallow it, and even if they make themselves eat, cannot hold the food down but keep bringing it up.[334]

However, just like Hippocrates, Galen commonly uses the concept *asitia* (or *inedia*) in his large work to denote abstinence from food.

The work of the Byzantine compilers gives a good impression of the views of anorexia in Classical medicine. Although several of them pay attention to anorexia, we will only go into detail about the rather extensive description of Alexander of Tralles (or Trallianus: 525–605). The work of this Greek physician was largely based on his own observations – an unusual practice within Byzantine medicine – though it undeniably betrays Galen's influences. He introduces his chapter *peri anorexias* (on the lack of appetite) as follows: 'It should be considered well known that anorexia is based on either a dyscrasia (a disturbed balance of humours) or an accumulation of humours in the stomach.'[305] His treatment is directed towards these humours: their composition should be either altered or they have to be removed by means of vomiting or evacuation of the bowels. To stimulate vomiting he recommends emetics, humid foods and drinks like lukewarm water. In cases of severe vomiting a laxative is recommended, for which Alexander adds a recipe. If anorexia originates from tough humours, he prescribes, according to the character of the affliction, diluting and cleaning potions. The different forms of dyscrasia (hot or cold) have to be fought, apart from medication, by certain foods like pigeon broth or raisins. The Classical view of anorexia, as depicted by Alexander of Tralles, is still apparent from the late mediaeval *Boec van Medicinen in Dietsche*.[327] In this Dutch treatise the herb 'menta-almente' is prescribed to raise appetite, when this has been disturbed by cold humours at the top of the stomach. An ointment of mint, cinnamon, pepper and vinegar would restore the appetite. Not only the cause of anorexia ('cold humours'), but also all ingredients of the ointment are to be found in Alexander's description.

In the early modern period, in which Classical medicine initially still remained an essential source of knowledge, the concept of anorexia was widely used. It is even to be found in several English dictionaries. Cockeram's dictionary of 1658, for instance, incorporated an entry on anorexia, denoting 'a queesin-esse of stomack'.[362] Around 1700 a remarkable number of doctoral theses entitled *De Anorexia* appeared at different medical faculties in Europe. In many of these treatises all sorts of explanations are provided for the lack of appetite: *Causae sunt Multae* (causes are numerous), writes Jacobus Willerus in 1715.[389] In accordance with the Classical sources, especially physical (gastric) afflictions are put forward, although emotional factors are not neglected. Take for instance the monograph from 1703 by the physician Harderus, who incriminates the stomach as the main source of mischief.[342] Harderus points out that either a defective stimulation of the gastric nerves or the injurious composition of the humours bathing the organ are responsible. Furthermore, the *animus pathemata* or disturbances in the spirit and feelings – especially anger, fear, and sadness – play a part. Scholars in particular had to be on the alert since the most deleterious influences were said to be undue study and meditation. Anorexia in 'mad' individuals was attributed by Harderus to the brain's insensitivity to influences from the stomach.

Although the influence of antique medicine was waning in the eighteenth century, many descriptions of anorexia still bear its marks. This is apparent from Zedlers *Grosses Vollständiges Universal Lexikon*.[392] In this comprehensive encyclopaedia from the first part of the century, hunger is attributed to the mind, 'for it is well known that sorrow, fear, deep thoughts among others may decrease or immediately chase away the appetite'. In the passage on anorexia, however, such psychic factors are lacking and virtually all causes mentioned have to do with the functioning of the stomach. Similar characterizations of anorexia are to be found in the work of the prominent early eighteenth-century Dutch physician Herman Boerhaave,[316] the famous French *Encyclopédie* by Diderot and d'Alembert,[329] the widely read medical handbook of the German Christian Gottlieb Selle (1748–1800),[370] and several eighteenth-century medical lexicons.[321] Anorexia, originating from a derangement of the stomach, also features in the works of several famous eighteenth-century nosologists, who tried to classify all familiar diseases after the model and principle of the classificatory botanical studies of Carolus Linnaeus (1707–78). One of the most prominent among them was François Boissier de Sauvages. In his *Nosologia Methodica*, anorexia belongs to the *anepithymiae*, a class of disorders in which the desire (like sexual appetite or hunger) is totally or partially extinguished.[317] According to Boissier, anorexia's predominant symptom is the partial or complete loss of appetite, often accompanied by aversion to food. The French physician distinguished no fewer than thirteen forms of anorexia.

Beside those linked with diseases like melancholia and specific forms like protracted abstinence ('anorexia mirabilis'), most of them are related to disturbances of the stomach.

At the end of the 18th century Philippe Pinel (1745–1826), a pioneer in the history of psychiatry, published another extended classificatory medical system. This French physician, whose name is closely linked with the struggle for a humane treatment of the mentally ill, hoped by publishing his *Nosographie Philosophique* (1798) to improve the classification of diseases, from which patients in his view might derive much benefit.[364] In this influential work Pinel expatiated on the *névroses*, a class of diseases, caused by physical as well as psychical factors. In one chapter he pays attention to the 'neuroses of digestion', to which belong bulimia, pica and anorexia. According to Pinel the latter is a gastric neurosis, which occurs 'extraordinarily frequently'. But strikingly enough he does not even touch on its causes, while he systematically elaborates the causes and symptoms of other neuroses of digestion. Pinel confines himself to one short case history, quoted (without any reference) from the work of Georg Ernst Stahl (1660–1734) concerning a 30-year-old woman 'of a lymphatic and melancholic temperament', who suffered for two days from nausea and vomiting. When the distress abated, her appetite did not return. The little food she took, brought about a slight aversion towards eating: 'fading' and wasting were the consequences.[364] Pinel concludes his section on anorexia with a formerly much quoted (but by himself distrusted) account of a people near Moscow, the Lucomoria, who were said to hibernate for months. Finally he refers to the *Elementa Physiologiae* of Albrecht von Haller (1708–77), wherein in his view more reliable instances of prolonged fasting can be found.[383]

More elaborate on the topic than his contemporary Pinel, is Erasmus Darwin (1731–1802). The grandfather of the famous Charles Darwin (1809–82) published at the end of the eighteenth century a book entitled *Zoonomia*, comprising an extensive classificatory system of all sorts of diseases.[328] In the class of 'diseases of sensation' a short reflection on anorexia is to be found, which obviously betrays Darwin's physiological orientation. In his view 'some elderly people and those debilitated by fermented liquors' are liable to lose their appetite for animal food. He attributes this to the deficiency of gastric acid as well as to the general decay of the system. At times want of appetite is produced by the putrid matter from decaying teeth, which affects taste and digestion. As physical strength is derived from the quantity of digested food, 'a total debility of the system' frequently follows the want of appetite. His next conclusion is quite striking:

> Some young ladies I have observed to fall into this general debility, so as but just to be able to walk about, which I have sometimes ascribed to their voluntary fasting, when they believed themselves too plump; and who have thus lost both health and beauty by too great abstinence, which could never be restored.

In a certain form, called *anorexia epileptica*, loss of appetite was accompanied by 'epileptic fits' and was relieved by the use of opium.

As well as opium physicians used other remedies for anorexia. The famous German physician Johann Schenck von Grafenberg (1530–98) induced a patient to eat by pinching his ring finger and by threatening to break it if he would not eat his soup. The same physician tells of a woman who was cured from food abstinence by an admonition.[200] But commonly more orthodox therapies were used. Dependent upon the supposed cause a number of remedies was recommended: diet, physical exercise and wine, besides bloodletting and medicines like analeptics, stomachics and emetics. However, in *An Essay on Health and Long Life* the Scottish physician George Cheyne (1671–1743), well known for his book on *The English Malady*, made a plea to physicians for a restrained attitude. In his opinion one can hardly approve of appetite being evoked by medicines, except in severe and sad afflictions. In general, abstinence, a regular motion and bodily exercise will always restore the loss of appetite.[323]

The view of anorexia by prominent nosologists, as a distinct clinical entity within medical nomenclature, found little response at the beginning of the nineteenth century. Rees' *Cyclopaedia* from 1819, for instance, pointed out that anorexia was seldom an idiopathic disease, 'but a frequent attendant on many'. It could be caused by various physical illnesses or by sudden shock, 'distressing news, depressing passions'.[362] In the authoritative *Dictionnaire de Médecine* a similar view was expressed. One Blache establishes, that *anorexie* occurs in different gradations –

from simple decreased appetite to the most complete *inappétence* – and is accompanied by chronic as well as acute diseases.[315] It is particularly symptomatic of several stomach disorders. However, its diagnostic significance should not be exaggerated, as it may have been present for a long time without any deficiency being shown at a post mortem, whereas the reverse also occurs. Blache does not deny that in afflictions such as hypochondriasis and nervous vomiting, appetite is also frequently disturbed, but it is seldom completely lost, unless it accompanies 'another pathological lesion'. Since complete anorexia as a symptom of other nervous stomach disorders rarely occurs, 'essential anorexia' (i.e. lack of appetite independent of another affliction) must be even more exceptional, so that he attached little value to the literature on this topic.

In accordance with this view Blache advises treatment of those illnesses of which anorexia is supposed to be the symptom; in his opinion lack of appetite is indicative of an inability of the stomach to receive food and it may be a useful warning of nature to refrain from food. Instead of medication, patients would derive more benefit from delicious sweet food, moderate exercise in the open air, bitter or slightly aerated potions, in short every remedy to instigate the process of nutrition. Similar remedies should be prescribed when anorexia occurs among those who are exhausted by sexual debauches or masturbation. Should the lack of appetite originate from intellectual work, too little exercise, 'lively passions' or deep sorrow, then cessation of intellectual activities, pleasant distraction, riding horseback and environmental change are recommended. Finally, according to Blache, the intake of tepid potions and opiates should be stopped immediately, when anorexia cannot be attributed to causes other than the abuse of these substances.[315]

Atrophia nervosa or nervous consumption

From the beginning of the century almost every historical survey of anorexia nervosa mentions the British physician Richard Morton (1637–98). His depiction of atrophia or phthisis nervosa in 1689 is credited as the first detailed medical description of current anorexia nervosa, and for many the history of this syndrome begins with Morton's treatise.[355;356] Before outlining his atrophia, we will first provide some biographical details of this physician.

As vicar of Kinver in 1662 Morton refused to give his genuine assent to the proclaimed Act of Uniformity with its requirement of comprehensive approval of the Book of Common Prayer. Ejected for this reason from his benefice and deprived of his income, the 25-year-old Morton decided to enter the field of medicine. This was probably not totally strange to him, for in Morton's days, clergymen in country districts often had to act as physicians in addition to their pastoral work. By the nomination of William III, Prince of Orange, he was created doctor of medicine at Oxford in 1670. Thereafter he made a successful career: he settled in practice in London and was admitted to the illustrious 'College of Physicians' on 20 March 1676. His crowning glory, however, was his appointment as physician in ordinary to William III, who had meanwhile become King of England. Only a few years before his death Morton began to publish and the *Phthisiologia seu Exercitationes de phthisi* published in 1689 was his *magnum opus*. This work, dedicated to William III, established his reputation at home and abroad for over a century and is still considered to be one of the first systematic treatises on phthisis or consumption. By his keen observations and lucid description of the disease he earned a permanent place in the history of tuberculosis.

As usual in the medical sciences of those days, Morton adopted the concepts of *atrophia* and *phthisis* from Classical Graeco-Roman medicine. In this context the work of Aulus Cornelius Celsus (30 BC–AD 45) is especially relevant. In *De Re Medica*, a compilation of Greek medicine, Celsus describes the *tabes*, denoting consumption or wasting, of which he distinguishes three forms.[322] In the first the body is not fed properly because with excretion matter leaves the body, whereas from the food nothing new is absorbed. Extreme thinness being the consequence, the affliction will be fatal if no treatment is offered. According to Celsus, Greeks called this sort of tabes *atrophia: commonly she has two causes. Either through great fear somebody takes too little, or from too much greediness more than necessary, and doing so the body is weakened by lack of food or the abundantly-present food is tainted.* In cases of reduced intake of food, Celsus advises the patient to take gradually more food, for if the body is suddenly overloaded with a large quantity of food, digestion is disordered. Those accustomed to overeating have to fast for a day, then restart with a small quantity of food, which is daily increased until the proper quantity is achieved. Furthermore Celsus advises such patients walks, gymnastics, anointings, massages, baths, wine and nourishing foods of easy digestion.

The second kind of tabes is called *cachexia* by the Greeks. The patient's condition is bad, which causes putrefaction of all foods. *Cachexia* is predominantly observed in patients whose body has been exhausted by a chronic disease, who have taken wrong medicines, uncommon or injurious foods or who have lived under deplorable conditions. Apart from emaciation, the skin is sometimes inflamed, because of pimples and sores or some limbs swell. According to Celsus this disease should be treated with fasting, followed by administration of an enema and then feeding, exercise, anointings, massages, wine, baths and blood-letting if necessary.

In Celsus' view the third form of tabes, called *phthisis* by the Greeks, is by far the most dangerous. The disease starts in the head and then afflicts the lungs, which causes fever, frequent coughs, vomiting of pus and sometimes bloody phlegms. In all probability this is what we now call tuberculosis. Although Celsus particularly elaborates on the therapy of phthisis, we will not go further into the topic, as in this context the two other forms of *tabes* are of more importance. Strikingly, Celsus distinguishes *atrophia* from a disease originating from illness, intake of injurious matter or other mishap. Apparently, he acknowledged the existence of a form of emaciation, in which such somatic factors do not play a predominant part. The causes of *atrophia* are psychogenic ('too great fear or greediness'), but are not elaborated further by Celsus.[25]

In the history of anorexia nervosa Morton might have remained unmentioned if phthisis only denoted tuberculosis. To him, it comprised also wasting because of diseases like chronic jaundice and gout. Using the word consumption in its literal meaning – a wasting of the body from any cause – Morton recognizes two basic types:[356] 'original' and 'symptomatical', the latter depending upon some other preceding disease and resembling Celsus' *cachexia*. An original consumption, by contrast, arises 'purely from a Morbid Disposition of the Blood, or

Animal Spirits, which reside in the System of the Nerves and Fibres, and is not the effect of any other preceding Disease'. Original consumptions are divided into two sorts: 'an Atrophy' and 'a Consumption of the Lungs', which reminds us again of Celsus' classification. Atrophies could be nervous (i.e. due to 'an ill and morbid state of the Spirits') or due to a defect in or loss of 'nutritious juice'.[313]

In the first chapter of his *Phthisiologia* Morton mentions the so-called 'nervous consumption' (also named by him and epigones *atrophia nervosa*, 'nervous atrophy' or *phthisis nervosa*). He describes it as

> a wasting of Body without any remarkable Fever, Cough, or Shortness of Breath; but it is accompanied by a want of Appetite, and a bad Digestion, upon which there follows a Languishing Weakness of Nature, and a falling away of the Flesh every day more and more.[356]

Morton is silent on the sex ratio of the disease and surprisingly enough he observed the affliction most frequently among former residents of Virginia who had returned to England. In the beginning the body appears oedematous and bloated, the stomach loathes everything but liquids, the urine changes colour, the face is pale, while the patient, even before the emaciation starts, is almost always confined to his bed because of feebleness. The nervous consumption is very hard to cure, especially if a physician is not consulted early enough. Particularly in the more advanced stages, when the body swells and patients begin to suffer from 'some difficulty and trouble in breathing', there is hardly any hope for the patient. For a physician 'there is nothing more to be done for his Cure than giving him some ease, whereby his Miserable Life may be lengthened for some days.'

Morton attributes this kind of consumption to 'the intemperate drinking of Spirituous Liquors, and an unwholsom Air', but the immediate cause is 'in the System of the Nerves proceeding from a Preternatural state of the Animal Spirits, and the destruction of the Tone of the Nerves.' This is detrimental to the working of stomach, appetite and digestion. Nevertheless, Morton also has an eye for psychological factors. One of the predisposing causes of nervous consumption is 'violent Passions of the Mind', which he specified later as 'Sadness and anxious

Cares'. Morton's almost psychosomatic approach of nervous consumption is reflected in his recommended treatment. Morton advises a formidable pharmacopoiea directed towards nerves, stomach and appetite. Beyond this, he adds the following therapeutic admonition:

> Let the patient endeavour to divert and make his Mind cheerful by Exercise, and the Conversation of his Friends. For this Disease does almost always proceed from Sadness and anxious Cares. Let him also enjoy the benefit of an open, clear, and very good Air, which does very much relieve the Nerves and Spirits. And because the Stomack in this Distemper is principally affected, a delicious Diet will be convenient, and the Stomack ought not to be too long accustomed to one sort of Food.

After this general reflection on *atrophia nervosa*, Morton concludes his chapter with two case histories of nervous consumption. The first concerns the 18-year-old 'Mr. Duke's daughter in St. Mary Axe', who in 1684 'fell into a total suppression of her Monthly Courses from a multitude of Cares and Passions of her Mind, but without any Symptom of the Green-Sickness following upon it'. Her appetite began to abate and she became emaciated. Notwithstanding the 'extream and memorable cold Weather which happened the Winter following' she continued her diligent nightly studies. In doing so she exposed herself, according to Morton, 'to the injuries of the Air, which was at that time extreamly cold, not without some manifest Prejudice to the System of her Nerves'. In the spring of 1685 some medicines were prescribed without effect and from that time on she resisted this kind of therapy. For two years she wholly neglected the care of herself 'till at last being brought to the last degree of a Marasmus, or Consumption, and thereupon subject to frequent Fainting Fits, she apply'd her self to me for Advice'. Morton was perplexed:

> I do not remember that I did ever in all my Practice see one, that was conversant with the Living so much wasted with the greatest degree of a Consumption, (like a Skeleton only clad with skin) yet there was no Fever, but on the contrary a coldness of the whole Body; no Cough, or difficulty of Breathing, nor an appearance of any other Distemper of the Lungs, or of any other Entrail.

Morton could only establish a diminished appetite, frequently recurring fainting fits, and an 'uneasie' digestion. He prescribed her various medicines,

> Upon the Use of which she seemed to be much better, but being quickly tired with Medicines, she beg'd that the whole Affair might be committed again to Nature, whereupon consuming every day more and more, she was after three Months taken with a Fainting Fit and dyed.[356]

The second case history pertains to 'the Son of the Reverend Minister Steele', who

> about the Sixteenth Year of his Age, fell gradually into a total want of Appetite, occasioned by his studying too hard, and the Passions of his Mind, and upon that into an Universal Atrophy, pining away more and more for the space of two Years, without any Cough, Fever, or any other Symptom of any Distemper of his Lungs, or any other Entrail; as also without a Looseness, or Diabetes, or any other sign of a Colliquation, or Preternatural Evacuation. And therefore I judg'd this Consumption to be Nervous, and to have its seat in the whole Habit of the Body, and to arise from the System of Nerves being distemper'd.

Initially Morton treated the boy pharmaceutically and only after this therapy appeared to be unsuccessful, did he seek other treatments. From this it is apparent that Morton placed relatively less value on psychic factors, as only in the end did he advise the boy to abandon his studies, go into the country air, ride horseback, and follow a milk diet. On this regimen the boy recovered markedly, 'though he is not yet perfectly freed from a Consumptive state; and what will be the event of this Method, does not yet plainly appear.'

Morton's work has been translated and reprinted repeatedly in many countries. However, even though Hieronymus Cardanus (1501–76) had already mentioned a case of nervous consumption (*phthoe falsa*), the disorder concerned did not develop into a well-known medical entity in early modern Europe.[381] Yet various eighteenth-century medical sources mention this particular form of phthisis and some clearly resemble Morton's depiction. Examples are the famous nosological works of François Boissier de Sauvages (1763) and William Cullen (1769) and the *Encyclopaedia Britannica* from 1771. A more elaborate description is to be found in a work of Robert Whytt (1714–66), First

Physician to the King in Scotland. In his famous *Observations on the Nature, Causes, and Cure of those Disorders which have been Commonly called Nervous, Hypochondriac or Hysteric* (1764), he devotes a few pages to 'a nervous atrophy'.[387]

Writing seventy-five years after Morton's *Phthisiologia* and without referring to his work, Whytt states: 'A marasmus, or sensible wasting of the body, not attended with sweatings, any considerable increase of the excretions by urine or stool, a quick pulse, or feverish heat, may deserve the name of nervous . . . ' In his view, this particular kind of atrophy may be so called because it often seems to proceed from

> an unnatural or morbid state of the nerves, of the stomach, and intestines (. . .) Further, the watching or want of refreshing rest, and low spirits or melancholia, which generally accompany this disease, may contribute to prevent the proper nutrition of the body.

Sometimes, without any apparent cause, the affliction takes a sudden turn: 'The patient, who had little inclination to eat, has an uncommon craving and quick digestion.' In addition to a quick physical recovery, low spirits give place to cheerfulness, and the patient daily grows stronger and plumper. This kind of nervous atrophy is illustrated by a case history of a 14-year-old boy.

During the nineteenth century several physicians still made reference to the notion of nervous consumption. But whereas Morton clearly distinguished nervous consumption from tuberculosis, this distinction faded more and more. When the concept of anorexia nervosa was introduced into medical literature, the London physician Samuel Fenwick (1821–1902) made a connection with anorexia nervosa and Whytt's 'nervous atrophy'.[414] But it was not until 1900, that the famous William Osler (1849–1919) in a lecture on Morton's *Phthisiologia* stated almost in passing: 'Under what he terms nervous consumption, I think we may recognize Gull's anorexia nervosa, particularly in the history of the two cases which he narrates.'[360] Two years later, nervous consumption was mentioned again in relation to anorexia nervosa. The English physician Samuel Jones Gee (1839–1911) entitled one of his lectures: 'Nervous atrophy (Atrophia nervosa; Anorexia nervosa)'.[336] As suggested by the title he used the terms atrophia nervosa and anorexia nervosa interchangeably. He gives a clear picture of the latter disease as it existed at the turn of the century, but preferred the concept of atrophia nervosa to label this clinical picture. It is not that he still attached great value to its original meaning in Morton's or Whytt's work, but in particular because he considered the term in its literal sense more adequate. According to Gee the illness is not the result of mere anorexia, for if patients take food it by no means follows that they soon recover: it may happen that the marasmus, constipation, amenorrhoea and melancholia persist. Using a concept like anorexia, Gee asserts, wrongly emphasizes loss of appetite instead of weight loss. However, his plea was in vain and 'nervous atrophy' remained forgotten in the annals of medical history.

Hysteria

With hysteria we enter into a comprehensive and complex part of the history of psychiatry.[304;382] Traditionally the affliction has been related to the condition or malposition of the womb or uterus (in Greek *hystera*). From ancient Egyptian medicine until well into the nineteenth century a wide variety of symptoms have been attributed to this organ. Hippocrates pointed out the detrimental effects of displacement of the uterus, for which he introduced the term hysteria. In his view the 'wandering womb' was found primarily in mature women deprived of sexual relations. The uterus dries up in those women, loses weight and rises to the organs, where it inflicts mischief causing all kinds of diseases.

Hippocrates' theory was quite influential as is evident from the work of several Graeco-Roman authors. Even the other coryphaeus of ancient medicine, Galen, was no exception to this rule. Nevertheless he rejected − just like his contemporary Soranus of Ephesus − the Hippocratic notion of the wandering womb. In his view the womb maintained its own place and produced a secretion analogous to the semen of the male. Retention of this substance (as a result of sexual abstinence) and to a lesser extent suppression of the menses would lead to a corruption of the blood and eventually to hysteria. Males might also fall prey to hysteria due to retention of sperm. Some of them, Galen continues, 'were seized by despair and sadness without reason; and because of their distaste for food they develop poor digestion.' In ancient medicine therapy for this affliction was dependent upon the supposed cause. For those who retained their seed, marriage was considered beneficial, whereas increased sexual intercourse was recommended to married people. Those suffering from retention of the menses should be treated pharmaceutically. The ascending uterus had to be restored to its proper place by means of foul, pungent odours in the nose and pleasant aromas brought in the genital tract. The views of Hippocrates and Galen laid the foundation for the theory of hysteria that recurred for centuries in numerous variants.

If we confine ourselves to the great physicians in the history of hysteria, like Galen several of them put forward eating problems as one of its symptoms. Trotula of Salerno (thirteenth century), one of the most famous of the few women authors in the history of medicine, devoted a passage to hysteria in her book on *The Diseases of Women*.[382] It is evident that she accepted Galen's theories about the retention of semen as the cause of hysteria. Nevertheless she did not reject the notion of the wandering womb. The latter could result, among other things, in fainting, loss of sight, speech and appetite. From the early modern period the work of Thomas Sydenham (1624–89) is noteworthy. Whereas others supposed demonic possession, the famous London physician relied upon natural causes. Honoured by his contemporaries with the designation 'English Hippocrates', Sydenham went beyond his Graeco-Roman ancestors. He primarily attributed hysteria to 'the irregularity of the spirits', but particularly considered 'over-ordinate commotions of the mind' to be the remote or external cause. Although in Sydenham's days his view was less appreciated, retrospectively his contribution was a landmark in the history of hysteria: the affliction was transformed into a psychosomatic disease. Long-standing hysteria might lead to cachexia, anorexia and chlorosis, according to Sydenham.[382]

The Italian physician Giorgio Baglivi (1668–1706), a great admirer of Sydenham, extended his theories.[310] He pointed out that numerous physical diseases were of psychogenic origin and that hysteria was caused by 'passions of the mind'. Along with his contemporaries, Baglivi held that mental diseases would sooner or later be manifest in gastrointestinal symptoms, largely brought about by decreasing appetite and disinterest in food. The latter symptoms he observed especially among young women unrequited in love. It is evident from Sydenham's and Baglivi's writings that seventeenth-century clinicians did not confine themselves merely to Classical theories. From this period on physicians progressively turned away from the Classical body of thought. The theory of the wandering womb was increasingly disputed, whereas attention gradually shifted to the brain as the 'seat' of hysteric affections. None the less, in several works from the eighteenth and nineteenth centuries eating problems remained to be mentioned as hysterical symptoms. No less a person than Albrecht von Haller, founder of experimental physiology, concluded after a discussion about several cases of prodigious abstinence that hysterics were among them; but others also pointed out a relationship between eating problems and hysteria.[383]

The relatively obscure French physician Joseph Raulin (1708–84) escaped from oblivion due to an original treatise on hysteria from 1758. He discarded the traditional beliefs in the uterine function and expressed the view that males were also subject to *affections vaporeuses*. His following statement is remarkable:

> Sometimes stomach-complaints, loss of appetite and aversion to food occur, which are so considerable, that during the entire illness it is impossible to ingest the least piece of food. Yet these patients do not emaciate and mostly preserve their natural colour.[366]

Raulin's contemporary and compatriot Jean Astruc (1684–1766) established in his highly esteemed treatise of women's diseases from 1761 that hysteria is commonly accompanied by 'disturbance or suppression of the menses'. Small wonder, according to Astruc, that in hysteria symptoms of disturbed menses also occur such as aversion from food, forms of disturbed appetite and a bad digestion.[307] From the eighteenth century the afore-mentioned work of Philippe Pinel should be quoted again. His *Nosographie Philosophique* from 1798 contains some striking passages on hysteria.[364] Just like the earlier-mentioned 'anorexia', this affliction belonged to the neuroses, though now to the *névroses de la génération*. In his depiction of hysteria Pinel evidently had an eye for its psychogenic character (among others 'severe and repeated emotions') and the major role of sexuality (for instance 'the lack of the pleasures of love').

The peculiar picture of the illness was presented characteristically in one of the cases of hysteria Pinel had observed. It concerns a girl of healthy constitution, who succumbed at the age of 17, without any known cause, to some form of mania. She talked to herself, jumped about, took off her clothes and threw them into the fire. This state continued for five months and disappeared during the summer as a result of various distractions and frequent journeys into the country, which was followed by her menarche. After three months, however, in which her periods did not recur, her hysterical symptoms returned once a month. At first she showed annoyance with her everyday activities, along with a tendency to cry without provocation, sombre and taciturn behaviour. Shortly afterwards, the rest of her body was drawn taut in a kind of tetanic rigidity, she lost the use of speech, could not open her mouth, had feelings of strangulation and complained of constipation. These symptoms persisted for three or four days, when in addition she was noted to abstain altogether from food. Afterwards a voracious appetite set in and all her functions returned to normal. This calm continued for about a week, but afterwards the attacks resumed with the same vehemence. In spite of Pinel's remedies the girl remained sombre and taciturn, refused to stay in bed and abstained from food, except for toast soaked in sugar and wine. Pinel recommended frequent trips to the country in an open carriage, to get the maximum fresh air. Partly as a result of this regime she regained her physical and mental health. The way Pinel concludes the case history is completely on the lines given by Hippocrates: ' to prevent any relapse, I insisted on the absolute necessity of her marrying by early winter; in this manner a substantial cure was achieved while simultaneously fulfilling the will of nature.'[379]

This case history – a typical sample according to the author – suggests that Pinel considered food abstinence to be one of the essential symptoms of hysteria. However, this conclusion is rather premature, for in the section 'General description of hysteria' eating disorders go unmentioned. This is characteristic of the position of these phenomena within the clinical picture of hysteria. Eating disorders did not belong to the most essential characteristics of the affliction, but nevertheless several prominent physicians from the history of hysteria often referred to them as part of a wide variety of symptoms. Before the nineteenth century we are only familiar with one publication in which food abstinence as a hysterical symptom played a predominant part. This is a case history, published in 1789 by a French physician whose name is not only lacking in the annals of hysteria, but also in medical–historical biographies. Of this great unknown, Charles(?) Naudeau, we only know that this *docteur en médecine* at the university of Montpellier and correspondent of the Parisian Royal Society of Medicine, was living in Saint-Etienne en Forez. One article of scarcely four pages, 'Observation sur une maladie nerveuse, accompagnée d'un dégoût extraordinaire pour les alimens', saved him from oblivion: many a historical survey of anorexia nervosa makes mention of it.[358]

In August 1787 Naudeau saw a 35-year-old woman who awoke one morning with 'sharp pains in the epigastric region'. The pains soon spread throughout her body, in consequence of which she lost her appetite. A consulted surgeon recommended blood-letting, purgation and an emetic, but the woman refused. Her aversion to medicines, solid and liquid food was extraordinary and she fell ultimately into 'inanition to the point of collapse'. The surgeon persuaded her to take some milk. She regained strength, but from that moment on she threw up thick and sticky phlegm. When her physical condition worsened, Naudeau was consulted. He found his patient frightened and restless and with a 'small, rapid and intermittent pulse'. He could not establish any obvious cause for her affliction and concluded it was 'une affection histérique'. He prescribed her medicines and advised rubbing her body with cloths and taking cold baths. In his view particularly the latter attributed to her recovery:

> Following this treatment her body and mind promptly recovered the equilibrium of her functions; I persuaded the patient, who took her potions more willingly, to the intake of lemonade, and I accomplished the cure with clear whey, diluted with watercress.

Only at the end of the previous century, after the introduction of anorexia nervosa, was Naudeau's article rescued from oblivion. Although his description went unnoticed for about a

hundred years, by the early nineteenth century other authors
were linking food abstinence to hysteria. After Von Haller
several sources point out that there were hysterics among the
prolonged fasters. The unknown German physician Von Rein,
for instance, described a case of hysteria in which food abstinence
was one of the most prominent symptoms.[385] It concerns a 19-
year-old girl ('Karoline M. from K.') who suffered in 1829 from
absence of the menses, headache and stomach ache. These complaints arose after she had suppressed her menses successfully by
drinking vinegar in order to be able to take part in a dancing-
party. In the beginning of the year 1832 she was plagued by
stomach ache, a dry cough, oppression, fainting fits, eructation,
globus hystericus (a 'ball' in her throat) and loss of appetite. She
was visibly wasting away, and therapies were of no avail. In
April 1832 she stopped taking food, as cramps in her throat and
gullet impeded her swallowing. According to Von Rein the girl
suffered from a form of hysteria linked with an increased
irritation of the total nervous system. The wilfully suppressed
menses had caused an induration and thus a swelling of milt and
ovaries, which in turn was an important factor in the cause of
the cramps. He gave an explanation of the food abstinence
(designated by the Classical term *inedia*) which was not uncommon in his days: it was a fasting cure originating from nature in
reaction to the induration of milt and ovaries. For this reason he
regarded any persuasion to take food as injurious and needless,
as evidenced by the absence of any emaciation.

Despite von Rein's magnetic treatment, her complaints persisted. The patient continued to renounce all food: 'She liked to
see, however, when others were eating and desired eaters sitting
in her locality. She seemed to refresh herself by the smell of
foods.' At the beginning of May she could not even smell or see
food any longer, and felt a severe pain in her breast. Although,
according to Von Rein, there was no reason to suspect her of
fraudulent fasting, she had been watched continuously by physicians for three days 'to establish this formally'. Imposture was
not uncovered. In July the patient began to cough up blood and
an inflammation on the right lung was discovered. The more
the latter developed, the more obviously her attacks of cramps
and food abstinence decreased. However, she was visibly emaciat-
ing, became feverish and also began to cough up pus. On

23 August 1832 she rattlingly breathed her last. A post-mortem showed a lung full of small 'tubercles'.

In an afterword Von Rein devotes much attention to the food abstinence. However, surprisingly enough he does not go into the question of whether tuberculosis might be the cause. After a reflection on the way hibernating animals and apparently dead people stay alive, he points out that *inedia* also occurs in maniacs and melancholics as well as ascetics. He attributes this to an overactivity of the brain or a part of the nervous system, a disturbed self-consciousness (*Gemeingefühl*), but also to a defect in the gastrointestinal system. Besides this, he remarks that in rutting animals hunger is worsened by the sexual instinct: 'This condition may occur likewise in early pubertal persons under stormy development of the sexual organs, or also at more advanced age due to increased irritation of the sexual system in hysteria and hypochondriasis.' The condition of 'highest sensibility' might have enabled the girl to feed herself in a peculiar way. Matter added to the air might be absorbed by lungs and skin and thus replacing food and drink. Therefore the smell of food initially may have been enough to refresh her.

Several elements in Von Rein's article have been mentioned before: the extensive watch to elucidate deceit, the comparison between prolonged fasters and hibernating animals, the hypothesis about living on nutritive elements in the air. The combination of these age-old themes with the diagnosis of hysteria is a new development. As such Von Rein was a precursor of an important evolution in the second part of the nineteenth century, in which contemporary physicians were increasingly confronted with 'hysterical' young women who would not eat. In 1840 Thomas Laycock of York, for example, said of anorexia:

> In no chronic disease is this symptom so constant and so strongly marked as in hysteria . . . Nothing is more true than that a hysterical girl will live and look fat on an incredibly small quantity of food, and that exclusively vegetable.[445]

With the introduction of the *anorexie hystérique* in 1873 the history of hysterical fasting reached its climax as well as its end.

Melancholia

A fourth illness of which emaciation and eating disorders were traditionally considered symptomatic was melancholia. This affliction, nowadays closely linked to depression, was originally more rooted in physiology than psychology. In Classical antiquity melancholia was a chronic disease, caused by black bile (*melas* = black, *cholè* = bile), one of the four humours – the others being yellow bile, phlegm and blood – considered at the time to be of crucial importance for health and disease. An excess of black bile caused melancholia, in which the brain was affected directly or indirectly. In Classical literature three types of melancholia were distinguished. Rufus of Ephesus (early second century) seems to have been the originator of this classification, though it was spread particularly via Galen's works.[368] In the first form 'the whole body is full of a melancholia blood', whereas in the second 'only the brain has been invaded'. The third form starts in the hypochondria (a region below the lower ribs), which gives off smoky vapours ascending to the brain (*melancholia hypochondriaca*). The extreme influence of the black bile manifests itself in a variety of symptoms: melancholia was accompanied by dejection, fears, restlessness, insomnia, misanthropy, delusions and gastrointestinal difficulties. As attendant melancholic symptoms Soranus of Ephesus mentioned considerable weight loss, whereas Hippocrates and Rufus of Ephesus referred to aversion to food.[308;343] But in antique medicine unanimity on this topic was lacking. Aretaeus of Cappadocia (around AD 150), for instance, noted that in more advanced stages melancholics are 'voracious, indeed, yet emaciated; for in them sleep does not brace their limbs either by what they have eaten or drunk, but watchfulness diffuses and determines them outwardly.'[347]

As these Classical authorities served as a frame of reference well into the early modern era, similar descriptions recurred repeatedly. A combination of symptoms derived from Classical sources is to be found in the flourishing Arabic mediaeval medicine.[347] The Islamic physician Ishaq ibn Imran (early tenth century) from Baghdad considered weight loss to be characteristic of the three types of melancholia. The 'sort that only occurs in the brain' is characterized by sleeplessness and 'burning hunger, or on the other hand, loss of appetite'. In the hypochondriacal type many vomited an acid, black-bilious juice. A famous Arabic physician, whose *Liber Canonis* was singularly influential even well into the seventeenth century, was Avicenna (or Ibn Sina; 980–1037). This physician and philosopher mentioned, among other things, delusions and loss of appetite as symptoms of melancholia. He illustrates this with the story of a young melancholic prince having the delusion that he had turned into a cow. Everyday he would constantly scream: 'Kill me so that a good stew may be made from my flesh.' He was eating nothing and gradually wasting away; the physicians were unable to treat him further. Finally the relatives of the patient pleaded with the king to instruct Avicenna – at that time prime minister – to treat the young prince. Avicenna accepted the case and said: 'Give the youth the happy news that the butcher is going to come to slaughter him'. Then he paid a visit to the prince, who was very jubilant upon hearing the news. Avicenna had a butcher's knife in his hand and said aloud: 'Where is this cow so I can slaughter it?' He sat down and put his hand by the side of the patient as was the custom of the butchers. Then he said: 'Ah! What a thin cow! It is not worth killing! Give it grass to be fattened.' Then Avicenna left and told the people: 'Untie him and any food (and medicine) I prescribe take to him and tell him – eat so that you will be fattened soon.' Avicenna's advice was strictly followed and it took a month to regain the prince's health.[371]

Of course, this is a peculiar case with an exceptional therapy, which today would be called an example of 'paradoxical therapy'. Traditionally, the treatment of melancholia was directed at the supposed excess of black bile. For ages, in order to restore the balance between the humours, the most applied therapies were bloodletting, emetics, purgatives, diets, massages, warm baths, bodily exercise and distraction. Even when the views of melancholia progressively dissociated themselves from the Graeco-Roman body of thought, these forms of therapy largely remained in use. The late seventeenth century brought important conceptual changes regarding melancholia.[347] To replace the theory of the humours, scientists, inspired by mechanical principles, developed theories about a disturbed circulation of blood, lymph or nerve fluids. Melancholia at that time turned out to be a popular affliction: it was regarded as a sign of intellectual and moral superiority, if not genius. Thinness and eating problems continued to be common symptoms.

In 1621 Robert Burton (1557–1640) presented an extensive and representative survey of the traditional views in his well-known book *The Anatomy of Melancholy*.[320] He acknowledged that melancholics 'be commonly leane', but referring to Aretaeus he simultaneously points out that 'they doe eat much'. The third form, the 'windy or hypocondriacall melancholy', was accompanied by leanness, but dependent upon the primarily affected stomach region, vomiting, excessive, little or no appetite may occur. The earlier mentioned Leyden professor Herman Boerhaave detached himself somewhat from the traditional humoral theory. His view of the human body as a machine in which mechanical laws are operative induced him to seek the causes of melancholia in the circulation and composition of blood. He considered the three traditional forms of melancholia to be different degrees of one affliction. In the first degree of melancholic illness he noticed among others: 'a lessen'd Appetite; a Leanness'.[347] As noted before, another coryphaeus from this era, the great scholar Albrecht von Haller, mentioned in his *Elementa Physiologiae* a number of cases of prolonged food abstinence. In his view many of these cases, were, apart from hysterics, nothing else but melancholics.[383] The famous nosologist Boissier de Sauvages found enough arguments to designate one of the many forms of anorexia as 'anorexia melancholia'.[317]

At the same time Robert Willan (1757–1812) described 'a young man of a studious and melancholic turn of mind'.[388] Although Willan became known as the father of English dermatology, he acquired a permanent place in the history of anorexia nervosa with the following description. In 1786 he was asked by a 'respectable clergyman in the neighbourhood' to assist a young man, who was starving himself. The patient embarked on a severe course of abstinence allegedly in the hope of relieving his disagreeable digestive complaints. Willan, however, suggests that the fasting was the result of 'some mistaken notions in religion'. Withdrawn from society, he exclusively permitted himself some water. After sixty-one days of fasting, Willan was consulted and he described him in the following way: 'His whole appearance suggested the idea of a skeleton, prepared by drying the muscles upon it'. This did not prevent the young man from copying the bible in shorthand, which had progressed almost to the Second Book of Kings. Willan prescribed him a fluid diet consisting of barleywater, mutton tea and mutton-broth. Three days later, in his nurse's absence, he ate a great quantity of bread and butter. The patient seemed to be doing well, but shortly afterwards he developed memory lapses and became frantic and unmanageable. Despite treatments of a purgative draught and two clysters, the young man died quite exhausted in the morning of 9 April, 1786. According to Willan the duration of the fast (seventy-eight days) was longer than any recorded in the annals of medicine. 'He could scarcely have been supported through it, except from an enthusiastic turn of mind, nearly bordering on insanity', Willan concluded.

When in the seventeenth century melancholia gradually lost its connection with black bile, from the hypochondriacal variant a new illness developed: hypochondriasis.[332] This turned out to be a fashionable complaint, especially in England ('English malady'). It was the most widespread affliction or, put it more properly, the most popular diagnosis in those days, a favourite topic of numerous essays, books and letters, as much for physicians as for the general public. Despite the great interest in it, its exact status was unclear. Today hypochondriasis denotes excessive preoccupation with suffering from a serious disease despite the fact that numerous and repeated medical examinations cannot establish any defect. In the past, however, the term hypochondriasis implied a totally different clinical picture. Some considered it to be the forerunner of melancholia, synonymous with melancholia hypochondriaca or traditional hysteria. Unanimity about causes and symptoms was totally lacking. Those who distinguished hypochondriasis as a separate clinical picture, suggested as a cause a defect in the nervous system or in one of the hypochondriacal organs like milt, stomach and entrails. *Grosso modo* this particularly resembled antique melancholia. As typical characteristics of hypochondriasis many of the melancholic symptoms appeared in the eighteenth century, which had been already described by Aretaeus. In particular gastrointestinal disorders were prominent symptoms, just as in the hypochondriacal form of classical melancholia: constipation, diarrhoea, flatulence, stomach aches, nausea and eructations. It should be no surprise that some physicians pointed out loss of appetite (whether or not in conjunction with voracity or bulimia) as a symptom of hypochondriasis, whereas others regarded eating disorders as of no, or merely secondary, importance. Only in the middle of the nineteenth century, when hypochondriasis acquired its current denotation, was a description published for the first and last time, in which eating disorders took a prominent place in the hypochondriacal clinical picture (see Chapter 8).

Although some of the characteristics of melancholia were accommodated by hypochondriasis, at the beginning of the nineteenth century thinness and eating disorders continued to be associated with melancholia. The influential German psychiatrist and psychologist Johann Christian Heinroth (1773–1843), for instance, mentioned lack of appetite and weight loss as features of the onset of melancholia, which had to be cured by sending the patient on holiday.[347] In a treatise on protracted food abstinence Léon Rostan (1790–1866), a pupil of Pinel, pointed out that 'la mélancolie' is undoubtedly the disease which best endures prolonged fasting.[367] Another indication of a relationship between thinness, eating disorders and melancholia is to be found in the work of another pupil of Pinel who was also an influential figure in the history of psychiatry: Jean-Etienne-Dominique Esquirol (1772–1840).

Like his teacher, Esquirol was an advocate of humane treatment of the mentally ill. Theoretically, however, he was a rival of his teacher. His *Des Maladies Mentales* from 1838, a summary of the clinical lectures he provided for more than twenty years, attests to his keen clinical observations.[331] In this textbook Esquirol discusses the *lypémanie* or *mélancolie*, of which he presented several case histories. One of them concerns the 23-year-old Mademoiselle M., who was brought to the renowned Salpêtrière hospital in 1812. She suffered, among other things, from irregular menstruation and obstinate constipation and scorbutic spots were observed on her lower extremities. She refused to move and did not want to leave her bed. Efforts to induce her to take nourishment were of no avail and only cold water triumphed over this repugnance. Occasionally she still manifested her unwillingness to take nourishment, though with less obstinacy. However, food had to be brought to her and she had to be pressed to partake of it. During the four years she had been in the Salpêtrière she spoke only a few words, 'which, however, indicated to us, that fear absorbed all her faculties', the more so as she had been excessively frightened by soldiers in the past.

Esquirol concludes his case history as follows: 'We never succeeded in overcoming the silence of this female, nor her aversion
to motion. She never had an attack of fury. She died of phthisis
at the age of twenty-nine years.' According to Esquirol's writing,
dejection and fear were far more important within the clinical
picture of melancholia than eating disorders and thinness. Nevertheless, the latter symptoms traditionally belonged to the large
group of marginal but constant signs of melancholia. This
association came to an end neither with the introduction of
anorexia nervosa, thirty-five years after Esquirol's description
nor after the age-old concept of melancholia had been supplanted
by 'modern' depression.

Love-sickness and chlorosis

As sadness and pangs of love may be closely related, it is no
great leap from melancholia to 'love-sickness'.[314;338] Love, an
inexhaustible source of inspiration to artists, was also an important and age-old theme in medical treatises. From Classical
antiquity on, the drawbacks of love and its detrimental effects
on body and mind have repeatedly been pointed out. In some
cases the sickly effects of love were viewed as so harmful that
consultation with a physician had been necessary. There was no
agreement, however, about the exact character of the *mal
d'amour*. The affliction might vary from innocent amorousness
and despair for unrequited love to insatiable (sexual) lust.

A well-known love affair from the Classical period, in which a
physician played a predominant part, occurred at the court of
Seleucus I, King of Syria (about 358–280 BC). Here we follow the
affair on the basis of an account by Plutarch (about 50–125).[365]
The story began when Prince Antiochus fell in love with his
young stepmother Stratonice, who was already mother of a
little boy by Seleucus. Antiochus was distressed and even desperately determined to seek a way of escape from life. He completely
neglected himself, abstained from food pretending to have some
wasting disease. However, his physician, the famous Erasistratus,
perceived quite easily that he was in love, but he had not the
faintest idea whom he loved so passionately. To solve this problem
he spent some days in the young man's chamber. Nothing
exceptional occurred, until Stratonice came to see him, then

those tell-tale signs of which Sappho sings were all there in him – stammering speech, fiery flushes, darkened vision, sudden sweats, irregular palpitations of the heart and finally, as his soul was taken by storm, helplessness, stupor, and pallor.

Furthermore, Erasistratus argued, had he loved any other woman, he would not have persisted to the death in refusing to speak about it. The physician told Seleucus that love was the young man's trouble, love that could neither be satisfied nor cured. The king was amazed, and asked for an explanation. Erasistratus said: 'Because, indeed he is in love with my wife.' With that Seleucus entreated him to meet his son's desire. Then Erasistratus replied that the king himself, though being Antiochus' father, 'wouldst not have done so if Antiochus had set his affections on Stratonice'. When Seleucus assured him that he would gladly let his kingdom go, if he might keep his son, Erasistratus stated that he was able to cure his own son. Shortly afterwards the king declared it to be his wish that Antiochus and Stratonice became husband and wife and so it indeed came to pass.

Galen mentions a similar case from his own practice.[334] This time the lover is a female. He noticed that her pulse became extremely irregular when someone mentioned the name of Pylades. Galen concluded that the illness was caused by love and pointed out that lovers may emaciate, become pale and feverish, and may suffer from sleeplessness. Others before him would also have established this. The earliest preserved treatise on love-sickness as a separate affliction is featured by Oribasius of Pergamum (325–403).[359] He described, beside symptoms such as dejection and insomnia, that the lover seems to be filled with voluptuousness despite a weakened body. He did not mention thinness or food abstinence as signs. In the work of another Byzantine physician, Paul of Aegina (625–90), love-sickness is discussed in a similar way.[363]

Arab physicians from the mediaeval period predominantly drew on these Byzantine sources, yet there are differences. Together with disproportionate passion they put forward physical causes like an excess of seed or in females a congestion of menstrual blood. They warned that proper treatment is necessary, as otherwise the affliction may deteriorate into mania, melancholia and wasting. Diverging from Byzantine sources, Ad Damîrî (second half of the fourteenth century), for instance, described in an extensive treatise on love-sickness that 'the imagination of the ardent lover is never free from the object of his ardent love . . . and the lover is prevented from eating and drinking'. In Western Europe similar observations were reported at the end of the thirteenth century by Arnaldus of Villanova and Bernard of Gordon from Montpellier.[353]

As far as therapy is concerned physicians from antiquity and the Middle Ages prescribed among other things, bloodletting, medicines, distraction and frequent sexual intercourse with another, other than the beloved. Bernard of Gordon even advised:

> Find an ugly looking old hag with long teeth and a beard . . . When the lovesick patient arrives, let her vilify his beloved by saying that she is fat and has enormous warts on her body, that she is drunk and an epileptic and has foul breath, that she wets her bed and has worms, and all the other horrible things in which old wives are specialists.

If success with this 'therapy' eluded them, some physicians ultimately advised uniting the patient with the beloved. In the early modern period the symptomatology shifted. The formerly predominantly platonic character of passion gradually transformed into love with a greater sexual impact. As well as frenzy and epilepsy, unsatisfied voluptuousness, obscenity and obtrusiveness were added to the picture of love-sickness. Love-sickness preeminently developed more and more into a women's disease. Parallel with this evolution confusion arose about the exact character of love-sickness.

In the mediaeval period the affliction had already been put forward as a form of melancholia.[347] The great Arab physician Avicenna, for instance, considered love-sickness to be closely related to the melancholic affliction. This view was underlined in Western Europe, for instance by Bernard of Gordon. Numerous early modern physicians followed their example. Influential medical writers like André du Laurens (1560?–1609), Daniel Sennert (1572–1637) and Thomas Willis (1621–75) inserted love-sickness into their treatises on melancholia.[347] In Robert Burton's famous *The Anatomy of Melancholy* about a quarter is devoted to 'love-melancholy'. Classical symptoms like food abstinence, leanness and paleness also characterized his melancholic form of love-sickness. From the eighteenth century onwards, when interest in the affliction was waning, beside *melancholia amatoria*, the concept of *erotomania* became fashionable. In this way platonic love found its way back into medical literature.

In the nineteenth century love continued to attract attention in psychiatric literature. As well as being a mental disorder it was considered an important factor in the causation of consumptive diseases like tuberculosis. The link with classical love-sickness, however, became increasingly obscure. The last prominent physician to describe the affliction in a way which strongly resembled the past was the Frenchman Esquirol.[331] He distinguished erotomania from classical melancholia and placed it in the category of monomania. The clinical picture with features like paleness and lack of appetite remained unchanged. After Esquirol some still stressed the platonic character of the affliction, while it was transformed by others into a kind of hypersexuality. Many nineteenth-century clinicians, however, did not pay any attention at all to erotomania. It was increasingly doubted whether love pangs were indeed a distinct clinical entity. Ultimately erotomania acquired a discrete place in the margin of psychiatric literature, as one of the passional delusions, depicted by Gaétan Gatian de Clérambault (1872–1934). Today erotomania or De Clérambault's syndrome denotes a rare pychotic state without depressive signs, in which a woman has the deluded belief that a particular man is very much in love with her.

Melancholia was not the most important, let alone the only, disease which assimilated love-sickness and caused its demise. The rise of chlorosis or green-sickness seems to be more responsible for this. This affliction appeared for the first time in the early modern period under that label, flourished particularly during the eighteenth and nineteenth centuries, decreased in incidence dramatically from the turn of the century on and then mysteriously disappeared in the 1920s.[344;378] Johannes Lange (1485–1565) was the first to give a clear description of green-sickness under the label of *morbus virgineus* or virgins' disease. He mentioned, among other things, paleness, aversion to food and absence of the menses as its characteristic symptoms. Not uncommon in those days, he attributed the cause to 'suppression of the menses' and the spread of impure menstrual blood afflicting the brain.[333]

The Frenchman Ambroise Paré (1517?–90), father of modern surgery, generally underlined Lange's observations. Girls who fall in love and start to menstruate, but whose marriage is too long delayed, are particulary liable to *palles couleurs*. Like Lange, Paré recommended marriage as the cure. Although he did not underestimate the role of the retention of 'menstrual discharge', he predominantly attributed the affliction to the female 'seed' remaining too long in the womb. This led to brooding, loss of appetite, insomnia, pallor and in extreme cases to death. Conditions of life were the explanation for the fact that girls from the city were more susceptible to the affliction than those from the country with their meagre and laborious livelihood.[361]

The namer of chlorosis, Jean Varandal (1563?–1617) from Montpellier, did not have much to add to either description. His remark about the observed pallor of chlorotics is interesting: he pointed out that chlorosis occurred 'almost endemically' in beautiful young girls of noble birth. Convinced of the notion that love is synonymous with pallor 'young girls and weak unmarried women try by every artificial means to make themselves more pale, in order that they may seem more beautiful'.[378] The French physician probably referred here to the use of cosmetics, but he may also have meant pica – i.e. the intake of inedible substances like lime, clay, wood, etc. – eventually aimed at suppressing the appetite. Nevertheless several of Varandal's contemporaries put pica forward as a frequently used method to achieve the desired attractive pallor. The descriptions of Lange, Paré and Varandal had broadly outlined the classical picture of chlorosis for a long time: until well into the nineteenth century its description and explanation were reminiscent of those early works.

Despite of – or due to? – its vague boundaries, chlorosis developed, particularly from the eighteenth century onwards, into a 'fashionable' disease. The many great physicians dealing with the affliction and hundreds of dissertations on the subject attest to this.[354] However, just like love-sickness, which was partly transformed into chlorosis, the latter came smoothly to an end. At the beginning of the previous century, when the number of chlorotic cases were still on the increase, disputes arose about the absence of the menses as cause, and numerous alternative theories were developed. Possibly under the influence of Broussais' doctrine of gastrointestinal 'irritation' (see Chapter 8) or due to the role of eating disorders within the clinical picture, some physicians considered a dysfunction of the digestive organs to be the cause of green-sickness. Others attributed the affliction to malfunctioning of certain organs (such as heart, liver or genitals), a disturbed nervous system, constipation, psychical factors (for instance fear of sexuality), badly ventilated or unhygienic rooms, etc. All these fairly speculative theories could not prevent chlorosis from becoming a deficiency disorder, resulting from a lack of iron, i.e. nothing but anaemia. Although by the third decade of the nineteenth century some physicians were already pointing out the change in the composition of blood which resulted from chlorosis, it would be some decades longer before this view was widely supported.[333]

Important nineteenth-century developments in haematology, like the ability to quantify haemoglobin, contributed to a more accurate insight into the composition of blood. Yet, this acquired knowledge did not provide a definite answer to whether impoverishment of the blood was the consequence or cause of chlorosis. This confusion is apparent, for instance, from the fact that in France green-sickness was viewed for some time as a form of neurosis associated with anaemia. About 1890, however, it was widely acknowledged that there were but two causes of chlorosis: loss of blood and an iron-deficient diet. Now, green-sickness was definitively equated with anaemia.[344] Blood tests had become the criterion of diagnosis of chlorosis and administration of iron its most adequate therapy.

In descriptions of chlorosis attention was completely focused on typically anaemic symptoms such as tiredness, palpitations and dyspnoea. Traditional chlorotic characteristics which did not fit with anaemia so well, like pica, lack of appetite and amenorrhoea, received much less attention. This reduction of chlorosis heralded the beginning of the end, though initially things looked different: it was at the end of the nineteenth century chlorosis reached its apotheosis. However, shortly thereafter a striking decrease set in: already by the 1930s the once popular chlorosis had become a medical rarity without any diagnostic significance.[357] Possible explanations of the peculiar decline of this age-old disease will be discussed in Chapter 11.

8

Who Was the First to Describe Anorexia Nervosa?

In the nineteenth century the foundation was laid for modern medicine, while psychiatry developed into a distinct medical discipline. Doctrines and traditions from previous centuries, however, were not easily cast out and the influence of former medical theories waned only gradually. Concepts like hysteria, melancholia and hypochondriasis appeared to be as ineradicable as if they were holy relics from an age-old medical inheritance. The often colourful theories hidden within these concepts, could not, however, make headway against the natural scientific climate which dominated nineteenth-century medicine. Rationalism and empiricism were highly esteemed by physicians: everything had to be carefully observed and compared. In specialist literature detailed case histories flourished, frequently associated with a passionate dispute about the proper diagnosis. Newly discovered syndromes, often provided with a Latin or Greek neologism, were numerous. In this way the 'discoverer' as well as the 'novelty' was immortalized via a term, created by himself, which then acquired a place within the ever more complicated classificatory systems of diseases. This would also occur in uncommon forms of emaciation and fasting: more prominently than ever they manifested themselves in the pantheon of medicine.

The 'discovery' of anorexia nervosa in the nineteenth century may be a fact of cultural-historical significance (as we will elaborate in Chapter 10). Yet we firstly have to put this development within the tradition of medical thinking. Even the Classical Greeks, Plato in particular, were fascinated by the question as to where the soul is situated in the human body. It had been assigned a place in the diaphragm and the heart. Both were designated by the Greek term *phren*, which became synonymous with 'spirit' or all the psychic capacities which man possesses. After traversing throughout the body, ultimately – by the beginning of the nineteenth century – the psyche was finally located in the brain. The notion of diverse psychical functions being each located in particular parts of the brain was developed by Franz Joseph Gall (1758–1828) into a new science, the doctrine of cerebral localization. He had been convinced of a direct link between the form of the skull and typical character traits. Gall called his doctrine craniology or cranioscopy, but it became popular under the label of 'phrenology', a term created by his pupil Johann Caspar Spurzheim (1776–1832). Today it amuses us to see in phrenology books representations of skulls, locating all sorts of human qualities and weaknesses – from patriotism to jealousy – each on their own well-delineated spot. Yet, at the basis of phrenology was the firm conviction that body and mind were closely related: the belief that the structure of the human mind is manifested in the architecture of the human body. Scientifically, phrenology gave a major impetus to brain research and physiological psychology. As such, the way was indirectly prepared for psychosomatic medicine in general and the discovery of anorexia nervosa in particular.[32]

Precursors of a 'new' illness

In the first half of the nineteenth century phrenology was very popular in France. Gall had emigrated from Vienna to Paris and his phrenological textbook had made the leading physiologist Broussais his ardent supporter. The same Broussais, however, was far better known as the promoter of physiological medicine, which instead of merely recording and arranging symptoms looked for the causes of pathological phenomena. All diseases, including mental disorders, were viewed by Broussais as organic dysfunctions, caused by a physiological process of 'inflammation'. He believed that inflammation of the stomach and entrails explained all pathological phenomena; he therefore advocated fasting as one of the cures. Although his views were both applauded and criticized by many, Broussais' work is typical of contemporary medical thinking, in particular as far as mental diseases (and more precisely hysteria) are concerned. On the one hand its cause was sought in certain disturbed organs ('peripheral' theories), whereas on the other increasing value was attached to the role of brain functions ('central' theories). The latter view predominated and developed into a physiological psychiatry, with the German Wilhelm Griesinger (1817–69) as its most influential advocate. Griesinger's motto 'mental diseases are brain diseases' completely dominated nineteenth-century neuropsychiatry.[584]

Against this background we will focus now on the work of the French physician Fleury Imbert (1795–1851), a rather obscure physiologist and phrenologist. He worked in particular in Lyon, where he was physician at the 'Hôtel Dieu' and also director of the Charité hospital. He was a member of the local 'Académie des Sciences, Belles-Lettres et Arts'. In 1834 he published a neurophysiological study on the sensations of hunger and thirst and also in the same year a historical-phrenological book on Napoleon and Descartes. Imbert defends medicine as a distinct science unrelated to metaphysics, philosophy, spiritualism or vitalism: medical practice, from observation to experiment, is fed by a physiological theory wherein the brain fulfils an essential role. The brain contains all vegetal, intellectual, affective, moral and psychic functions or capacities. Other organs only have to execute the orders received from the brain. It is along these lines that the soul may provoke disorders. Hence, we do better to replace 'soul' by 'brain', Imbert proposed.

In 1840 Imbert's book *Traité Théorique et Pratique des Maladies des Femmes* appeared.[436] Under the label 'neuroses of the stomach', he describes three eating disorders: anorexia, bulimia and pica. In the extensive chapter on the first disorder, two types of anorexia are suggested: 'anorexie gastrique' and 'anorexie nerveuse'. Unlike the former, the latter form of anorexia is caused directly by the brain and consequently also called 'primary' or 'idiopathic'. In view of the different localizations of the disease, medication varied correspondingly: in the case of 'anorexie gastrique' the stomach is treated, whereas in 'anorexie nerveuse' medication is directed at the brain functions. Typical of patients with 'anorexie nerveuse' is the loss of appetite (the appetite is no longer excited by the brain). Hence, they often refuse to eat and consequently emaciate. Furthermore, such patients display all sorts of neurotic symptoms, particularly a change of temperament, i.e. they become melancholic, angry and/or frightened. All these symptoms are caused by a dysfunction in the encephalon's grey matter. Other organic disorders, for instance of the stomach, are lacking. Strikingly enough – as it concerns a book on women's diseases – Imbert is totally silent on menstrual irregularities in these patients.

Like Broussais, Imbert tried to integrate physiology and phrenology within a positivistic-scientific medicine, which reduced the functioning of the human mind to metabolic processes in the brain. How the brain might exert its influence – directly or indirectly – and why certain organic disorders occur at one time and not at another, still remained to be answered in those days. However, it is peculiar that Imbert in his description of eating disorders does not mention hysteria. The association of a symptom (*anorexie*) with an unspecified brain dysfunction (*nerveuse*) was rather uncommon at the beginning of the nineteenth century. Perhaps this was the major reason why Imbert's notion of *anorexie nerveuse* found no response and his work totally fell into oblivion, even despite the fact that half a century later the term *anorexie mentale* acquired a permanent place within French medicine (see below). However, neither with respect to his interest in eating disorders, nor regarding the oblivion into which Imbert fell, was he an exception.

Louis-Victor Marcé (1828–64) was better known during his lifetime than Imbert, though he had also been largely forgotten at the turn of the century. Nevertheless, in his short career as a psychiatrist he had been uncommonly active.[462] After receiving his MD degree in 1856 at the University of Paris, he was soon requested to take charge of a large asylum. In 1858 he published his *Traité de la Folie des Femmes Enceintes, des Nouvelles Accouchées et des Nourrices*, a book now considered to be a classic, it being the first extensive treatise on childbirth psychosis. Four years later his *magnum opus* appeared: *Traité Pratique des Maladies Mentales*, a voluminous handbook in the tradition of the flourishing nineteenth-century French psychiatry. Meanwhile he became associated with the Parisian hospitals Ferme Sainte Anne and the Bicêtre, had a successful private practice, gave lectures and clinical demonstrations for students, wrote numerous articles and was a member of the editorial board of the *Dictionnaire de Médecine et Chirurgie*. His abundant activities may have contributed to the sudden termination of his promising career by his premature death in 1864 at the age of 36.

In a recent historical study of anorexia nervosa[462] attention was focused on a completely neglected article Marcé published in 1860 and of which appeared an abbreviated English translation in the same year. In this report Marcé depicts a particular form of hypochondriacal delirium, which is chiefly characterized by food refusal and occurs especially in pubertal girls. The author has observed several patients surviving for months or even longer on extremely small amounts of food. Some of them literally died of hunger and he accurately describes their wasted condition: all traces of adipose tissue had disappeared; the patients were reduced to skeletons and the abdominal coat was so contracted as to touch the vertebral column; the pulse was filiform and insensible and the weakness soon became so great that patients could hardly walk a few steps without being seized with fainting. However, most typical is that

> all the intellectual energy centres round the functions of the stomach; incapable of the slightest exertion or of sustaining the least conversation beyond their delirious ideas, these unhappy patients only regain some amount of energy in order to resist attempts at alimentation, and very often the physician beats a retreat before their desperate resistance.[448]

In Marcé's view the disease is not to be cured by the traditional medical treatments directed at the condition of the stomach (bitters, tonics, iron, exercise and hydrotherapeutics). When the disease is in an advanced stage, these remedies are of little use as the disease is not a disturbance of the stomach: this organ suffers only from want of food. It is not the stomach that demands attention, as Marcé emphatically states, but 'it is the delirious idea which constitutes, henceforth, the point of departure, and in which lies the essence of the malady; *the patients are no longer dyspeptics – they are insane*'. Marcé considered it to be 'indispensable to change the habitation and surrounding circumstances, and to entrust the patients to the care of strangers': thus the family is liberated from the patient's obstinate resistance and incessant lamentation about stomach ache, and the physician is able to act with full liberty and may obtain the necessary moral ascendancy. Each day the nourishment should be gradually increased. However, if the food refusal continues, the physician should employ intimidation and even force, ultimately Marcé does not hesitate to recommend the use of the oesophagus probe. The serious risk to life necessitates rigorous measures, the author argues. The original paper in French is completed by two rather extensive case histories: the 12-year-old Mademoiselle A.B. and the 14-year-old Mademoiselle X.

Mademoiselle A.B. was a spoilt child who at the age of eight fell ill with typhus and several stomach complaints, which also plagued her in advanced age. When she was 12 years old, she fell ill and developed an aversion to food. She was very depressive and desperate and threatened to commit suicide. She gradually lost her appetite and became emaciated. A year later, in October 1857, she had lost thirty-five pounds and during the subsequent winter her condition deteriorated to such an extent that people expected her imminent death. Every meal was accompanied by scenes of violence and threats of suicide, during which pieces of crockery were smashed. In despair it was decided to separate her from her family and to entrust her to the care of strangers, who might exert 'a certain moral authority' over her. In July 1858 Marcé found her in a condition of extreme emaciation; she barely weighed 50 pounds and looked like a living skeleton. That very day Marcé proceeded to action: he violently opened her mouth, put a feeding-bottle filled with broth, and held her nose to prevent her from throwing up everything. His 'therapy' was successful: 'Some draughts of liquid were easily swallowed, and soon the patient, obviously moved and intimidated by this unexpected struggle, requested to feed herself the rest of the broth.' The following days, despite the patient's objections, he succeeded in making her eat. After a month she ate four times a day and had become less obsessed by her illness. A few months later she again weighed 84 pounds and ate without coercion. Yet she continued to abhor food and often managed to cleverly conceal food in her clothing. She recovered and going home in 1859 she was in excellent physical and intellectual health, although her periods had not yet returned. A year later, she was still healthy, although the regularity of her daily meals needed some attention.

The second case history concerns Mademoiselle X., who developed an aversion to food shortly after her menarche. She gradually reduced her intake of food and ultimately took only a few spoons of soup reluctantly and hesitatingly. When Marcé was consulted in June 1858, the signs of emaciation were obvious, but apart from her stubborn food refusal not a single *trouble intellectuel* could be established. Initially Marcé succeeded in persuading her to eat, but after a few months she was content with extremely small amounts of food. In March 1859 Marcé found her totally wasted: she looked worse, could hardly stand up and felt continuously cold. Her nourishment consisted only of a few spoons of soup, whereas during meals she only showed *une foule de manies*. The patient was aware of her condition, but considered herself to be unable to conquer her aversion to food. Every promise, wrested from her under moral pressure, was ineffective as soon as she was with her family. Probably for this reason Marcé withdrew her from her family and put her under the supervision of someone who took care that the physician's prescriptions were observed. Gradually it was possible to increase her food intake, even of food she had previously loathed. By the end of May 1859 she was freed from her mania and largely recovered.

> But, having returned to her home environment, where she was totally lacking moral guidance, Mademoiselle X. still displays in her pattern of feeding caprices and bizarreries, and I would not be able to assure that she is secured from every relapse.[448]

Marcé's striking description has been completely forgotten and even went unnoticed in his own days. It may be unclear what sort of patients Imbert observed, but Marcé gives a precise description of his patients' behaviour. To the modern diagnostic eye there seems to be no doubt: it is anorexia nervosa. That his report found no response at all is even more peculiar, given that Marcé, not only in his description of the disease but also in the recommended treatment, almost literally prefigured the 'discoverers' of anorexia nervosa more than ten years later! We could attribute the lack of response to the author's choice of the rather inadequate term 'hypochondriacal delirium'. Would Marcé have encountered more response if he had used the term 'hysteria', that prototypical nineteenth-century psychiatric disease? Presumably not, when we realize that a year before this report two studies on food refusal in hysterical women also went unnoticed.

The first occurs in an interesting article by William Stout Chipley (1810–80), chief medical officer of the Eastern Lunatic Asylum of Kentucky.[402] Around the mid-nineteenth century, many physicians working in such asylums were quite familiar with the problems of wasting diseases, undernutrition and food refusal in the insane. In 1859 Chipley addresses the causes and treatment of 'sitomania', an intense dread of eating or aversion to food, in those days usually labelled as 'sitophobia'. He regarded food refusal as a secondary symptom in various forms of insanity, usually being caused by either mental or digestive derangement. 'The most fruitful cause of sitomania is some morbid condition of the brain giving rise to hallucination' and 'amongst the most common delusions is the fear of poison'. Along with these rather well-known forms of food refusal, Chipley found another type:

> I allude to those cases in which a morbid desire for notoriety leads to protracted abstinence from food, in spite of the pangs of hunger, until finally all sustenance is refused. I have never witnessed a case of this kind except in females predisposed to hysteria. These cases are remarkable, because they are almost peculiar to well-educated, sensible people, belonging to the higher walks of society (. . .) . This is another phase of that terrible malady, hysteria, which so often incites its high-born and accomplished victims to most curious attempts at imposition on those around them.

For Chipley the motive of food refusal in these hysterical females can undoubtedly be attributed to their craving for attention from those surrounding them. He illustrates this with a case of an 'amiable' and 'delicate' young woman, who 'was not slow in perceiving that wonder and amazement grew inversely to the amount of food taken'. In spite of every effort 'to wean her from her folly, she died'. Chipley's description met the destiny of other publications: oblivion.

In exactly the same year Pierre Briquet (1796–1881) published a work which was also relatively soon forgotten, though it turned out to be in retrospect a milestone in the investigation of hysteria. At present his name is again familiar to psychiatrists. He was rediscovered by a group of American psychiatrists who labelled a form of hysteria accompanied by physical complaints as 'Briquet's syndrome'. Briquet was not a psychiatrist but an internist, who for years dealt with the study and prevention of epidemics (especially cholera). Almost by accident he came across hysterical patients when he was appointed as head of a ward in the Parisian Charité hospital. Probably his epidemiological interest induced him to observe and study disorders or clinical pictures in their different components and then to represent them in sober figures. At any rate his matter of fact empirical approach resulted in a, at the time, highly unusual book: *Traité Clinique et Thérapeutique de l'Hystérie*, published in 1859.[398] As far as both style and content are concerned, this monumental publication is extraordinary, looking strikingly 'modern' for its time: instead of merely echoing classical views and theoretical reflections, interspersed with illustrating case histories, for ten years Briquet – aided by numerous assistants – systematically gathered data on 430 hysterical patients. His method was: first observe, then conclude. He soon found out that hysteria, as he analysed it numerically, strongly deviated from the traditional views (called by him the 'classical' theory of hysteria) which had been considered unassailable since Hippocrates and Galen. Briquet clearly demonstrated with figures that hysteria might also occur among men, albeit only in a ratio of 1 to 20 females (the latter being qualified as extremely 'impressionable'). From this, along with other observations, Briquet concluded that hysteria should not be located in the womb, as had been supposed for centuries, but in the 'affective part' (to be distinguished from the intellectual part) of the brain.

Briquet was the first to explicitly renounce the until then popular theory that frustrated sexual instincts or insatiable erotic desires played a major part in the causation of hysteria. Once again Briquet supported his opinion by 'hard' figures: he argued that hysteria was hardly ever observed in nuns, whereas the disease was very frequent among Parisian prostitutes. Charcot, and later also Janet, agreed with Briquet's views and rejected the notion of hysteria as a sexual neurosis. Yet, such convictions were never completely abandoned. After 1860 most neurologists tended to agree with Briquet and Charcot, while gynaecologists stuck with the idea of the sexual psychogenesis of hysteria. Psychoanalysts, Freud first of all, would spread the latter view in all kinds of varieties of 'unconsciously curbed sexual expression'.

In Part 2 of his book Briquet describes a whole series of hysterical symptoms, among them 'hyperaesthesia of digestion' and more in particular 'gastralgia'.[398] In this section he emphasizes that hysterical patients frequently display a number of pains

and derangements of the stomach. This is even the first symptom
in women whose hysteria develops slowly and gradually. Often
this symptom is already to be found before the age of 13 and
before menarche. In a number of young girls, plagued by an
irregular menstruation in conjunction with chlorosis, appetite is
gradually lost. Accordingly, as hysteria develops slowly, in
hysterical women (and extremely rarely in men) it is typical that
an aversion towards ordinary food and a sometimes bizarre
appetite occurs, or even that patients have a hysterical attack
whenever they take a certain kind of food. Briquet provides
several colourful examples of this, like the princess of Naples
who fainted whenever she brought some food to her mouth.
When young individuals – and they specifically suffer from
'capricious gastralgia' – are over particular in the choice of their
food, they gradually waste away: they lose their strength,
become pale-complexioned and are predestined to lead the life
of sick women and to die at an early age.

Although gastralgia, accompanied by vomiting as its most
predominant symptom, is the most acute kind of hysterical
hyperaesthesia of digestion, we may consider this to be the least
harmful, as it can be treated well by proper medication. It is
peculiar, Briquet concludes, that despite frequent vomiting some
of these women succeed in staying 'fresh' and even stout. Some
of them have an insatiable hunger 'so that their day passes,
literally speaking, by eating in order to replace what they had
just vomited, and by vomiting in order to deliver what they had
just eaten.' In other cases appetite is completely lost, coupled
with an aversion to every sort of food. Then even the smallest
amounts, whether liquid or solid food, will induce a horrible
stomach ache. This form of gastralgia is the worst of all, because
it leads to progressive emaciation, through which patients
become exhausted and die totally weakened and wasted. Briquet
illustrates the peculiar mental state of these patients by the
example of a 20-year-old, highly intelligent woman, who spent
most part of the day on the one hand preparing *pot-au-feu* of
which she intended only to take the broth, and on the other
continuously adding water to dilute it. Briquet warns parents
and physicians against this kind of gastralgia: if it is not rapidly
and at any price terminated, death is inevitable. But whatever
kind of hysteria it may be, it is always directly influenced by the

affections morales: unpleasant experiences and emotions aggravate the condition, whereas pleasant circumstances and experiences lead to relief or even disappearance of the stomach complaints. To be sure of this, it suffices to place the patients in a better environment than that to which they are accustomed. However, it should be noted that the sudden disappearance of gastralgia may only be related to the emergence of another hysterical symptom.

How comparable the phenomena described by Briquet are to anorexia nervosa is not as obvious as in Marcé's report. It cannot be ruled out that such patients were among those he studied, but his book was primarily meant to be a comprehensive study of hysteria in its diverse manifestations. Consequently he did not intend to describe 'new' syndromes by means of extensive case studies. It looks as if he considered the eating disorders as fairly well known to those who were familiar with hysterical patients. If his depiction of 'hysterical gastralgia' had been indeed the description of a special clinical picture, it would still have gone unnoticed, as did his whole book. It was overshadowed within a few decades by Charcot's work and thus quickly fell into oblivion. When it was rediscovered a century later on the other side of the Atlantic Ocean, every psychiatrist had already for a long time been familiar with a term which saw the light even before Briquet's death: anorexia nervosa.

Gull and Lasègue

It is an idle dream of many a physician with academic ambitions to be recorded in the history of medicine as the discoverer of a new syndrome, preferably named after the illustrious scholar so that his name be immortalized. However, when several scientists simultaneously claim the 'discovery' for themselves, it becomes essentially a struggle over who was actually the first. The time of publication in specialist literature is often the decisive criterion. In the case of anorexia nervosa it is a competition between the Englishman Gull and the Frenchman Lasègue. Cultural affinities and linguistic chauvinism often decide on whom the honour is bestowed. Hence it is quite comprehensible that shortly after Lasègue's decease his compatriots considered him to be the discoverer, while across the Channel priority was naturally claimed for Gull. Before answering the question of who deserves the honour of being credited with the first description of the anorexia nervosa syndrome in modern medical literature, we will first introduce the 'competitors'.[477]

William Withey Gull (1816–90) was one of the most prominent English physicians of the second half of the nineteenth century. He was an extraordinary man in many respects. First of all, he was renowned in scientific circles as an excellent clinician with a shrewd capacity for observation. His numerous publications show how strongly he emphasized the importance of the clinical examination and this especially at a time when medicine was developing modes of scientific enquiry which were moving away from everyday clinical practice and patient care. Gull was a leading and influential physician in Great Britain, as witnessed by his professional reputation and the many honours he received. After a brilliant medical career, he quickly achieved academic promotion. His greatest fame came in 1871, when he successfully treated the Prince of Wales (later King Edward VII) for typhoid fever. In the following year he was knighted by Queen Victoria, who subsequently appointed him her Physician Extraordinary and later even Physician Ordinary to the Queen. No wonder that Sir William Gull became a 'fashionable physician', whose extensive private practice was made up of the most prominent members of British high society and many wealthy people in the London area. Whereas Gull started his medical career with a salary of £15 per year, after his death he left an inheritance of no less than £344,000, an amount never earned before by a British physician!

About fifteen years ago Gull's name was unexpectedly mentioned in relation to the notorious 'Jack the Ripper' case, the unsolved series of murders of five prostitutes in London's East End in 1888. This murder case is one of the most intriguing mysteries in the history of criminality. In 1973 the BBC devoted a sensational series to Jack the Ripper. Its final episode put forward the view, that the court at the time of Queen Victoria had been closely involved. The journalist Stephen Knight made thorough investigations into the case and published a sensational book providing the 'definitive solution' of the mystery.[442] To prevent a scandal arising from Prince Eddy's consorting with prostitutes (the prince was a son of the Prince of Wales and grandson of Queen Victoria), the court – via connections with the influential company of freemasons – supported a secret conspiracy to make a number of prostitutes 'disappear'. A series of horrible ritual murders followed, in which Sir William Gull, again according to Knight, would have played a central and highly morbid role. Although this all seems very unlikely, Knight's (fascinating) book provides information on Gull's personality which might be relevant to our own 'detective story': who was the first, Gull or Lasègue? Before answering this question, we will briefly portray Gull's opponent.

Born in the same year as Gull, Ernest Charles Lasègue (1816–83) did not earn so high a reputation, a fact which may account in part for the frequent misspelling of his name in Anglo-American literature. Lasègue ranks as one of the great French mid-nineteenth-century psychiatrists – together with Bénedict-Augustin Morel (1809–73) and Valentin Magnan (1835–1916) – but he was overshadowed by the famous Jean-Martin Charcot (1825–93), the 'Napoleon of the Neuroses'. Although Lasègue was not as renowned as Gull or Charcot, his scientific contributions are no less important. His list of publications is impressive and embraces internal medicine, psychiatry, neurology, and the history of medicine. As well as reports on hysteria, melancholy, catalepsy and alcoholism, Lasègue wrote seminal papers on delusions of persecution, *folie à deux*, kleptomania, and exhibitionism.

Lasègue's early training and work as a teacher of philosophy and rhetoric – the poet Charles Baudelaire (1821–67) was one of his pupils – influenced much of his further career in neuropsychiatry. The young teacher made friends with Claude Bernard (1813–78), the pioneering physiologist who worked at the Salpêtrière Hospital and persuaded him to start studying medicine. Though for the rest of his career greatly influenced by Bernard, Lasègue always remained something of a philosopher, critically questioning the fundamentals of medicine and appearing averse to any kind of dogmatism, either organic or psychological. His oeuvre certainly shared one important characteristic with Gull: the observation of facts as the cornerstone of scientific endeavour. However, Lasègue's academic career developed more slowly: when Gull was already a full professor, in 1853, Lasègue's career was just beginning and only some fourteen years later did he become Professor of General Pathology, finally, in 1869, he took up the prestigious Chair of Clinical Medicine in La Pitié Hospital. Lasègue was not intent upon titles or honours and although elected a member of the French Academy of Medicine in 1876, he remained devoted to his clinical work and to his many teaching functions at the Faculty of Medicine in Paris, even when suffering from severe diabetes. He died shortly at the age of 67 on 20 March 1883.[477]

Let us return to our initial question. With a few exceptions, up until now Gull's and Lasègue's publications have not been systematically analysed to establish who in fact was the first. The matter has often been decided in favour of Gull, because in 1868 (five years before Lasègue's article) he had mentioned the 'new' syndrome. A careful analysis of the respective publications, however, undermines this conclusion.

It was and still is a great honour to be invited for the 'Address in Medicine', the major speech at the annual meeting of the British Medical Association. In 1868 at the Oxford meeting the honour was granted to William Gull, who simultaneously received an honorary degree from Oxford University. This important 'state of the art' address was published shortly after the meeting in the authoritative medical journal *The Lancet*. It is an eloquent and lengthy – sometimes too ponderous and verbose – plea for patient care in clinical medicine as the foundation of a physician's task. Gull strongly emphasized the importance of diagnoses being based on a clinical examination of the patient and, if possible, on a knowledge of the pathology, though this might often be impossible since the explanation of many diseases was obscure. The diagnostic process was thus mainly 'negative', reached by the exclusion of other pathological processes. It is in this context that Gull wrote the famous passage supposedly making him the first person to refer to the 'new' syndrome:

> At present our diagnosis is mostly one of inference, from our knowledge of the liability of the several organs to particular lesions; thus we avoid the error of supposing the presence of mesenteric disease in young women emaciated to the last degree through hysteric apepsia by our knowledge of the latter affection, and by the absence of tubercular disease elsewhere.[425]

Should this brief and cryptic note, constituting approximately

0.5 per cent of the whole lecture, stand as the first description of a new syndrome? It seems to us and others a far-reaching interpretation, which was used by Gull himself as main evidence to support his claim for priority, though during the subsequent five years until 1873 he made no mention of his 'discovery'.

In April 1873 Dr Lasègue published a French article 'De l'anorexie hystérique' in the *Archives Générales de Médecine,* almost the official mouthpiece of the Parisian medical faculty. He began his article by underscoring the importance of his contribution:

> The object of this memoir is to make known one of the forms of hysteria of the gastric centre which is of sufficient frequency for its description not to be, as too readily happens, the artificial generalisation of a particular case, and constant enough in its symptoms to allow physicians who have met with it controlling the accuracy of the description, and to prevent those who have yet to meet with it in their practice being taken unawares. The term 'anorexia' might have been replaced by 'hysterical inanition', which would better represent the most characteristic of the accidents; but I have preferred the former term, without otherwise defending it, precisely because it refers to a phenomenology which is less superficial, more delicate, and also more medical.[443]

Then follows a splendid description. Lasègue mentions that his report is based on eight cases, all female, the youngest being 18 and the eldest 32. 'Although these cases are few in number', Lasègue admits modestly, 'they so much resemble each other that the latter ones found me in no indecision in regard either to diagnosis or prognosis, and, in fact, all passed on according to rule.' For this reason he decided, instead of describing each case separately, to provide 'a somewhat diagrammatic sketch of the disease'. Finally it is noteworthy that Lasègue nowhere refers to any other source but his own observations which took him some years to gather.

Soon after its publication this paper must have caught the attention of one or more British physicians, for barely five months later, on 6 and 27 September of the same year, a bipartite English translation entitled 'On hysterical anorexia' appeared in *The Medical Times and Gazette.*[443;478] Translations of French articles were then not uncommon and remind us that the British academic world was not isolated from the Continent. It would be interesting to know who took the initiative to

translate Lasègue's article. We may assume that the translation
was initiated by someone who must have been closely related to
the editorial board of the journal, who could read French and
was able to judge the quality and originality of the article. It is
peculiar that a colleague – probably from Gull's own academic
circle (editorial membership is often an honour granted to
prominent scientists) – was acquainted with Lasègue's original
article, yet the top physician Gull alleged that he did not know
of it, implying as it does that he was unacquainted with the most
important French medical literature. Even more so, he additionally asserted that during the preparation of his own lecture on
'anorexia hysterica', he would not even have noticed the English
translation until it was brought to his notice by one Dr Francis
Webb. It is rather peculiar that a leading physician, a month
before his lecture, does not even read an important specialist
paper or, if he did, does not pay attention to an extensive article
dealing with the same topic as his lecture! *The Medical Times and
Gazette* was not merely a specialist paper with scientific contributions. This fortnightly magazine published all kinds of news
from the medical scene as well as the accounts of the meeting of
the Clinical Society of London to which Gull had delivered a
lecture. In other words, it was the obvious source for keeping
abreast of things within medical circles. Should we conclude
from Gull's assertion that he did not read this journal frequently?
It is one of the several peculiarities in Gull's account.

On 24 October 1873, more than a month after the publication
of Lasègue's translated article, Sir William Gull presented two
lectures at the meeting of the Clinical Society of London. We
will confine our analysis to the first lecture: 'Anorexia Hysterica
(Apepsia Hysterica)', of which two reports exist,[426;427] followed
by the publication of the full paper in 1874.[428] After having
placed his article from 1868 in the spotlight, Gull makes a
specific reference to Lasègue's article. The abbreviated account
of the lecture states:

> In the paper now brought forward, the word anorexia had been
> preferred to apepsia, as more fairly expressing the facts, since
> what food is taken, except in the extreme stages of the disease, is
> well digested. Dr Lasègue, of La Pitié Hospital, Paris, in April last
> published remarks on this state . . . which he also called anorexia
> hysterica. Dr Lasègue seems not to have known of the reference to

this morbid condition which was made by the author of the paper at the time named; therefore Dr Lasègue's observations are the more confirmatory, having been made from an independent point of view.[427]

In the paper of 1874 Gull writes:

> It is plain that Dr Lasègue and I have the same malady in mind, though the forms of our illustrations are different. Dr Lasègue does not refer to my address at Oxford, and it is most likely he knew nothing of it. There is, therefore, the more value in his Paper, as our observations have been made independently. We have both selected the same expression to characterise the malady. In the address at Oxford, I used the term Apepsia hysterica, but before seeing Dr Lasègue's Paper, it had equally occurred to me that Anorexia would be more correct.[428]

This passage is preceded by his peculiar 'defence' wherein he states: 'After these remarks were penned, Dr Francis Webb directed my attention to the Paper of Dr Lasègue . . . '

However, twenty years after his 'discovery' Gull no longer seems so closely attached to his Oxford address. In 1888 he published his final scientific contribution in *The Lancet*.[429] It is a simple and brief case report, which in fact contains no novelty, but became well known for its depiction of a 14-year-old wasted patient. Strikingly, the medical journal paid much attention to his short contribution, coming at a time when clinicians were familiar with the clinical picture.[461] Furthermore, it is noteworthy that at the end of his article Gull refers to 'my first paper', without a detailed reference. From the context – Gull is speaking of hyperactivity despite extreme emaciation – it is evident that he meant his paper of 1874. Although he does not mention Lasègue, who with equal emphasis had described the paradoxical hyperactivity of anorexic patients, Gull no longer felt the need to claim priority in describing the new illness. Had his great age put him in a mild mood and made him realize the relativity of his life-work? Or had his name meanwhile been firmly established as 'the discoverer of anorexia nervosa'?

When we leave Gull's article of 1888 out of consideration, we dispose of several indications that he somewhat too emphatically claimed 'parenthood' of anorexia nervosa.[477] Our interpretations of the facts may be coloured to a certain extent by the less favourable impression which Gull makes upon us. Sir William seems the prototype of the ambitious physician and the successful academician. He radiated great self-confidence and authority to the point of arrogance. He was known for his

> adamantine determination to proceed with a course of action entirely in his own way. He had always been hard-headed to the point that it was said his resemblance to Napoleon went beyond physical appearance.[442]

By contrast, in his attitude towards his patients he was very attentive, friendly and patient. The same attitude was not presented to his colleagues unless they could match his academic rank and intelligence, for 'of all evils, he looked upon ignorance as the worst.' The memorial tablet in the chapel at Guy's Hospital records that 'few have exceeded him in the depth and accuracy of his knowledge'. In short, his lifestyle did not conform to the Scripture text which adorns his gravestone in Thorpe-le Soken (Essex): 'What doth the Lord require of thee, but to do justly, and to love mercy, and to walk humbly with thy God?'

The image of Charles Lasègue stands out in sharp contrast to that of William Gull. The former seemed to be a calm person of inconspicuous appearance, who carefully weighed his words. He was much loved by both his colleagues and students. Both in appearance and writings, he always remained a rather humble man. In scientific circles he was known as a shrewd sceptic who did not easily propagandize new ideas. Sufficiently acquainted with the major English and German literature, he also knew the history of neuropsychiatry quite well. But he himself was not eager to have his name connected with some major scientific discovery, though he could not refrain from delivering a mordant and rather sardonic editorial riposte to Gull's lecture in 1873.[463]

Let us now answer the question: who was the first to discover anorexia nervosa, Gull or Lasègue? We could easily set this question aside by pointing out its irrelevance, since others – in particular Morton and probably contemporaries like Imbert, Marcé, Chipley and Briquet – had earlier described a similar syndrome. But the publications of these authors found no response, whereas in the last decades of the nineteenth century striking attention was paid to the phenomenon. In this sense the modern medical history of anorexia nervosa commences in 1873 with the independent 'parenthood' shared by Sir William Withey Gull and Dr Ernest Charles Lasègue. Both had already investigated a few cases before 1870, but being critical clinicians both waited some years before they confided their experiences to the scientific circle. Both decided this in the same period, which led the ambitious Gull to claim priority *a posteriori* based on dubious arguments. Let us drop the controversy in the annals of the *petites histoires*, a footnote in the history of science. After all it was only a storm in a tea-cup though the fact that English tea is concerned perhaps makes all the difference . . . However, ultimately the content of the respective publications is far more important than disputes on the 'proprietary rights' of a discovery.

Chapter 9
Self-Starvation in the Hands of Physicians

In 1873 anorexia nervosa acquired an acknowledged place in the pantheon of medicine. Although almost two centuries had passed since Morton's *Phthisiologia* Gull and Lasègue had not added much that was new to the description of their seventeenth-century predecessor. The affliction, however, is interpreted in a totally different way from Morton's approach. Yet this does not imply that nineteenth century physicians were in complete agreement on this topic. Nor are they today!

Characteristics of the 'new' illness

Comparing the writings of Morton, Gull and Lasègue, a remarkable similarity in the clinical description of the illness is evident:

1 It primarily occurs in girls and young women (especially between 15 and 20 years of age).
2 Physically a striking emaciation or inanition (cachexia) is to be found, as a consequence of markedly decreased intake of food, often accompanied by constipation and absence of the menses (amenorrhoea).
3 Physically or mentally the urge to move (physical restlessness or hyperactivity) and a lack of insight into the illness, coupled with an occasionally persistent resistance towards treatment, are remarkable.
4 No physical causes of the symptoms can be found so that the picture must be considered one of nervous or mental origin.

As far as style is concerned the descriptions, however, betray different approaches.

Gull remains the cool observer in his case histories, often only enumerating – almost telegraphically – the principal symptoms and clinical findings. He rightly points out that typical phenomena like amenorrhoea, slow pulse and slow breathing are consequences of starvation. Gull is surprised at the striking restlessness of anorexic patients, despite their occasionally extreme emaciation and physical weakness. He writes about Miss A.:

> The patient complained of no pain, but was restless and active. This was in fact a striking expression of the nervous state, for it seemed hardly possible that a body so wasted could undergo the exercise which seemed agreeable.[428]

Apart from the urge to move, Gull observes that patients always feel well and often display stubborn behaviour.

Lasègue describes the same characteristics, but far more extensively and with a feeling for snappy details.[478] In his article it is obviously the psychiatrist who is speaking, depicting a colourful picture in splendid French sentences. Lasègue particularly stresses the physical hyperactivity, which may be explained by the fact that he gathered his observations of anorexic patients during the famine in Paris due to the German siege in the winter of 1870–71. With his medically trained eye he could clearly observe the behavioural differences between the self-starved anorexics and the forcibly starved Parisians: the former show a remarkable liveliness and hyperactivity, whereas the latter are languid and inactive. Immediately he adds a striking observation of anorexia: 'Another ascertained fact is, that so far from muscular power being diminished, this abstinence tends to increase the aptitude for movement.'[443] Although Gull mentions a fatal case, both he and Lasègue are fairly optimistic about prognosis. Nevertheless, both point to certain difficulties in treatment. Gull underlines the fact that the restless activity is often difficult to control and he warns against a lax attitude of physicians:

> In the earlier and less severe stages, it is not unusual for the medical attendant to say, in reply to the anxious solicitude of the parents, 'let her do as she likes. Don't force food'. Formerly, I thought such advice admissible and proper, but large experience has shown plainly the danger of allowing the starvation process to go on.[428]

Soon Gull had discovered that medication for the appetite and digestion was largely useless. Instead, food should be adminis-

tered in increasing amounts and under different 'moral conditions': 'The patients should be fed at regular intervals and
surrounded by persons who would have moral control over
them, relations and friends being generally worst attendants.'
This conviction induced Gull to have some of his patients taken
care of by a nurse instead of relatives.

Lasègue's therapeutic reflections, like the description of the
disorder, resemble Gull's strikingly. The French neuropsychiatrist
underlines the fact that the whole variety of medicines to
stimulate appetite and digestion are inefficacious. He also repeatedly points to the lack of cooperation by patients, who do not
'sigh for recovery'. Notwithstanding, they possess 'an inexhaustible optimism, against which supplications and menaces are alike
of no avail'. Lasègue gives a keen description of the increasing
helplessness of the family and its extreme manipulation by the patient:

> The family has but two methods at its service which it always
> exhausts – entreaties and menaces (. . .) The delicacies of the table are
> multiplied in the hope of stimulating the appetite; but the more the
> solicitude increases the more the appetite diminishes. The patient
> disdainfully tastes the new viands, and after having thus shown her
> willingness, holds herself absolved from any obligation to do more.
> She is besought, as a favour, and as a sovereign proof of affection, to
> consent to add even an additional mouthful to what she has taken;
> but this excess of insistence begets an excess of resistance.[443]

Lasègue does not explicitly provide concrete implications for
treatment. He does underline that the physician must possess of a
certain authority without being authoritarian: he should manage
his patients carefully and avoid intimidation. To Lasègue the
connection between the patient's behaviour and the reactions of
those surrounding her is essential: 'we should acquire an erroneous
idea of the disease by confining ourselves to an examination of
the patient'. Although Lasègue nowhere explicitly makes a plea
for 'parentectomy' – a therapeutic separation of the patient from
the family (for example via hospitalization) – this was shortly
concluded afterwards from his views by other clinicians.[474]

Gull's and Lasègue's views on the genesis of the clinical
picture are partially apparent from these therapeutic advices.
Their explanations of the cause of anorexia nervosa have to be

put in the historical context of medical thinking. Both are of the opinion that anorexia nervosa/hysterica is not rooted in a somatic affliction. As both underline, it is certainly not a disturbance of the stomach or digestion in general. For this reason Gull drops the earlier label 'apepsia' in favour of 'lack of appetite' (the literal meaning of anorexia). Lasègue follows a similar reasoning, though he immediately considered the term *inanition hystérique* to be more adequate. Gull is careful in his remarks on cause and genesis of anorexia nervosa. Initially he refers to 'a morbid mental state' and 'mental perversity', whereas his final publication concludes with the statement: 'perversions of the "ego" being the cause and determining the course of the malady'.[429] Underscoring his preference for 'the more general term' anorexia nervosa, Gull wants to avoid the adjective 'hysterical': 'we might call the state hysterical without committing ourselves to the etymological value of the word, or maintaining that the subjects of it have the common symptoms' of hysteria.'[428] Lasègue, on the contrary, also mentions 'perversion mentale' and 'perversion intellectuelle', but consistently speaks of hysterical patients. In his view it is only as far as the localization of hysteria is concerned – here 'gastric hysteria' – that hysterical anorexia differs from other forms of hysteria.

A century after Gull and Lasègue the principal signs of anorexia nervosa have not essentially changed (see Chapter 1). Particularly in the French literature a well-known symptom triad was isolated from Lasègue's description, the so-called three A's (*anorexie, amaigrissement, aménorrhée*), which would serve for many generations of medical students as a memory aid in identifying the syndrome. However, it remains peculiar that the clinical picture is accepted as a medical entity only at the end of the nineteenth century. In contrast to earlier descriptions of a similar illness, the publications of Gull and Lasègue acquired an almost immediate and widespread acceptance within medical circles.

Nervosa or hysterica?

Gull's lecture of 1873 induced many reactions from listeners. Although it aroused scepticism in some, the majority of the reactions attested to a positive interest in the new clinical picture, which a few colleagues recognized from their own experience.[426;427] The major point of discussion concerned the causal explanation, and obviously Gull himself does not seem content with the term 'hysterical'. Many others in his day had great difficulty with his concept, which etymologically refers to an affliction of the uterus (*hystera*). Two months after Gull's address, the London physician Dennis De Berdt Hovell devotes a strikingly critical reflection to the 'abuse' of the notion of hysteria.[405] Referring to Gull's address, he considers the term *anorexia puellaris* to be more correct. Furthermore, this term divests the illness of its mystifying designation, for in his view it is 'a morbid psychological state' which is connected with the nervous system rather than the uterus. It is a neurosis with moral and physical aspects. As the latter is predominantly caused by undernutrition, adequate medicines and nourishment should be administered – if necessary under coercion – whereafter 'moral treatment must be instituted as indispensable to recovery'. Hovell concludes his reflection with a sharp outburst at physicians who continuously refer to hysteria, but do not understand it and treat patients wrongly. In his view, these physicians are perhaps even more the subject of a 'morbus hystericus' than their patients!

It is apparent from numerous commentaries appearing in the subsequent editions of *The Lancet* that not everyone agreed about the disappearance of the notion of anorexia hysterica, but that at the end of the nineteenth century British physicians did not doubt the existence of a particular illness called anorexia nervosa. In the fifteen years after the contributions of Gull and Lasègue – the period 1873–88 – the British medical press only occasionally paid attention to the 'new' illness. One of the striking exceptions was a lengthy report on anorexia nervosa published in 1880 by the London physician Samuel Fenwick, who made the gastrointestinal tract the subject of his life's work.[464] In a fairly accurate description, illustrated by several case histories, he attributes the disorder to 'either anaesthesia or a perversion of the sensibility of the nerves distributed to the stomach, analogous to what we sometimes observe with respect to the cutaneous nerves in hysterical females'.[414]

Furthermore, after the notorious history of Sarah Jacob (see Chapter 4), some short and often critical reports on 'fasting girls' appeared, but only a few of them made the link with anorexia nervosa. However, between 1888 and 1900 several cases were described and from that moment on the stream of publications in English continued to increase. The same holds for the French medical press which contained the more pertinent case reports, owing to the French psychiatric tradition of detailed clinical observation and attentiveness towards the psychology of patients.[431]

Lasègue's original article had been published in 1873 in the leading journal *Archives Générales de Médecine*, of which he himself was the editor. As we noted before, his article was rapidly translated into English. In the subsequent years there were only few French publications on the new clinical picture. In his dissertation on obesity, L.S. Worthington reported an interesting case of a 15-year-old girl who considered herself to be overweight and became severely emaciated as a result of a strict diet. Although this looks like a typical case of anorexia nervosa, the author was apparently not familiar with the publications of Gull and Lasègue.[483] The first report in French specifically dealing with Lasègue's clinical picture is only to be found in a Swiss journal in 1878. Dr Adrien(?) Rist fairly extensively describes the history of a 16-year-old girl, who displayed all the behavioural characteristics observed by Lasègue. However, Rist underlines the fact that she does not show any other hysterical symptoms and that he could find no reason to call her hysterical (hence the term *anorexie idiopathique*). Then he wonders, whether the girl – considering herself to be fat – has reduced her food intake in order to lose weight. Nevertheless, it is 'une véritable maladie mentale' which has nothing to do with the food refusal of the insane, melancholic or hypochondriacal patient. One might consider it to be an 'isolated syndrome' or even associate it with hysteria, but in fact such questions of classification are accidental, Rist concludes.[457]

In France the stream of publications only gradually started from 1883 on (but still five years earlier than in Great Britain). In historical surveys, the year 1883 is often defined as the moment when the currently still used French term *anorexie mentale* would have been introduced by Henri Huchard (1844–1910) in his revision of Axenfeld's *Traité des Névroses*.[397] But nowhere in this book can the term be found. Huchard only speaks of *anorexie hystérique* (referring to Gull and Lasègue), but

does underline that this kind of anorexia is particularly characterised by 'un état mental particulier'. In fact, the concept of
anorexie mentale turns up for the first time in the dissertation of
L. Deniau in 1883. He distinguishes two kinds of anorexia. The
anorexie gastrique is a digestive disorder which secondarily disturbs
the appetite, but is not attended with striking emaciation. *Anorexie mentale*, however, is not a digestive disorder, but rather a
'trouble mental'.[409] Yet, since Deniau admits that he derived
this distraction from his teacher Huchard, we may grant the
latter the parenthood of the term *anorexie mentale*. The new
terminology was not directly widely used; only in 1895 is the
concept to be found for the first time as title of a French publication.[467]

The period 1883–95 would be dominated by the work of
Jean-Martin Charcot, whose name is closely connected with the
studies of hysteria at the School of the Salpêtrière. Through his
interest in hysteria and hypnotism, this 'Napoleon of the Neuroses' became an important inspiration for the work of Sigmund
Freud. Charcot's major contribution to hysterical anorexia is a
plea for 'isolation' of the patient, 'removal from the place where
the disease originated'. He viewed this as the principal component
of 'moral or psychical treatment'.[400] Somewhat triumphantly
Charcot illustrates his authoritarian method with an example of
a girl, who had to confess to him:

> As long as papa and mamma had not gone – in other words, as long
> as you had not triumphed (for I saw that you wished to shut me
> up), I was afraid that my illness was not serious, and as I had a
> horror of eating, I did not eat. *But when I saw that you were
> determined to be master, I was afraid*, and in spite of my repugnance I
> tried to eat, and I was able to, little by little [italics in the original].

It is striking that Charcot, apart from hysterical anorexia (*anorexie
hystérique*), occasionally speaks of nervous anorexia (*anorexie
nerveuse*). In a lesson from 1887, he even seems to use the latter
term to designate a serious form of hysterical anorexia under the
label of *anorexie nerveuse primitive*.[401]

Perhaps this tendency to distinguish variants of anorexia –
parallel with a growing doubt about the hysterical nature of the
disorder – may have originated partially from one of Charcot's
pupils. While his teacher was still living, Georges Gilles de la

Tourette (1857–1904) expressed his critical view – be it in carefully chosen words – that he had not yet observed a 'pure' case of *anorexie hystérique*. In his monumental book *Traité Clinique et Thérapeutique de l'Hystérie*, of which Part 3 would appear after Charcot's death, Gilles de la Tourette emphasizes the term *anorexie primitive*.[423] This primary form of *anorexie hystérique* had to be distinguished from secondary variants such as *anorexie gastrique* from food refusal in psychotic or melancholic patients. This diagnostic differentiation had been inspired in particular by the work of Paul Sollier, with whom we enter into the last decade of the nineteenth century.

The stream of French language publications started seriously only from 1890 on. Beginning with an extensive paper from 1891 Sollier would show his particular interest in anorexia nervosa in several publications for a couple of years. His writings are exemplary for the discussions about classification and nomenclature in psychiatry at the turn of the century. He distinguishes two forms of anorexia: *anorexie primitive* is the most serious form because it is based on an *idée fixe*, whereas *anorexie secondaire* is often of a temporary nature and may occur in whatever hysterical picture. The major difference concerns the psychical condition of the patient, more precisely her attention, which becomes fixed in the first form and is easily diverted in the latter. The causes are similar in both forms and can be divided according to Sollier into four groups: (a) *causes morales*, like coquetry, the desire for slenderness, weariness of life or obstinacy; (b) *anorexie*, i.e. the loss of appetite or sensation of hunger; (c) *accidents nerveux* like spasm of the gullet, stomach ache caused by oversensitivity of the mucous membrane or vomiting; (d) *illusions sensorales* and more precisely macropsy or the inclination to perceive the magnitude of certain objects bigger, e.g. the quantity of food which has to be digested. Following Charcot's recommendations the crucial element of the treatment in each of these cases is 'isolation': Sollier emphasizes that simply and solely the physician has to be in command.[466]

Where Sollier initially uses the terms *anorexie nerveuse* and *anorexie hystérique* interchangeably, from 1895 on he speaks about *anorexie mentale* which should be clearly distinguished from *anorexie hystérique primitive* and *dyspepsie nerveuse*.[467] The former offers a far more serious clinical picture – without signs of hysteria and more similar to neurasthenia and hypochondriasis – with a chronic course and often bad prognosis. But apparently Sollier became confused by his own terminology, for in later writings he uses *anorexie hystérique* and *anorexie nerveuse* once again interchangeably. Moreover, he shifts his attention to the absent sensation of hunger – reflecting a kind of anaesthesia of the stomach – as being the essential element of the disorder which he now groups under the label *psychopathies gastriques*. Although there was great confusion and disagreement about the nomenclature and associated views on cause and therapy, the last decade of the nineteenth century at least shows that French psychiatrists had a lively interest in the clinical picture.

Psychasthenia and neurasthenia

Parallel to the disputes on terminology *nervosa* versus *hysterica*, a polemic arose on explanatory theories and corresponding therapies. At the turn of the century this was part of the conflict between several psychiatric schools, of which the opinions on both sides of the Atlantic Ocean often varied considerably. A representative example with which we may end our discussion of the French nineteenth-century psychiatric writings on anorexia is the important work of the psychiatrist and psychologist Pierre Janet (1859–1947). His immense oeuvre fell into oblivion for a long time, but in recent years is has been rediscovered, presumably through the renewed interest in hypnosis and dissociative phenomena (such as multiple personalities). Janet's first reference to hysterical anorexia is to be found in his bipartite work *État Mental des Hystériques* (1893–94). It concerns a rather oblique discussion of food refusal in patients with an extensive history of all sorts of hysterical phenomena.[438] He only elaborates his own view on anorexia nervosa a few years later.

At the end of 1906 Pierre Janet pays a second visit to the United States. His lectures on hysteria at Boston's Harvard University had been published a year later: *The Major Symptoms of Hysteria*. Herein he discusses the hysterical phenomena as mental fragments which are dissociated or disconnected from the conscious, wilful control. The section on 'hysterical anorexy' is predominantly a discussion of the views of Charcot and Lasègue, more precisely their – according to Janet, exaggerated

– emphasis on the *idée fixe* which would induce these patients to wilful starvation.

> The following observation of Charcot is famous: while undressing a patient of this kind, he found that she wore on her skin, fastened very tight around her waist, a rose-coloured ribbon. He obtained the following confidence; the ribbon was a measure which the waist was not to exceed. 'I prefer dying of hunger to becoming big as mamma.' Coquetries of this kind are very frequent; (. . .) The authors who have observed such ideas seem to me to be inclined to exaggerate their importance. This is what certainly happened to Charcot, who used to seek everywhere for his rose-coloured ribbon and the idea of obesity.[440]

For the same reason Janet criticizes contemporary explanations of the striking hyperactivity of anorexic patients. He quotes the article of Dr Gabriel (?) Wallet, who argued that these patients walk so much in order to emaciate or to compensate for the food they have to take.[481] In Janet's view, one should not generalize such an explanation. He emphasizes that such activity is primary suppression of the feeling of tiredness. This is accompanied by a general condition of excitement: 'The exaltation of the strength, the feeling of euphoria, as it is known in the ecstatic saints, for instance, does away with the need of eating.' Ultimately, in Janet's view, this represents an extreme 'dissociation' on the psychological side of the nutritional regulation in the brain. In hysterical anorexia this system seems to be paralysed, as if it suffered from loss of memory: the nutritional function escapes from the watching consciousness: 'Alimentation has become, as it were, a somnambulistic phenomenon.' This new concept of 'functional dissociation' – so typical of Janet's thinking – would predominate in his later work.

In his Harvard lectures, Janet had already remarked that 'refusals of food are not always a phenomenon of the hysterical neurosis; they belong at least as often to the psychasthenic neurosis.'[440] Though he is still rather vague in his book *Les Névroses* (1909), a distinction between hysterical and psychasthenic anorexia is clearly more apparent.[441] Yet he remained interested for a long time in the hysterical form but gradually also became interested in obsessional phenomena (compulsive acts and thoughts, tics, phobias), as exemplified in his influential book *Les Obsessions et la Psychasthénie*.[439] A patient called Nadia induced Janet to bring up hysterical anorexia for discussion. This 27-year-old woman showed many behavioural characteristics as described by Lasègue, but her small food intake – ever since puberty – proceeded according to Janet from a dominant fixed idea: she was obsessed by the fear of looking ugly and being expelled for this reason. She took pains to hide her body as much as possible from the glances of others. In fact this was not so much to do with a fear of being or becoming fat, according to Janet, but with the desire to stay a little girl and not to grow up, as Nadia admitted herself: 'I didn't want to gain weight or grow or look like a woman because I would have liked to stay always a little girl.' This may create the impression that Janet considered anorexia nervosa essentially to be an obsessive-compulsive disorder. Although some followed his ideas, in the course of time 'compulsiveness' (obsessions, perfectionism, anancasm) became more and more viewed as a personality characteristic – possibly accentuated by starvation itself – in a large number of anorexia nervosa patients. Perhaps Janet has made the classification problem at the turn of the century even more complex and confusing. Nevertheless, his interest in the obsessional 'aversion to one's own body' elucidated an essential problem, which today is also viewed as an important factor in anorexia nervosa: the fear, excited by puberty, of growing up and maturing sexually.

But how did anorexia nervosa develop in countries other than Great Britain and France? Despite the fact that German-speaking academicians during the 1800s were well acquainted with medical publications from both countries, for a long time medical literature in Germany and Austria showed a remarkable silence regarding the 'new' illness.[479] It was more than a decade before the first extensive writings on anorexia nervosa appeared in German, predominantly outside the field of psychiatry. By the German-Austrian School of *Mageñarzte* (stomach specialists), particularly Berthold Stiller (1837–1922) from Budapest and the Viennese professor of 'electrotherapy' Moriz Rosenthal (1833–89), anorexia nervosa was conceived primarily as a form of gastric neurosis, more specifically a sensory neurosis, character-ized by a deficiency in hunger sensation.[458;472] Similar notions had been put forward by the above mentioned Imbert en

Fenwick. But in fact, this view was a modern continuation of age-old medical theories about anorexia, in which the stomach was primarily incriminated as the source of mischief. In the late nineteenth century this 'gastric anorexia' was not only influential in Germany and Austria, but also found some response in countries like America (see below), France, Belgium and Holland.[480] But although from 1892 on, some important German contributions on anorexia nervosa appeared, at the end of the nineteenth century leading German textbooks of psychiatry still did not refer to anorexia nervosa at all. This may reflect a lack of interest in anorexia nervosa on the part of German-speaking physicians, as also witnessed by Sigmund Freud's attitude towards the 'new' disorder.

Freud must have been familiar with the clinical picture of hysterical anorexia through the works of Charcot. He visited the renowned neurologist in Paris from October 1885 to February 1886 and translated a collection of his now legendary lectures into German. Nevertheless, Freud himself was not much interested in the disorder. If the term anorexia appears in his works, it usually refers to lack of appetite or distaste for food as one of the characteristics of hysteria, and has nothing to do with the typical syndrome of anorexia nervosa. A well-known example is the case of Frau Emmy von N., described in his *Studies on Hysteria*, the book Freud published with Josef Breuer (1842–1925).[420] Around the same time, 1895, Freud was developing his own ideas and sent drafts to his friend, Wilhelm Fliess (1858–1928), with whom he exchanged a prolific correspondence. In one of these manuscripts, Freud developed his ideas on melancholia:

> The nutritional neurosis parallel to melancholia is anorexia. The famous *anorexia nervosa* of young girls seems to me (on careful observation) to be a melancholia where sexuality is undeveloped. The patient asserted that she had not eaten, simply because she had *no appetite*, and for no other reason. Loss of appetite – in sexual terms – loss of libido.[417]

Freud illustrates his theory with a 'schematic diagram of sexuality', according to which 'anaesthesia' or insensitivity plays an important role in the development of melancholia. In the case of 'anxious melancholia', Freud supposed that 'sexual tension is diverted from the psychical sexual group' because of its 'being linked in another direction (with disgust – defence): this is hysterical anaesthesia, which is entirely analogous to hysterical anorexia (disgust)'. From these passages it remains unclear whether Freud made a distinction between anorexia nervosa and hysterical anorexia.

In Freud's later oeuvre anorexia nervosa received only passing reference. In a lecture 'On psychotherapy' for Viennese physicians in 1904, he remarks: 'Psycho-analysis should not be attempted when the speedy removal of dangerous symptoms is required, as, for example, in a case of hysterical anorexia.'[418] Only many years later, in 1918, does Freud refer for the last time and almost in passing to anorexia (nervosa) in his famous case history of 'the Wolf Man'.[419] It is an account of a young Russian who was extremely frightened of wolves and suffered from severe depressions. He had been in psychoanalysis with Freud, who particularly analysed his sexual experiences and fantasies from childhood. The report contains a short episode on loss of appetite, which Freud immediately considers to be the first expression of a disturbed sexual development – especially in the oral or cannibalistic phase:

> It is well known that there is a neurosis in girls which occurs at a much later age, at the time of puberty or soon afterwards, and which expresses aversion to sexuality by means of anorexia. This neurosis will have to be brought into relation with the oral phase of sexual life.

When Freud, in 1895, spoke about the 'famous' anorexia nervosa, it cannot but refer to what he learnt in Paris. For in both Austria and Germany it is difficult to find traces of this acquaintance with anorexia nervosa until World War I. From 1914 on, particularly in Germany, another period of diagnostic confusion started, when anorexia nervosa was confounded with pituitary insufficiency or Simmonds' disease (see next section). For this reason, it would take several decades before the German-speaking physicians learnt what *Magersucht* (pursuit of thinness) really is![432]

Initially the interest in anorexia nervosa in other countries was even more marginal. In Italy, for example, hardly any interest was shown in it. The first known Italian case report on the illness was published as late as 1937.[434] This fact is still more astonishing considering the description of an anorexic-like syndrome published in 1875 by Giovanni Brugnoli (1814–94). Unaware of Gull's and Lasègue's publications, this professor of medicine from Bologna reports on two obvious anorexic girls.[399] Although he, like many other contemporary clinicians, is silent on the intense fear of fatness of anorexic patients, he does observe symptoms like denial of illness and overactivity despite emaciation without any obvious physical cause being ascertainable. Recognizing the unique nature of the clinical picture he describes, Brugnoli makes a plea for the re-establishment of *anoressia* not just as a symptom, but as a syndrome in its own right. Unfortunately, due to reports of Gull and Lasègue, his plea came two years too late and his striking clinical observation was even ignored until the 1960s.[434]

Though indifference was less extreme than in Italy, in the USA it was also several years before substantial interest in the medical press was recognizable. Even the Australians, with Astles' (1882) article,[396] were far ahead of the Americans.[475] Although cases of 'extraordinary fasting' aroused considerable attention at the time,[7] anorexia nervosa had been initially almost unknown in the United States. American physicians would only much later participate in the scientific debates on this syndrome.[476] How may this be explained? Take, for instance, the 'fasting girl' Mollie Fancher from Brooklyn. As we have reported in Chapter 4, the man who risked his personal fame by challenging this alleged miracle was the renowned New York physician William Alexander Hammond. In the Civil War he had acquired the prestigious position of Surgeon-General and as an authoritative neurologist he fiercely defended a strictly somatic view of mental diseases. Hammond had a dislike of psychological theories and used the diagnosis of 'hysteria' to disqualify all sorts of 'supernatural' phenomena as a kind of sick craving for sensation. This is apparent from his grim battle against the 'cheating' of Mollie Fancher. His book *Fasting Girls: Their Physiology and Pathology* from 1879 shows that he was acquainted with the work of Lasègue and Charcot.[172]

Hammond himself described the case of a 23-year-old woman who

became hysterical in consequence of domestic troubles, and losing all
her desire for food, took nothing daily but a single cup of chocolate.
She persevered in this restricted diet for twenty-nine days, although
during the last eight or ten she gave decided evidences of starvation.

She became emaciated and her menstruation ceased. From the
thirtieth day on she started to eat more and more, as she was
afraid of dying. Although this example follows on the notice of
Lasègue's *anorexie hystérique*, Hammond does not make his conclusion explicit. We have seen in Chapter 5 that Hammond also
played a role in Tanner's famous hunger exploit. Perhaps this
made some American physicians of the time believe that food
abstinence was more a voluntary and wilful (whether or not
'fraudulent') phenomenon. In any case, the diagnosis of anorexia
nervosa was far from popular.

A second explanation is suggested by James Hendrie Lloyd in
1893. After a description of a 26-year-old anorexic patient, this
physician from Philadelphia remarks: 'The case which I have to
report is a rare one, at least in this country, where the grave
forms of hysteria are either not as common, or not as carefully
observed, as in Europe.'[446] Indeed, in late nineteenth-century
America the diagnosis of 'neurasthenia' was far more popular
than hysteria. The former concept had been introduced by the
New York neurologist George Miller Beard (1839–83), who
used it to characterize a condition of 'nervous exhaustion', a
kind of overexertion due to the transition of modern civilization,
with its enormous pressures and demands for constant work.
Soon the term became the scientific synonym to 'American
nervousness', which would reach epidemic proportions. Being
one of the many symptoms of such a condition of exhaustion,
digestive disorders and bad appetite in particular were often mentioned.[510;584]

What had been known formerly as 'nervous dyspepsia', was
now called 'neurasthenia dyspeptica' (neurasthenia gastrica).[459]
Its most effective therapy was the rest cure (consisting of bed
rest and solid food) by which the neurologist Silas Weir Mitchell
(1829–1914) firmly established his enormous reputation. In his
day he was one of the most popular American clinicians and
known as the foremost expert on neurasthenia, whose writings
were quoted as a 'medical bible'. Notwithstanding this his views

were fairly simple, as appears from the title of his influential book *Fat and Blood, and How to Make Them* (1877). He paid much attention to his patients' appetite, but preferred to avoid the term 'anorexia', for it did not refer to a lack of appetite, but to an 'annihilation of appetite'. Although he depicted some cases of 'self-starvation' and was acquainted with the work of Charcot, Mitchell did not explicitly refer to anorexia nervosa, probably because of its hysterical connotation.[450]

Indeed, the differences in medical jargon and the fact that many young women were supposed to suffer from the almost epidemic neurasthenia, may explain the delay in American interest in anorexia nervosa. In 1886, for instance, the New York City physician Margaret A. Cleaves reported a case of an 18-year-old girl who suffered from amenorrhoea, poor appetite, emaciation, backache, headache and vomiting.[403] She recovered markedly after 'the most minute instructions' as to rest, sleep, diet, dress, and the activities which were to occupy the patient's time. The doctor was convinced that the girl suffered from 'a profound nervous exhaustion' and that the local symptoms were the effect of neurasthenia. Cleaves did not mention a word about anorexia nervosa. Three years later, the disorder was explicitly discussed in an article on 'gastric neurasthenia' by the Boston instructor in clinical medicine G.M. Garland. Referring to several German-Austrian 'gastric specialists' he considers anorexia nervosa to be a 'sensory neurosis' and concludes that 'the occurrence of these cases without at least a background of hysteria is very rare'.[421] He provides a rather atypical case-history of anorexia nervosa of a 63-year-old widow, which betrays only rudimentary understanding of the clinical picture of anorexia nervosa among American physicians at the time. Even as late as 1898 John C. Hemmeter (1863–1931), the clinical professor of medicine in Baltimore, stated that 'nervous anorexia' is based upon neurasthenia, hysteria, anaemia, chlorosis and certain neuroses of the stomach:

> It is found in those addicted to the excessive abuse of alcohol and tobacco, and as a symptom of the morphin habit. It is, therefore, not a disease peculiar to itself, not a typical morbid entity, but rather a sequence.[435]

Nevertheless, a slowly growing interest in anorexia nervosa had emerged in the American press of the 1890s. As we noted before, in 1893 James Hendrie Lloyd reports on a case of anorexia nervosa, referring to Gull's work and to Lasègue's 'classic essay on hysterical anorexia'. Characteristically enough, although he appears to be quite familiar with the literature on anorexia nervosa, Lloyd does not quote any American author in connection with this syndrome. In the same year the leading physician William Osler mentions the illness in his classic text-book *Practice of Medicine*.[454] Shortly afterwards medical journals started to publish short abstracts of European articles on anorexia nervosa and in the more popular medical publications the 'new' disorder also set in.

So, shortly before the turning of the century, the American medical profession, just like many of their colleagues from other countries, seemed to accept little by little, the existence of a peculiar form of self-starvation.[476] Where in the Anglo-Saxon countries Gull's term of anorexia nervosa was understandably adopted, the French terminology – initially hysterical anorexia (*anorexie hystérique*) and later nervous anorexia (*anorexie mentale*) – spread in Russia and afterwards also in other Eastern European countries. The Italians too chose the term of *anoressia mentale*, whereas in Dutch speaking countries clinicians still refer to anorexia nervosa.

Ebb and flood of theories

Having arrived at the twentieth century, the syndrome was flowing through medicine and psychiatry. At the turn of the century the concept of anorexia nervosa was widely used by physicians. This does not imply, however, unanimity among clinicians on the explanation of the affliction. It was considered a psychic illness, but its true character was disputed. The reason for food refusal or emaciation was interpreted differently according to the place assigned to the syndrome within current psychiatric pathology: a delusion, an obsessive idea or an hysterical reaction. Regardless of these diverging interpretations, the view of Morton, Gull and Lasègue was prominent: anorexia nervosa is a psychogenic self-starvation accompanied by several, occasionally fatal, physical disturbances which result from undernutrition and inanition. Therapy predominantly consisted of restoring the nutritional condition and body weight in various ways (mostly by forced feeding). However, in 1914 this view began to waver and anorexia nervosa became involved in scientific controversies which have hitherto remained unsolved.

When Morris Simmonds (1855–1925), a pathologist at the General Hospital St Georg in Hamburg, published in 1914 a paper on a fatal case of 'pituitary cachexia', he could not suspect what a misunderstanding he would arouse.[465] That the patient involved had died in an extremely wasted condition, was not necessarily linked to the atrophy of the anterior lobe of the pituitary that was observed at autopsy. But due to this rather accidental association the lately discovered 'Simmonds' disease' or 'pituitary cachexia' was put forward by a number of physicians – particularly in Germany, France and Scandinavia – as a possible cause of numerous forms of uncommon emaciation. As such anorexia nervosa moved from the psychiatric to the internist handbook. Although the equalling of anorexia nervosa with Simmonds' disease was based on scant scientific research, numerous specialists were convinced that anorexia nervosa was nothing but an endocrine affliction. In their 'blindness' to all flaws of their theory and the growing evidence undermining their viewpoint, they continued to renounce any psychological or psychiatric view and advocated just one singular treatment: administration of hormones, in order to restore the supposed shortage, whether it was successful or not.

From the 1930s on, an increasing number of publications emphasized the difference between Simmonds' disease and anorexia nervosa as well as the psychogenic nature of the latter. In particular the work of the Scotsman Harold L. Sheehan (1900–88) marked an end to all confusion: he conclusively demonstrated that malnutrition was not typical of pituitary insufficiency and that the latter had been caused by a thrombosis (frequently in consequence of considerable bleeding at childbirth).[17] Thus after 1945 anorexia nervosa once again returned to the psychiatric handbooks, terminating more than a quarter of a century of confusion with pituitary cachexia. During those years the 'mistake' had not been without dramatic consequences. For thirty years many cases of 'endocrine emaciation' have been described, which in retrospect appeared to be cases of anorexia nervosa. The strictly biological view had led to experimentation with all sorts of hormonal therapies: animal extracts of pituitary glands, thyroid gland, ovaries and adrenal gland were administered and propagated as 'successful'. That numerous patients had had their psychic needs misjudged and wrongly treated, throws a dark shadow on this episode in the history of anorexia nervosa. A positive consequence of the persistent misunderstanding may have been that the endocrinological and physiological research of starvation was stimulated and still inspires many researchers.[56]

After World War II the endocrinological view of anorexia nervosa made a rapid and smooth demise. Internist playing down of the psychological component now made room for psychiatric dramatization. In the period 1945–60 psychiatry was strongly dominated by psychoanalytic views. Traces of this are to be found in contemporary theories on anorexia nervosa: fear of food intake was linked to unconscious fear of oral impregnation.[30] The interest in anorexia nervosa was not particularly great. After 1960 this changed drastically due to the pioneering work of the psychiatrist and psychotherapist Hilde Bruch (1904–84), who focused attention on the lack of self-esteem and the distorted body image in anorexic patients.[5] With Bruch we arrive at the recent past of anorexia nervosa. Since then a variety of divergent views have passed in review. The rivalry between biological, psychodynamic, learning theory, feminist, family systems and other views still continues. Meanwhile in affluent Western countries anorexia nervosa has become a 'fashionable illness', though it is still considered a rather 'mysterious' disorder. In the next chapters we will try to unravel the roots of this phenomenon within its cultural–historical context.

10
The Victorian Roots of Anorexia Nervosa

After 1700 in Western Europe four revolutionary movements manifested themselves in labour relations, family life and politics: the higher agricultural production made possible by the agrarian revolution was responsible for the disappearance of large famines; the demographic revolution induced a population explosion because of a remarkable decrease in mortality; the Industrial Revolution created new mass products and means of production; the social–political revolution empowered the bourgeoisie. These societal revolutions were accompanied by two competitive world views: Enlightenment and Romanticism. From the eighteenth century on, the new human sciences arose out of the tension between these diversities, creating a territory of their own alongside, and gradually in imitation of, the natural sciences.

In this way psychology was able to acquire its right to exist within a Cartesian world. René Descartes (1596–1650) viewed man as a thinking machine. Parallel to his dualistic view of reality – mind and matter – he developed a new image of man with a separate body and soul. In doing so, he created the problem of the relationship between them, which would become the essential theme of psychology in subsequent years. The notion of the physical being influenced by the mental developed into the leading principle of psychosomatic medicine, which would put forward anorexia nervosa as show-piece or so-called paradigm.

Descartes had been dead for more than two centuries when this prototypical form of psychosomatic affliction was discovered by physicians. *Why as late as the last quarter of the nineteenth century?* On the basis of the characteristics of anorexia nervosa as a culture-bound syndrome we have described in Chapter 1, we would like to answer this question. The result of our historical research is inevitably a collection of snapshots of a hurried tourist, who has chosen in advance the places to visit on his whirlwind tour. In search of important traces of discontinuity in sociocultural history, we must impose strict limitations upon ourselves. For each of the cultural-historical themes we discuss our selective interest has been focused on: (1) striking shifts, (2) in higher social strata, (3) of Western European and North American societies, (4) in the second half of the nineteenth century. This itinerary establishes the direction and limitation of our further exploration. Looking at a historical episode as a link in the chain of time, anorexia nervosa is inviting us to link the present with the past. In previous chapters the phenomenon of self-starvation was differently labelled: as a wonder, a spectacle or an illness. Are fasting saints and miraculous maidens then comparable to modern anorexics? We started this book with that question and we will likewise finish it.

In 1939, on the basis of his clinical experience since World War I, the British physician John Alfred Ryle (1889–1950) was the first to predict a further increase of anorexia nervosa.[575] He associated this expectation with the popularity of the fashion for slenderness and the greater 'emotionality' in the life of young people. (These are two important themes which we will explore later). The idée fixe of longing for thinness can already be found in the first nineteenth-century depictions of anorexia nervosa, whereas this theme is totally lacking in earlier forms of self-starvation. How is this obsession with slenderness, now almost a century old, to be explained? Moreover, we cannot avoid the question of why it is of particular concern to girls or young women. 'What is wrong, then, with our youth?', Ryle rightly seems to ask more than half a century ago. For this reason problematic puberty and adolescence is another essential aspect whose historical roots we want to uncover. This inevitably leads us to the upbringing or the family conditions of young people. Early publications on anorexia nervosa suggested that something was wrong in these families. Today this theme remains very popular in professional circles, so that we have every reason to search for important historical shifts in family life.

Another, possibly essential element in our historical puzzle, was put forward by Sigmund Freud. It crops up in many varieties in more recent literature: conflictual sexuality. Presumably this is associated with the two previous themes and indirectly also with the fashion for slenderness, as we will discuss with regard to the question of why anorexia nervosa is mainly confined to women. Once again we meet here a 'modern' topic, which has become – parallel to the rise of feminism – a fiercely disputed issue. As the history of the women's movement leads us back to the end of the previous century, it will be no surprise to find that we have to imply in our exploration the possible importance of a changed image of women. This brings us directly to the fifth and final theme: to what extent are there indications that anorexia nervosa is a symptom of a changed ideal of beauty? Is anorexia nervosa a sign of a deranged obsession with thinness, the product of a new body culture, or the rejection of a consumer society? The answer has to throw some light on the meaning of self-starvation amidst abundance, a striking paradox only to be found in Western countries.

Analyzing these five aspects in the next sections, we had to face a number of restrictions. In Chapter 1 we warned against the relativity of our historiography and the selectivity of our hypotheses. A second restriction has literally to do with confinement: the approaching limitations on the size of this book, together with our own limited capabilities enforce us to only outline the five mentioned themes, each of which could easily comprise a book on its own. Finally, we once again emphasize what will be the final theme of this book: that our analysis does not aim to provide a definitive explanation of the rise of anorexia nervosa. For important biological and psychological factors are involved here, as well as the sociocultural variables we have discussed. A culture cannot be considered to be the 'germ' or 'procreator' of clinical pictures. This would be a simplistic denial of the complexity of human behaviour. Furthermore, it would imply a violation of rational logic by fitting something from one level of abstraction (society, culture) into the Procrustean bed of another (the medical model – illness in terms of cause/effect).

We do regard culture as an essential context for the meaning of (ab)normal human behaviour. Only against this background does a 'clinical picture' become a *Gestalt*, i.e. a figure acquiring a meaningful form and substance. In other words, culture is regarded as the soil from which self-starvation grows into a sign of sanctity, a kind of spectacle, or a specific illness. In short, we are dealing here with the eternal history of the interaction between nature and nurture (*le grain et le terrain*). Thus we also diligently or lavishly sow here without any certainty as to what the reader will reap. But enough excuses; let us return with our five guides to the birthplace of anorexia nervosa: the Western sociocultural milieu of the last quarter of the nineteenth century.

The powerlessness of the 'ideal' family

To many the nuclear family is still the cornerstone of society, a kind of social structure of atoms; being the smallest organizational unit it forms the essential building-block for greater molecular modes of cohabitation. The ideal of family life as the basis for upbringing and as a sociocultural link in a chain of generations, was the basis for the development of the middle- and upper-class bourgeois family from the seventeenth century on.[582]

Becoming imbued with middle-class ideas the bourgeois type of family gradually became in the eighteenth and nineteenth centuries the leading model for male-female relationships and social intercourse with children. Particularly in the last century this bourgeois family cultivated three important role patterns: the dominating position of the husband as breadwinner, the domestic function of the wife as spouse and mother, and the central place of the child as future torch-bearer of culture and progress.[495] In this power structure, patriarchy – the male 'vocation to responsibility' – became almost self-evidently associated with the cult of domesticity, originating from the female's 'natural predestination' towards maternity. In the middle-class family men created the material conditions of domesticity, whereas women were responsible for the affective role. In this way the appropriate moral lifescript could be engraved on the blank tablet – *tabula rasa* – of every child's mind. This heavy responsibility had already been stressed two hundred years earlier in the enlightened 'thoughts concerning education' of the English philosopher John Locke (1632–1704).

At a time when children had to be morally protected (see next section), the nineteenth-century bourgeois type of family was a 'haven in a heartless world'.[600] The boundaries between the public and the private were carried to extremes. The traditional family of the early modern period (an extended family which also consisted of non-relatives) was still closely interwoven with the rest of society at large and thus displayed a less clear-cut communion of working and living. In subsequent centuries the family retired into its own world of relationships, which were finally confined merely to the two-generation or nuclear family. In nineteenth-century middle-class circles the latter grew into a kind of bastion, a refuge within a society full of tension and threats. This evolution from the seventeenth century on has been attributed to various sociocultural changes such as the progressive loss of traditional values, the rise of industrial capitalism, and especially the shift in the cultural-psychological image of man, designated as the growth of affective individualism.[593]

From the eighteenth century onwards individuality, self-fulfilment and intimacy were progressively emphasized. Simultaneously the appreciation of affectivity and emotional development increased. The affective relationship between husbands and wives – the bonds of love – was considered to be of growing significance. The domestic circle became a centre of romanticism, sentimentality and privacy. Increasing appreciation of the emotional aspect in interpersonal relationships and more explicit recognition of the uniqueness of each individual led to greater care for and a more specific interest in the human being-in-development: the child. Within the security of domesticity family relationships were imbued with sentiment. In the previous century the romantic love between husband and wife became the ideal of affective bond and communicative openness. However:

> Between husband and wife, and between parents and children new feelings of involvement *and simultaneously also of a new distance* were growing. The extension of being young creates the no-man's-land of puberty; the postponed maturity turns sexual joys more and more into a provisionally forbidden fruit. Bodiliness, physical maturation and menstruation become topics which one initially should not talk about in the presence of children and which later on are not to be mentioned at all. Hence, the discovery of the unicity of each human being and of the different nature of children demands a fairly unexpected price: man and wife being different or, more exactly, the inability to communicate about that difference.[495]

In the Victorian bourgeoisie it was not merely a double moral standard regarding sexuality that prevailed. The pursuit of a high morality – in contrast to the decadence of the impoverished city – served to raise the middle class marriage beyond a merely procreative purpose. However, the latter function led to a cult of motherhood which inevitably implied a moral repression of women and children. The Victorian family as moral bastion turned out to be mainly a prison for everyone who lived there, except the father who was deemed morally strong enough to move freely in the outside world. In fact, the emotional character of this 'peaceful and stable' family was one of *explosive intimacy*.[545] Behind the screens of middle-class decency and devotion to duty, within the privacy of home comfort and cosy intimacy, the members of the family were 'intimately' attached to each other by psychological, social and economic bonds. Unconditional loyalty does not allow personal autonomy, romantic love does not tolerate open conflicts, moral self-discipline represses every frustration.

> In this way the 19th-century middle class family can develop into an ambiguous breeding-place of closer emotional bonds between the members of the family as well as of an inarticulate repugnance of woman against man, children against parents.[495]

Legislation as well as Protestant and Catholic doctrine reinforced the bourgeois aversion to non-conjugal sexuality, the exceptional esteem in which marriage was held and preference for the patriarchal family. The Victorian bourgeois family was characterized by an intense emotional involvement and a religiously inspired care for the moral well-being of its members. This moral reveille, which flourished between 1770 and 1870, was accompanied by a strengthening of patriarchy and a repression of sexuality (for women and children). The climate of upbringing in such mid-nineteenth-century families was predominantly characterized by strict rules of manners and a system of punishment aimed at cultivating diligence, a sense of duty and moderation. Upbringing was largely synonymous with moral training (with an overalertness towards sexuality); formation of conscience, discipline and subjection to authority were major themes. That such a 'bringing up by keeping down' was frequently attended with psychological as well as physical cruelty is clearly

apparent from the nineteenth-century witch hunt against masturbation (see below). Yet in the previous century the practice of
upbringing gradually shifted from physical to mental punishment, from brute force to subtle manipulation. Favourite methods of control were frequently connected with food: children
were supposed to eat everything mother dished up for them,
open aversion to particular foods was punished by an additional
portion and a violation of the house rules often meant that they
had to go to bed without food.

More than any other ritual of domestic life, the family meal
became a metaphor for this peculiar blend of intimacy and
hierarchy and acted as a model of showing both affection and
discipline. From the nineteenth century on, in bourgeois families
the dining-room became the centre of the cult of the family and
the ritual reunion of all the family around the table reached a
degree of sacredness as never before.

> In the French bourgeoisie of the nineteenth century, the ritual of the
> family meal seems to have been particularly important, and this
> probably has some connection with the high standard attained by
> French cuisine at that time, and the prestige, among Frenchman
> today, of 'bourgeois cuisine'. (. . .) Our bourgeois tables are normally
> adapted to the dimensions of a stable family group, and they remind
> old couples afterwards of the departure of their offspring.[517]

In relation to the rearing practices around the dinner-table, we
will briefly dwell on the meaning of eating in stories and books
aimed at inducing morality in children. The problem of famine
and the mortality in children of early modern France is recognizable in the well-known fairy tale of Mother Goose. Undernutrition, neglect and maltreatment of children are themes in Tom
Thumb and Cinderella. To rural residents at that time eating
was synonymous with surviving, whereas being able to eat
unlimitedly was a luxury of which many fantasized. From the
eighteenth century onwards the care for the well-being of
children became a crucial parental duty (see below). The romanticization of juvenile literature is an exponent of this. In the mid-
nineteenth century – within a strongly moralistic, occasionally
spartan climate of upbringing – fairly horrible children's stories
are to be found.[574] The stories of Heinrich Hoffmann (1809–
94), director of the Frankfurt Insane Asylum became popular in

Europe. In 1844 he wrote a collection of tales (*Struwwelpeter*) as a Christmas present for his 3-year-old son Carl. Therein features the well-known story of *Suppenkaspar* (Soup Kaspar): a fat boy refused to eat his soup, became thin as a thread and died after five days! Food refusal as rebellion is a bad idea, so children were taught.[540]

Three decades later the first reports about the occurrence of possibly fatal anorexia nervosa appear. Oddly enough, the first descriptions of Gull and Lasègue already mention 'stubborn' or 'obstinate' patients. Strikingly, this behaviour is not interpreted as opposition to parents. Nevertheless, the latter are not considered able to improve the situation. Gull and Lasègue do imply a power struggle within the family, without labelling it as such. They underline the fact that the treatment of anorexic patients should preferably take place outside the family setting and under the guidance of an authority, physician or nurse, who temporarily adopts the parents' role. However, anorexia nervosa was not immediately viewed as a form of protest or rebellion. When the first medical reports appeared, the stubborn 'Soup Kaspar' was no longer a typical example of juvenile literature. At the end of the nineteenth century increasing attention was paid to the inner life of the 'innocent' child. Stories and fairy tales, such as those of the brothers Grimm or Mother Goose, were progressively infantilized and stripped of horrible scenes: disobedient children were no longer faced with a cruel punishment or death, but a gnawing conscience. At the turn of the century the concern not to 'traumatise' the child had become a theme in upbringing, at a time when Sigmund Freud came to the fore and child psychology/psychiatry started to claim its own right of existence.[507]

It was not easy for youngsters to break free of their families with such galling bonds. At the end of the nineteenth century girls in particular were confronted with conflicting role expectations: at home mother personified the traditional female image, whereas in the middle classes, the first wave of woman's emancipation had started. In bourgeois circles 'repressed sexuality' manifested itself in all kinds of neurotic ways (see below) and forms of sexual abuse or incest remained hidden for the outside world.[594] Whereas in the first part of the nineteenth century there was no place for the influence of family relationships on the development of mental disorders, fifty years later psychoanalysis introduced a radically new view of the parent–child relationship. Therefore it is striking that – even before Freud formulated his views – the first therapeutic advice with regard to the recently discovered anorexia nervosa considered the removal of the patient from her home environment of crucial importance. Initially this measure did not proceed from a specific theory; this would be developed much later.[474] In the eyes of a present-day family therapist an important cultural-historical root of anorexia nervosa has to do with the powerlessness of the 'ideal' bourgeois family, which was subject to radical changes from the end of the nineteenth century on: the child now holds a central instead of a peripheral position within the family, and the parents' educational responsibility (and thus the risk of failure) is more important than ever before.[51]

The growing-pains of puberty and adolescence

Psychological history was considerably stimulated by the historical interest in the position of the child. This interest on the part of historians cannot be but a twentieth-century phenomenon; not surprisingly since at the outset it had already been proclaimed by contemporaries as 'the century of the child'.[548] The French historian Philippe Ariès (1914–84) in particular has put forward the 'discovery of the child' as a historical fact.[488] According to Ariès, in the seventeenth and eighteenth centuries an obvious awareness of childhood arose, of the uniqueness of the children's world, to be distinguished and progressively also more separated from the adult world. A pioneer of this pedagogic revolution was the French philosopher Jean-Jacques Rousseau (1712–78), particularly in his book of 1762, *Émile ou de l'éducation*. In this comprehensive work he expounded his educational ideas from the imaginary example of a little boy, Émile. Rousseau fiercely opposed the contemporary attitude of treating children as adults. He strongly emphasized that the child was a vulnerable, naturally good, nonsexual and innocent human being. Rousseau made a plea for a pedagogic isolation of the child against the 'dangerous' outside world. The notion of a generational continuum – the unnoticeable overflowing of childhood into adulthood – underwent a rapid erosion, reaching a logical conclusion with the 'generation gap.'

In the decades after Rousseau there would develop in the upper bourgeoisie a particular 'sentiment of infancy', through which children ceased to be miniature adults. This implied the birth of a new phase of life, a transitional period between childhood and adulthood: adolescence. Rousseau himself spoke of puberty as the 'second birth' or the moment when individuals really enter life. Later, sociologists and historians would speak about the invention of adolescence;[563] adolescence would be a sociopsychological construct, a creation of the changed sociocultural conventions through which the social environment of adults became fenced off to non-adults.[526] At the root of the social definition and delimitation of adolescence lay an implicit notion of the ideal maturation from child to adult; at any price precocity had to be precluded. However, it was soon apparent that upbringing at home (propagated for so long in higher social strata) led to too much interaction between youngsters and parents, which was an inappropriate situation to encourage slow and steady 'natural maturation'.

In the nineteenth-century middle class the educational principle developed that young people would grow up better in peer groups: hence the popularity of boarding-schools. To youngsters the importance of being well-prepared for complex adult life was increasingly pointed out. In this way the boarding-school – particularly the English version – developed into an extreme materialization of adolescence as a moratorium (postponement of adulthood). During the course of the last century the school system became more and more standardized and bureaucratized by all kinds of government measures, with an ever-increasing tendency to assign pupils to peer groups. Leisure activities of young people were organized by adults: after 1890 the first important youth movements and organizations arose, but were always guided by adults – the Boy Scouts are the best known example.[526;547]

The societal organization of youth had a double effect: it realized the desired segregation from adults and provided adolescents – as a kind of compensation – with a status of their own. It is only possible to talk about a rising youth ideology or youth culture round about the turn of the century. The status of the adolescent is then a social fact; but at the same time it induces a great concern in adults who become progressively more aware of the dangers and possible derailments of this phase of life. The 'generation gap' and 'revolting youth' are not exclusively twentieth-century themes. Specific groups of youngsters, united in opposition to the ruling culture or society, can be found in the late mediaeval period. But such 'youth movements' only became established from the second half of the eighteenth, and even more obviously in the nineteenth century, though they continued to be a rather isolated phenomenon. Only in our century do they become the driving force of a 'youth culture', gradually spreading over all walks of life and seeking escape from the tension between opposition and adjustment, rebellion and conformity.[537]

The idea that youth is an early modern invention is not generally accepted, adolescence was also considered a distinct and specific stage in life in earlier periods. This assumption is predominantly based on literary sources: all kinds of (often autobiographical) writings demonstrate that adolescence as a typical phase of growth is a universal fact of all time. Yet adolescence as a central theme is hardly to be found in pre-1900 *belles lettres*. Although Rousseau had already emphasized two major features of adolescence (pubertal crisis and intellectual awakening), this was denied by the majority of Romanticists. Perhaps the French female writer George Sand (1804–76) was the first to point out this lacuna in 1854–55. Nevertheless we have to wait until the 1890s before the adolescent began to acquire a recognized place in French literature.[566] British *belles lettres* showed a similar trend. Yet Samuel Richardson (1689–1761) in 1740 wrote his *Pamela, or Virtue Rewarded* with the passion of youth as its leading motif. But in other literary creations ordinary adolescents developed harmoniously with romantic marriage as the happy end. The conflictual nature of adolescence on the one hand, and the ambivalence of adulthood on the other, are only to be found as literary themes in the second part of the nineteenth century and, of course, predominantly in twentieth-century literature.[591]

With the work of the American psychologist Granville Stanley Hall (1844–1924), the modern notion of adolescence, but also formally the problematization of this phase of life, has been born. Hall's voluminous book *Adolescence* from 1904 is considered to be the official exponent of this new view on the *Sturm und Drang* of young people. But the essence of this different view had already been heralded in the last decades of the nineteenth century. Hall's approach was linked to the work of the German physiologist Wilhelm Preyer (1842–97), who in 1882 published *Die Seele des Kindes* (The Mind of the Child). This mile-stone in developmental psychology was based on Preyer's diary notes while observing the daily development of his son from baby to 3-year-old toddler. In the nineteenth century more of these 'baby-diaries' or 'toddler-biographies' appeared, among them one by Charles Darwin who carefully took notes of his son's development. No wonder the development of the individual and the human race were linked to each other in Darwin's theory of evolution. This link gave an important impetus to the notion of stages in psychic development and thus lay at the basis of child psychology and psychiatry, which acquired a distinct profile of their own at the end of the nineteenth century. At the same time the way was smoothed for the study of adolescence: Hall started where Preyer left off.[508;509]

Hall's book *Adolescence* is a compilation of the nineteenth-century knowledge of the growth of youth, amplified with wide research of his own (a combination of anthropometrics and questionnaires about the social environment of youngsters). According to Hall, adolescence as a structural phase of development is biologically determined (in fact he refers to puberty) and from an anthropological point of view occurs universally and unchangeably. Hall was a social Darwinist whose psychological model of development was undeniably genetic–evolutionary in character. Its essential notion was the theory of recapitulation: each individual rehearses in his own phased development the most important steps in the (biological) evolution of the human race. Herein adolescence occupies a prominent place, because it recapitulates the most recent evolution of mankind. In adolescence the *Sturm und Drang* of a sensitive transitional period in societal development is revealed. At the beginning of the twentieth century mankind was at the threshold of important shifts and was characterized, like adolescence, by an enormous potential for growth and progress. But if not led into good channels, this might run aground.

In this context it is probably not accidental that the discovery of the adolescent as a constant source of concern for parents and society had been mainly a turn-of-the-century American crea-tion.[508] Perhaps it had to do with the rapid socioeconomic expansion of the United States, the immigration paradise with almost unlimited possibilities, where so many endorsed the liberal individualistic ideal of the successful 'self-made man'. On the eve of the twentieth century fame and fortune seemed to be easily obtainable through the wonder of progress as if every dream of the future appeared to be within reach. The 'magic word evolution' was not merely a scientific concept associated with Darwin's descent theory, but also moved beyond the fierce disputes between science and religion concerning the origins of mankind. It had as much to do with what mankind could yet achieve: progress was bringing the future ever closer.[487]

The Victorians developed a new notion of time and space: before the turn of the century velocity had already become the driving force of progression. Train, steamer and telephone proudly attested to this. But progress also implied the risk of decadence, as every hurried evolution could deteriorate into revolution. That was the horror of the bourgeoisie, encouraging industrial progress but simultaneously fearing moral derailment as a consequence. The upbringing of upper-class young people tried to avoid this dilemma by maintaining a strong distinction between the sexes: a boy was expected to acquire a successful career via study. This could only flourish within a 'happy family', the criterion of success for which a girl had to strive. Today in certain milieus a similar attitude is still to be recognized. Yet, the process of adolescence in socioeconomic terms – ending with material independence and the start of one's own family – essentially differs from the one of a century ago: currently young people leave their family of origin more rapidly and easily, though the step towards a professional career has become more difficult and complex.[559]

We have depicted adolescence as a sociocultural creation of an industrialized society. Without entering into the eternal 'nature/nurture' debate – is man a product of nature or a creation of culture? – we cannot ignore the view of adolescence as an universal phenomenon of all time, because the biological develop-ment from child to adult would show constant features in every period. Here we encounter a conceptual confusion which fre-quently occurs: puberty is essentially a biological phenomenon.

It refers to sexual maturation – *pubescere* means to mature, particularly sexually – as marked by the occurrence of the first menstruation in girls (menarche) and the first seminal emission in boys. Puberty is the beginning of the psychosocial maturation in adolescence – *adolescere* means to grow or to grow up – which can only manifest itself when biological maturation has been reached. In fact the notion of the universal occurrence of adolescence is based on the constant character of pubertal characteristics and leans on the premise that psychological development is necessarily rooted in the physiological maturation of the individual. There is obviously a connection but this does not necessarily imply a causal relationship: psychological development in general and adolescence in particular is also determined by sociocultural factors, by the historically and geographically changing social climate. Moreover, physiological phenomena in puberty may be constant as far as their 'content' is concerned; 'formally', however, they appear to be subject to historical changes and did not previously receive so much attention as they do today. As examples of the changing pubertal forms we will briefly discuss the menarche and growth spurt.

The rather sudden and significant acceleration of growth in puberty, especially a sharp increase in height, is nowadays so well known, that such a growth spurt is considered to be characteristic of puberty. Yet this phenomenon was not a scientifically established and recognized fact before 1880.[597] The history of this phenomenon incites intriguing questions such as why did physicians formerly show so little interest in the growth spurt? Was the adolescent spurt so inconspicuous as to be overlooked or was the phenomenon perhaps so commonly acknowledged that physicians did not consider it worth studying? These questions are even more pertinent if we realize that sporadic publications on the topic in the eighteenth century were then followed by a century of peculiar silence. The attitude of the Belgian scientist Adolphe Quetelet (1796–1874), the father of modern applied statistics, is remarkable in this respect. He acquired international fame through his anthropometric studies which demonstrated that the height in different populations varies according to a 'normal curve' (known as the Gaussian curve). Quetelet published a series of measurements of height and weight in boys and girls between 0 and 25 years of age. A look at these data clearly shows a peak in growth rates: between 12 and 14 years for girls and 13 and 15 years for boys. None the less he does not mention this phenomenon or interpret it as the proverbial exception proving his rule of 'normal' growth. Looking for natural laws of universal constancy, Quetelet 'enshrined in a rule' the monotonically descending velocity of growth, obliterating the adolescent spurt and confusing a number of later workers.[597] Only after Quetelet's death was his 'perfect' growth curve criticized and the pubertal growth spurt as a normal phenomenon of growth accepted. This coincided with the moment when the practical value of this knowledge – in the form of growth curves – entered into the textbooks of paediatrics. Thus the 'discovery' of the pubertal growth spurt may be considered to be one of the scientific ways along which the development from child to adult became problematic. The growth curve is additionally the expression of a typical inclination of scientists in the second part of the previous century to quantify all kinds of phenomena. It heralded a new scientific belief: measuring is knowing.

The nineteenth-century interest in female adolescence, more precisely in the age of the first menstruation (menarche) is also striking.[597] The first systematic study on this issue was published in 1795 by the German obstetrician Friedrich Benjamin Osiander (1759–1822), who mentioned an average age of 16.6 years. From that moment on numerous studies appeared in various European countries, revealing important differences: on the one hand geographically (earlier menarche in Southern European countries) and on the other with respect to social class (higher menarcheal age among working-class girls). In the nineteenth century, middle-class girls' first menses occurred on the average at about the age of 14 to 14.5 years (in working class children this was mostly one year later). A decrease was probably already apparent during the second part of the previous century, but in the subsequent hundred years this became particularly obvious: menarche accelerated with a velocity of three to four months per decade (the typical age of onset of anorexia nervosa has decreased likewise!).

Nowadays the age of menarche seems to have stabilized at about 13 years (with minimal differences between the social classes). This peculiar 'secular change', which also includes an increase in height, indicates a more rapid physical maturation of current children in comparison to their nineteenth-century peers. All kinds of explanations have been suggested for this.[583] Typically for a late Victorian mentality, it has been suggested that a stronger exposure to sexual stimuli might be responsible for the accelerated maturation (see below). The notion that the climate plays a decisive role continues to be an obstinate myth. The only plausible explanation of the 'secular change' is a generally improved nutrition, though the true nature of this influence is still obscure.

The affliction of the 'new woman'

The nineteenth century was undeniably the era of the bourgeoisie.[589] The bourgeoisie came to the fore during the new economic and industrial revolutions, which ushered in the nineteenth century. In the wake of fundamental shifts in labour conditions and family structure, the bourgeoisie had established an indisputable hegemony in the 1860s. However, at the turn of the century this social normative bastion was undermined. The power structures in society underwent important shifts as a consequence of the rearrangement of economic power through emerging capitalism, mass production by ever larger companies and the expansion of trade markets to national and international proportions. All this has been stimulated to a great extent by increasing transport facilities and the associated mobility of the population (especially in America). Against the background of a mobile and large-scale economy both the labour and the women's movements – reactions of suppressed majority groups – threatened the balance of power.

From the 1870s on, young middle class women began to seek a new self-image under the flag of intellectual self-fulfilment. The language of these 'new women' was self-conscious, assertive and with time also aggressive. Although not directly iconoclastic, this movement eroded the current model of the ideal woman-mother, who was the figurehead of the bourgeois family between 1820 and 1860. The sociocultural changes discussed above markedly influenced the development from child to adult, which was noticeable earlier among boys than among girls: in the first half of the nineteenth century for the former and only half a

century later for female adolescents.[536] This difference is mainly
due to the demarcation of ever stricter gender roles in the urban
middle class, where every effort was made to turn the girl into the
ideal 'woman at the fire-side', the loyal wife and devoted mother
who had to see that the family was a moral bastion to protect the
middle class values from the dangers of the decadent outside
world. From the mid-nineteenth century on girls had it drummed
into them that motherhood was the ultimate aim. In this 'cult of
true womanhood' motherhood was professionalized; being a
'profession' it was now irreconcilable with any other aspiration
'outside'.[606] Choosing a professional life outside the family implied a violation of the 'natural vocation' to motherhood. Every
intellectual or other ambition was condemned as counternatural
and consequently a reprehensible 'imitation of males'.

The turn of the century misogyny (hatred of women) was
primarily directed towards the 'new women', who disfigured
their 'nature' by unhealthy intellectual aspirations. Against this
risk of 'degeneration' of the female race the very popular social
Darwinist evolution theory was eagerly used as argument. The
prevailing medical view of physiology and sexuality supported
the conservative notion of women's homely and social roles.[533]
The mid-nineteenth-century 'cult of true womanhood' is reflected and strengthened in the medical opinions about the 'cycle
of femininity': from puberty to menopause reproductive processes determined the character and rhythm of women's lives.[589]
From the first to the final menses a woman's life is determined
by her biological clock, which reminds her every month that
the ebb and flow of her reproductive system is a divine natural
law she has to respect on pain of all kinds of afflictions and
disfigurements. Natural destination to reproduction – 'anatomy
as destiny'[546] – was women's highest asset, and simultaneously
explained her 'weaker' nature. In the second half of the nineteenth century the 'cult of true womanhood' became a medical
and scientific dogma, echoed in every shape and form in the
flourishing sex education literature for young girls.

To be sure, such a view of women's biology existed from
antiquity on, but never before had it been uplifted to a scientific
credo in such an emphatic and abundant way as between 1840
and 1890.[589] It was the period in which medical science acquired
a great reputation and wanted to adopt the role of 'moral

conscience' from the Church. But it was also a period in which women's role ('mother at the fireside') had to be defended ever more fiercely against the gradually growing criticism on this moral cornerstone of the bourgeois family. The medical profession – being itself a typical example of conservative male bourgeoisie – blazed out both in professional scientific publications as well as in popular advice literature. Girls had been taught that in puberty the physiological dictatorship of the ovaries began, to end only at the menopause. The way a girl passed through the storms of puberty was viewed as decisive for her entire life to come. Nature had created a completely different 'bodily economy' for both sexes.[573] Men had to limit their sexual activities in order to spare their mental energy; in women the energy stream had to be directed in the opposite way, from the brain into the pelvis. The limited energy which a girl possessed at the dawn of her femininity, had to be preserved at any price for the growth of her reproductive system. Such valuable energy could not with impunity be dissipated in sexual interest or activity or in *unfemale behaviour* such as intellectual efforts, sport, factory work and interest in non-homely activities. A whole catalogue of illnesses, nervous afflictions and even death was in store for those who were guilty of such activities.[511;512] Woe on the mothers who had not guarded and supported their maturing daughters at the crucial moment in their life: the first menstruation, that painful and traumatic unfolding of innocent girl into sexually mature woman.

But with the first menstruation awoke emotions and sexual feelings. With the uncontrollable monthly bleedings, the deeply rooted 'animal nature' in every woman threatened to break out. This was a (monthly) time bomb to every middle-class family, which was founded on the Victorian values of control, discipline and rationality. These biopsychological storms could best be kept in control by a good preparation for marriage and reproduction. Thus the point was to guide young people into the safe port of a new homely nest of their own. In that sense it was suitable that for the majority of the girls in the nineteenth century adolescence was relatively short, running from menarche at 14–15 years to marriage at 18–20 years of age. Yet this life-phase implied a threat to middle-class values, for in the female adolescent both the highest human asset as well as the lowest

animal danger was already present. Woman's biological weakness was immediately considered to be her moral strength. The
male adolescent had to face the inverse situation: in puberty his
strength and vitality developed explosively, but likewise the risk
of uncontrolled sexual drive was threatening.[532] The adults' fear
found expression in the repellent nineteenth-century antimastur-
bation crusade

Sexuality – certainly in females – had to be expressed within
marriage for reproductive purposes. From the 1870s on the birth-
rate declined in Western industrialized countries. The growing
interest in birth control at the end of the nineteenth century may
more plausibly be associated with economic conditions than with
the emerging women's movement.[514] In the eyes of conservative
social-Darwinists the declining birth-rate, however, was a threat
to the evolution of mankind and to the further progress of society.
People appealed to moral strength of women – who were
otherwise viewed as physically and mentally weak – not to deny
their natural vocation to motherhood. With this argument people
tried to cope with the new threat to the social order: the women's
movement claiming social and political emancipation.[552] When
the British philosopher John Stuart Mill (1806–73) published his
book about *The Subjection of Women* in 1869, the moment had
been carefully chosen. For in the 1860s the struggle for votes for
women had arisen and in Great Britain the first feminist organizations were formed. Mill became an influential advocate of
women's rights. This also fitted his liberal view that all individuals
should have the freedom to be themselves and to choose their own
individual life styles. In *The Subjection of Women* Mill refuted the
contemporary myth that women could not achieve great artistic
or philosophical success and were unfit for high posts in public
life. In the second half of the nineteenth century Mill's passionate
plea for women's political and societal equality became a pamphlet
and manifesto of the emerging women's movement.[552]

Although more militant feminists strived for female suffrage
as their primary aim – hence the name 'suffragettes' – the
women's movement soon produced a far-reaching undermining
of traditional Victorian values. The famous Seneca Falls Conven-
tion of July 1848 in the state of New York, the official start of
the first feminist revolt in the United States, resulted in a
'Declaration of Rights and Sentiments' wherein women claimed

equality in almost all public domains: from suffrage to divorce, from professional opportunities to full education.[542] It was only to be a few decades before women's 'sexual liberation' was also to be found on the feminists' agenda. The militant women's movement appeared on the streets with protests and petitions: they literally assumed the 'public role' they claimed for women. The formidable weapon of the hunger strike would only be applied around 1910 (see further on). Had the self-starvation of anorexic patients perhaps served as an example? Or had anorexia itself been an expression of silent protest within the walls of the Victorian bourgeois home? Was it one of those 'modern' afflictions to which 'new women' seemed so susceptible?

High was the emotional price nineteenth-century feminists had to pay for their efforts. Numerous advocates of the women's movement experienced a 'nervous breakdown', especially those who additionally ran the household.[512] Their emotional life was undermined by the contradiction a new generation of women had to cope with: the conflict of interests between their public and private roles. Growing girls were confronted with an intellectual and emotional dilemma: the choice between a family or a career. Haunted by these questions women themselves became a major concern, an alarming issue for the male world. None the less physicians had warned against the risks and now mobilized their scientific arsenal to treat the 'new afflictions'. Whereas male health had been particularly undermined by masturbation, the female gender was 'weak' because of the 'vulnerability' of its reproductive system. For this reason many illnesses were associated with the menses.[583] Chlorosis was one example, but the most typical afflictions were hysteria and neurasthenia.

Although hysteria has a venerable history, it was in particular the classic illness of the nineteenth century.[585] By then it had reached epidemic proportions and had numerous subtle variants. Apart from the more spectacular pictures such as hysterical paralyses, upper-class women displayed all kinds of mysterious phenomena, often manifesting themselves as a 'crisis': they became unwell, fainted or were plagued by severe oppression. These were the Victorian 'vapours'. The hysterical woman was the embodiment of hyper-femininity and her 'sick' behaviour a symptom of the stereotypical female ideal propagated in middle-class circles. An interaction of three factors transformed hysteria into a particular behavioural option for the Victorian woman. Upbringing conditioned many girls into psychologically vulnerable women with a deficient development of self-image or self-esteem. At the same time patterns of socialization and cultural values promoted hysteria as an acceptable and attractive alternative, and the hysterical role provided a secondary gain in terms of a strengthened position of authority within the family.[589]

Nineteenth-century physicians took pains to legitimate hysteria as a real illness. The affliction was considered to be especially biological in origin, and here a typical Victorian theme returns: women's constitutional weakness or impressionability.[573] Initially the classical view of hysteria – the 'sick' womb (see Chapter 7) – was embraced in all kinds of varieties, but after 1870 this theory fell into disrepute. The emergence of neurology was not unconnected with this. Hysteria was removed from the sphere of gynaecology and defined as the neurologist's territory: an 'oversensitive nervous system' now became the new theme. But whether neurological or gynaecological in origin, physicians frequently associated hysteria with a certain 'unfemale' life style or upbringing, which necessarily undermined a woman's fragile constitution. Here the typical ambivalence of nineteenth-century physicians towards their hysterical patients (or women in general) is noticeable: on the one hand the hysteric was protected by a biologically founded diagnosis, on the other she was accused of being herself responsible for the affliction.[510] Thus hysterical women could not expect any sympathy from physicians (in those days all males, of course, virtually without exception).

Essentially the attitude of physicians was similar towards that other typical nineteenth-century affliction, neurasthenia.[584] This is undeniably an American 'invention', whose year of birth – just like anorexia nervosa's – can be situated around 1870 (see Chapter 9). Strikingly enough this new illness had been immediately associated with the hurried life of the urban middle class of industrialized America. Its epidemic proportions were seen as suggestive of an illness of 'modern' civilization. The risk of 'nervous exhaustion' was the price of rapid progress, which was only achieved by 'brain work' for which the working class or the uncivilized were considered incapable. For men this was a respectable affliction, though the majority of the American neurasthenics were upper-class women. The list of their symp-

toms was even more impressive than in male 'victims' of neurasthenia: hardly any bodily function or organ remained unafflicted!
Everything was indicative of exhaustion: total weakness, dejection, irritability, headache, paleness, menstrual irregularities, constipation, loss of appetite, etc.[533]

The arsenal of possible therapies turned out to be just as
extensive: from revitalizing tonics to electric stimulation. The
prototypical therapy for neurasthenics was the 'rest cure'. The
recommendations were simple: much bed rest with massage
(preferably in a health resort, far away from all troubles) and
abundant nourishment.[510] The latter element is not unimportant
for our cultural-historical analysis. Nineteenth-century middle
class people – physicians as well as patients – became obsessed in
a peculiar way by food intake and weight regulation. But the
compulsory bed rest is an intriguing component in the light of
the restlessness and hyperactivity which are so characteristic of
anorexia nervosa. Finally, the advice again turns up to remove
the patient from the home environment. A hundred years later
all these ingredients can still be found in the recommended
therapies for anorexia nervosa! This highlights the fact that all
these illnesses of the 'new women' – both in form and content as
well as meaning – are interwoven with a Victorian cultural
pattern whose influences have infiltrated well into our century.

Both in description and explanation, as well as the therapy
proceeding from these, nineteenth-century hysteria and neurasthenia caricatured the 'weak' sex in the shape of childish women.[589]
Simultaneously, precisely this 'sickliness' offered many women a
chance to express their dissatisfaction with their lives in a covert
(passive–aggressive) way and to temporarily escape from the
family duties, imposed by the cult of true womanhood. By the
end of the nineteenth century physicians were more or less
aware of these mechanisms and their own powerlessness against
them: the temporary removal from the family was considered to
be a necessary step towards cure. Admission to a hospital or stay
in a health resort offered relief for both medical attendant and
husband: it constituted an 'honourable' retreat from a power
struggle which confronted both men with their frustrating powerlessness.[459] The approach to anorexic patients was quite similar:
away from home and forcible feeding if necessary. The 'price of
repression' was indeed high![524]

Discovery of the forbidden sexuality

In psychological historiography the concept 'Victorian' is almost always associated with a particular attitude towards sexuality. As expression of a mainly repressive sexual morality it is often reduced to a simplistic cliché. Initially the conditions of life in the nineteenth-century middle class were relatively stable and solid. By the end of the century they became very complex and confusing as a result of the radical changes we have noted above. Sexuality did not escape this development. Nevertheless, at the beginning of the previous century the civilizing process seemed to have led sexuality into clear channels. Control and domination were the behavioural codes by which the civilizing of social intercourse created a number of 'civilized' taboos. This process reached its climax in the first part of the nineteenth century, when sexuality became imbued with middle-class ideas.[604] In an increasingly organized society – which had its orgins in the late Middle Ages – people had learnt to curtail and control their emotional lives. The increasing feeling of shame and formation of conscience are typical expressions of this. In addition a shift had gradually become manifest from social control by means of society's behavioural codes (control from the outside or external coercion) to personal control via one's own rules of conscience (control from the inside or internal coercion).

At the beginning of the nineteenth century self-control had been the ideal of emotional domesticity. But it was still an affect control 'by order', a prohibition of sexual enjoyment in the name of 'social decency'. This was the ruling idea of every middle-class family that wanted to see its societal status confirmed, particularly in moral behavioural codes and rules of social intercourse. Sexual life has been restrained by a strict external censorship which gradually, via the development of conscience, was internalized to become self-censorship. However, by the turn of the century this Victorian structure of order had already been seriously undermined by the gradual fading away of societal restraints and inner conscientious restrictions on the relationship between men and women. A process of 'de-tabooization' set in: all kinds of taboos, certainly regarding sexuality, would perish within a period of hardly a hundred years – roughly between 1860 and 1970 – as 'sacrosanct beliefs' before the iconoclasm of the sexual revolution.[486] None the less, in the previous century the taboo on sexual expression seemed to have been unanimously and unwaveringly established by Church and state, morality and science. But it was precisely the extreme rigidity by which the formal aspects of sexuality were regularized, which betrayed the intense fear of the potentially dislocating power of repressed sexuality. In the era of the steam-engine scientists knew how strong the driving force of repressed energy could be. Psychoanalysis would reveal this mechanism in a way provocative to many Victorians.

A far-reaching example of sexual repression is the attitude towards masturbation in the nineteenth century, which implied a true horror.[564] The moral-religious, pedagogic and medical repression of 'self-defilement' has already started in the eighteenth century. It would reach a climax in the early Victorian era, which combated the 'secret sin' by all means possible. In particular the vitality of young people, more precisely of boys, was supposed to be in danger. Priests and physicians mobilized a nearly sadistic arsenal of horrible accusations: the 'self-abuser' awaited a series of terrifying vexations and illnesses. An alarming new illness emerged: 'spermatorrhoea'.[533] Through abundant loss of seed the onanist visibly wasted away. His nervous system pined away and insanity lay in wait. Anyone who wasted his seed outside marriage was undermining his masculinity. A similar reasoning was also followed in the condemnation of homosexuality. The inconsistency in argument is striking. For, even though masturbation implied a scandalous waste of natural forces, we should not conclude that sexuality was a source of energy for the productivity of citizens! On the other hand unanimity was lacking as to whether total sexual abstinence or sexual intercourse during marriage was the best remedy. By contrast, for girls and women the argument was identical: every form of sexual excitement might endanger their vulnerable reproductive system. Society did not even refrain from surgical resection of the clitoris in 'sick' female masturbators, though this was an exceptional measure as no sexual activity at all was expected of a well-bred woman.[573]

The 'angel of the house' was viewed as an asexual human being with the innocence of a child. Opposed to these madonna-like figures were the 'degenerated' or 'fallen' women, the whores.[491] The average Victorian middle-class man was well aware of this, for he often secretly sought comfort with prostitutes whom he publicly despised. The 'anti-sexual syndrome' of the nineteenth century did not imply simple repression. In fact social censorship condemned the overt expression of sexual desires. But whereas the latter were supposed to be non-existent in 'true' women, men – including the faithful husbands – were allowed a secret erotic exhaust-valve.[538] Marriage was based on romantic love, leaving no room for sexual passion. Therefore, instead of identifying Victorian mentality with pure sexual repression, it is to be characterized more properly as bourgeois hypocrisy, and in particular as a double moral standard. Strikingly, the feminist movement in the second part of the nineteenth century only partially exposed this double standard: it wanted to protect women primarily against the dangers of prostitution and adhered to the heterosexual model of marriage.[552] Only scant attention was paid to women's sexual lamentations, but instead another danger of sexuality was emphasized: undesired pregnancy. Initially the right to 'voluntary motherhood' was synonymous with the right to refuse sexual intercourse with the husband. Only after the turn of the century was birth control considered to be a means by which a woman could also claim the right to sexual pleasure.[514]

All this must have been quite confusing for a middle-class girl growing up in the last quarter of the previous century. She had been wedged between narrow family bonds, became increasingly aware of her own status between childhood and adulthood, and sought for her own identity as a 'new woman'. However, parallel to the problematic adolescence sexuality had also awoken in a body that became ever earlier mature. Contemporary sex education, wrapped up in all kinds of vague insinuations, was far from clarifying: the maturing girl was kept 'innocently' ignorant or sexuality was even more mysterious than before. In what tragedies this could result, was illustrated by an at the time sensational play of the German *avant garde* expressionist Frank Wedekind (1864–1918): *Frühlings Erwachen – Eine Kindertragödie* (Spring Awakening – A Tragedy of Childhood) from 1891. The play – which had to wait fifteen years for its premiere! – expresses the awakening of sexuality in a group of grammar-school pupils and their incapacity to deal with this, as programmed by a hypocritical society. Wedekind ridiculed in expressionist style the complete failure of the contemporary system of upbringing. The play is a satirical charge against bourgeois hypocrisy and dogmatic morality trying to restrain the awaking sexuality in young people by all kinds of rules and prohibitions, which make entry into the adult world a frightening experience. The play symbolized the *Sturm und Drang* of an ignorant adolescent who, confronted with sexual impulses, escapes into romantic day-dreaming or deeply unhappy flirting with thoughts of death.[609] *Spring Awakening* was the first play that explicitly dealt with pubertal crisis in a society which complicated growing up, but was at a loss when faced with the adolescent problems it had itself created.

However, for some the solution seemed to be simple. Who today realizes that the favourite breakfast of many Americans, now exported almost everywhere, was in fact meant as a remedy against 'sexual mischief'? Cornflakes, so beloved by numerous children, were indeed a product of the nineteenth-century reform-movement.[560] Like religiously inspired 'knights of purity' numerous organizations fought against the 'perdition' of society. Purity was 'total abstinence' from all carnal joys. Alcoholism, prostitution and abortion were the major symptoms of a 'moral tumour' which was particularly rampant in urban society. Its horror was expressed in the mental and physical degeneration of the insane and syphilitic patient. To be armed against this threatening 'degeneration' every citizen had to be taught how to remain in peak condition. At the beginning of the previous century Sylvester Graham (1794–1851) urged his fellow Americans to observe three health commands: wholemeal bread, bodily exercise, and sexual abstinence. The extremist preacher himself suffered from the American illness of 'dyspepsia' (see Chapter 7) and is remembered as the father of the Graham crackers.[578] Fifty years later, the physician John Harvey Kellogg (1852–1943) followed in his footsteps; his name adorns numerous breakfast tables today. His cornflakes – put on the market in 1898 – were to protect Americans against the excitement of sexual appetite arising from 'unhealthy' nourishment. Ironically enough, the crusty cornflakes only became popular after they had been coated in sugar, an offence against the 'cult of healthy food'. This is probably typical of the *Zeitgeist* at the turn of the century, when many Victorian commands and prohibitions appeared to be untenable in their orthodox formalism. The same happened to sexuality.

At the end of the nineteenth century 'repressed' sexuality gradually came to the surface. When 'stormy' adolescence could no longer be ignored and the 'age of the child' was heralded, Freud's 'discovery' of child's sexuality aroused a storm of Victorian indignation.[523;524] Interest in sex was no longer an expression of perverted minds in the obscure slums of pornography and prostitution. Sexuality became the public subject of study by honourable scientists; a new science was born: sexology.[607] Many physicians still fiercely opposed the discussion of sexual matters, but the question of 'sexual upbringing' could not remain unanswered. In the wake of the feminist movement ever more voices were heard demanding sexual emancipation. The increasing democratization of birth control severed the connection between love and reproduction. This drastic change provided married women especially with chances for new sexual experience: from procreation to re-creation or from load to lust. But meanwhile the 'new women' had discovered more than the joys of (mainly coital) sex within marriage. Behind velvet curtains and beneath silk hoop-petticoats erotic sensuality and tender passion had been frequently disguised. Victorian women have far too often been characterized as prudish and passionless human beings, who even in their most sentimental daydreams and romantic fantasies preserved a 'virtuous' distance.[503] The repressive antisexual atmosphere of the Victorian bourgeoisie is often considered to stand in sharp contrast to the sexual liberalization of the second half of the twentieth century. But the nineteenth century may have been much more tolerant and flexible towards the emotional and affective bonds between women.

The nineteenth-century bourgeois social climate was characterized by a strongly mutual commitment between women.[589] Occasionally this emotional bond or affective intimacy was very passionate and often eroticized (in our view anyway). The mother–daughter relationship was exemplary of the close and long-lasting friendship between women. Social intercourse between mother and daughter was marked by mutual sympathy, understanding and respect. Via role-modelling one generation brings up the other for the domestic role which the bourgeois family assigned to women. But the economic and intellectual changes in the last decades of the previous century provided bourgeois daughters with alternatives to their mothers' domestic role. Inevitably a generation conflict arose which was no longer compatible with intimacy between women who had before closely identified with each other in the closeness of the bourgeois family. By this generational rupture the 'new women' also incited a breach in the silently accepted bonds of love between women. Perhaps in response to the threats of feminism, male moralists and physicians proposed perverse and degenerate 'lesbian love' as a new medical theme. Male homosexuality, too, was still fiercely disputed and became a central theme of the emerging sexology. The medical world – bastion of society's patriarchal structure – took pains to keep control of the 'new women' and the 'liberated sexuality' within an ever more differentiated pathology, as if in a nosological straitjacket: from hysteria to neurasthenia, from agoraphobia to anorexia.[585]

Medicalization of all kinds of socially abnormal behaviour was the hallmark of a secularizing society, in which scientific determinism and social Darwinist evolutionary views reinforced one another.[487] This development culminated in a rage of classification: like animals and plants, human beings could be arranged according to hierarchical classes in all their (abnormal) varieties. Classifying and ranking were the prevailing 'words of order' by which (predominantly male) scientists wanted to arrange a changing and conflictual society, where traditional relationships both between the social classes as well as between the sexes were undermined ever more openly. Science prescribed the new norms. It not only established the boundaries between sick and healthy, but also dealt with (ab)normality of bodily forms and physical appearance. In the nineteenth century for the first time women's beauty had become a matter for physicians.

Beauty as a 'weighty' task

This brings us to the fifth and final theme of our exploration of the cultural-historical roots of modern anorexia nervosa. The reader may be surprised that we did not start earlier with this theme, for should anorexia nervosa not be primarily considered a caricature of the ideal of slenderness? This was noted before (Chapter 1) with respect to the 'epidemic' proportions of anorexia nervosa. Inevitably the question arises of to what extent a particular eating culture might be decisive. The conclusion that anorexia nervosa is hardly known in the Third World seemed to be an interesting point of departure. The tragic and occasionally hallucinant history of famine and undernutrition is impressive indeed. Shortage of food and hunger on a large scale have been repeated plagues up to the mid-nineteenth century. The industrial and agrarian revolution then resulted in a striking improvement in food supplies so that at the beginning of our century large-scale famine had almost disappeared in the Western world (at least in times of peace). But economic and demographic considerations do not carry us much further, though certain influences should not be underestimated: we have already mentioned the probably crucial role of nourishment in the 'secular change' in growth velocity and age of menarche.

The history of nutrition becomes more interesting when more cultural-psychological or social-anthropological meanings are involved. Then we are dealing with the psychosocial functions of food: its symbolic and religious significance; the aspect of hedonism and gastronomy; as a means of communication and exertion of power; a sign of identity and status.[527] A few aspects have been casually mentioned before: the place of food within the bourgeois family and the obsession of the Victorian health movement to banish 'sexually exciting' food. A particular link between food and sexuality had been suspected by physicians for centuries. All kinds of foods, diets and fasting rules were part of the therapeutic arsenal of healers and physicians from time immemorial (see Chapter 6). But more important than the physician's relationship to food is the – nowadays self-evident – meaning of food as source of pleasure: the gastronomic function. We looked for an answer to the question: can we find, historically, a recognizable alteration in appetite in the nineteenth-century bourgeoisie?

In placing the eating habits of the upper classes in a historical perspective, we write a history of eating-culture.[558;596] The alternating fasting and feasting of mediaeval people was closely linked to the unpredictability of food supplies and the general uncertainty or insecurity of life. The short life expectancy was still dominated by the concern to survive physically, a fate people did not have in their own hands. In the seventeenth and particularly the eighteenth centuries a more efficiently organized society gradually provided more security. The social superiority of the upper classes could no longer be expressed through the *quantity* of food they were able to consume. Now the *quality* of food had become an expression of social distinction. A refined taste was considered to be a sign of 'civilization' and the noble *haute cuisine* arrived. The civilizing of appetite was not only accompanied by an increasing formalism in eating behaviour - 'table manners' - but also required a certain degree of self-discipline. A connoisseur would never be guilty of gorging, however hungry he might be and however attractive food might appear. The bourgeoisie cultivated a real 'culinary art', the gastronomic aesthetics of the élitist *grande cuisine* as it had been dictated in the previous century by professionally run 'first class' restaurants. Luxurious eating had become a *folie bourgeoise*.[490] At home, however, the communal meal of the bourgeois family turned out to be a ritualized reflection of the rigid familial relations and formalized rules of social intercourse. It exuded discipline and control, decency and moderation. As never before self-control was the bourgeois adage: everything in moderation, including eating and weight.

In the nineteenth century, for the first time gastronomes associated their ideas about culinary art with the important concern to avoid corpulence.[558] The father of modern gastronomy, Jean-Anthelme Brillat-Savarin (1755–1826) devoted two chapters to corpulence in his famous book *La Physiologie du Goût* (The Physiology of Taste: 1826). This stout lawyer called himself a *médecin amateur* who, had he been a physician, would have started his scientific career with a substantial monography on corpulence. His well-known aphorism: 'Tell me what you eat and I will tell you who you are', referred to the distinction between the gourmet and the gourmand, the connoisseur and the glutton. No doubt, the latter would die earlier.[499] That corpulence in the previous century became an increasing concern in the upper classes is easy to infer from the simplification of menus, which influential gastronomes such as Georges August Escoffier (1847–1935) recommended: the number of courses was drastically reduced and lighter meals were prepared. The *nouvelle cuisine* was born.[558] Physicians, belonging themselves to the privileged clientele of the luxury restaurants, would translate this concern in scientific terms. Eighteenth-century physicians propagated a moderate lifestyle as a guarantee for health. Their nineteenth-century colleagues would transform this beneficial advice into strict prescriptions.

In the second part of the previous century it became the tendency to express normality and health in numbers. People diligently measured and weighed, counted and compared. Quetelet was the great inspirer of anthropometrics: expressing man in measures. An exceptional and many-sided exponent of this new rage – 'measuring is knowing' – was Sir Francis Galton (1822–1911). Strongly influenced by Darwin's evolutionism, he published in 1844 a study of three subsequent generations of British noblemen (born respectively between 1740 and 1769, 1770 and 1799, 1800 and 1829).[558] His study suggests that at the end of the nineteenth century young men in the highest stratum of English society were no longer putting on weight so rapidly as their fathers and grandfathers had done, though they reached the same average weight at the end of their life. Galton gathered his data from a prominent grocery and a wine-business in London, where a weighing scale was placed for the use and amusement of the customers. That was not uncommon in those days: by the end of the nineteenth century weighing scales were to be found in all kinds of public places.[578] Simultaneously physicians started to weigh their patients regularly and a number of theories had been developed about body weight as an indicator of a mental disorder or criminal constitution. Not merely one's eating behaviour, but also one's weight had become an important personal characteristic.

Studying body experience from a cultural-historical perspective, we can find in the nineteenth century a growing interest in the aesthetic and medical aspects of body size.[579] Parallel to this an increasing aversion to obesity is to be observed. For men in particular the preservation of health was used as an argument and placed within the evolutionism of the 'survival of the fittest': progress did not benefit from fat people and gluttons. For women gradually – particularly in the late-nineteenth-century upper classes – a new ideal of slenderness arose. Here the medical argumentation played a minor role (unless concerning the moderation of food intake), but in its place the aesthetic of female elegance started to develop new norms of body size. Although a certain plumpness still continued to be the prevailing norm, by the turn of the century the modern ideal of slenderness came into being. The 'battle against fatness' had started: obesity was the 'enemy' and physicians provided the 'weapons'.[530] Modern diet culture made an impressive advance (see also Chapter 11).

The history of beauty norms for women cannot be reduced to a chronicle of human aesthetics. Visual perception is in itself continuously susceptible to changes in our environment. Frequently we look with the eyes of others. When the influence of that other – a person, a group, a society – is great, beauty becomes an interactional fact through which one individual is acting in compliance with the influences (i.e power) of the other. For Naomi Wolf the current cultural fixation on female thinness should be viewed as an obsession with female obedience rather than with female beauty:

> The great weight shift must be understood as one of the major historical developments of the century, a direct solution to the dangers posed by the women's movement and economic and reproductive freedom. Dieting is the most potent political sedative in women's history; a quietly mad population is a tractable one.[610]

No wonder feminists speak about the 'politics of beauty'.[551]

Women's age-old subordinated position within a male-privileged society and their efforts to struggle free from it is reflected in contemporary ideals of beauty. From the fifteenth century on Western society idealized three types of female figures.[494] Until the seventeenth century the stomach-centred and – by present-day standards – rather plump woman was admired. This 'reproductive' type was then replaced by the 'hour-glass' model, with a narrow waist accentuating the full bosom and round bottom. The change occurring at the end of the nineteenth century can still be found today: although generally speaking men's preference is still for the maternal figure, twentieth-century women progressively idealized the lean, almost 'tubular' body type, deprived of the symbolic emphasis of fertility and motherhood. The thinness of the 'new woman' expressed her sexual liberation and rejection of the traditional female role.

Slenderness became the new shackles of women and thus became a substitute for the corset. Here history seems to be repeated in a peculiar way. The period 1810–60 was characterized by a striking revival of an earlier fashion: tight-lacing.[550] But now women applied themselves much more fanatically to the creation of a 'wasp-waist' or an 'hour-glass figure'. On the one hand a whole fashion and trade in corsets arose, while on the other physicians ever more fiercely warned against the dangers of this deforming habit. Most women made light of these warnings, which may be interpreted as a kind of opposition against the male medical establishment. But actually they transformed the 'maternal figure' – the beloved beauty ideal among most men – into a caricature by overemphasizing bosom and pelvis. The corset became the symbolic manifestation of the psychosocial 'straitjacket' in which women were supposed to live, laced and entangled within the traditional role pattern. The emerging women's movement found it hard to cope with the corset rage and the rapid changing fashion in clothes, which flourished in precisely the bourgeois circles from which the 'new women' proceeded. In their striving for 'liberation' these women rejected the corset: literally and figuratively they wanted more freedom of movement. Clothes should be adapted to an active lifestyle and with the desire for more physical exercise, women also wanted to play sport more frequently. Once admitted to this male territory women too fell under the spell of competition. These revolutions at the end of the previous century undeniably heralded a new trend: this 'new body' had to become slimmer!

Body control, competition and achievement were new elements of bourgeois coercion. Newspapers and magazines showed the model and advertised the means of reaching the desired goal.[493] The shaping of one's own body was essentially based on observation, comparison and correction. In nineteenth-century bourgeois houses mirrors were no longer an ornament but an indispensable part of the furniture. They fulfilled the function of critical judges and silent witnesses with which the woman held a dialogue in delight or dismay. Emerging photography increased the requirement of precision and correction as the camera relentlessly recorded every variation. For a long time the corset could squash the torso into the required sculpture and the crinoline might have hidden inequalities. The small and plump Empress Eugénie of France (1826–1920) wore a striking crinoline when she married Napoleon III in 1853. She had been the very picture of the round Victorian ideal of beauty, an exponent of the 'maternal figure'. But a competitive fashion rival came from Vienna. Elisabeth of Austria (1837–98), better known as Sisi, was also wearing the fashionable crinoline when she plighted her troth to the Austrian Emperor Franz Joseph in 1854. But what seemed to be a fairytale marriage turned out to be the tragic life history of an unhappy spouse and a sorely tried mother; her son, Crown Prince Rudolph, committed suicide and she herself was killed by an Italian anarchist. By her strikingly unconventional lifestyle – certainly considering her noble rank – Sisi presented herself as a 'new woman'. A real escape from the caricature of her façade marriage was impossible, so she sought an identity of her own, away from ceremonial obligations. She expected to find this in a special body culture which made her into the prototype of the modern rage of slenderness.[22;534]

In 1859 Empress Eugénie aroused a sensation by appearing for the first time at an official ceremony without the fashionable crinoline. Shortly afterwards the British Queen Victoria would also take off her hoop skirt. Yet the European court adhered to the fashion for some years hence. The end of the crinoline era was heralded by Sisi, who from 1864 could no longer be persuaded to wear the hoop-skirt. Two years later Eugénie, too, appeared for the last time in her crinoline. When the rivals met for the first time during a reception, in Salzburg in 1867, both empresses disappeared into a neighbouring room to inspect each other's beauty: standing in front of a mirror they compared their body sizes. Meanwhile Sisi had markedly simplified her clothes and was praised because of her overslender waist, which was very uncommon for a mother of four children. With her height at 5 ft 9 inches she was strikingly tall, but never weighed more than 100 pounds (the 'ideal' figure of a modern mannequin). Her life pattern was typically anorexic: she insisted on a rigid low calorie diet and gave herself hyperactively up to excessive sports and gymnastics (in her bedroom in the Viennese Hofburg the apparatuses on which she completed her daily fitness training can still be seen).[534] Her obsession with beauty is clearly recognizable from her special photo collection, containing portraits of the most beautiful women of that time![498]

Sisi had demonstrated that severe hunger cures and Spartan body culture made the corset superfluous. The lasting cultivation of the laced waist was replaced by the mythology of slenderness:

> The *size*, in the meaning of 'height, thickness and stature in relation to clothes', becomes a sneaky shackle, not a physical but a mental means of coercion, enforcing correction not physically, but mentally; a new boundary-line causing every woman who crosses to be denounced and stigmatized.[568]

With Sisi, the modern ideal of slenderness as a phenomenon of fashion had been born. The 'maternal type' had been gradually superseded by the slender and frail figure of the Victorian 'new woman'. In her pictorial ideal she took example from the ballet dancers in the Romantic period and from the myth around the English poet Lord Byron, who throughout his life had struggled against his appetite and controlled his weight obsessively by vinegar-cures, diets and laxatives (see Chapter 11). With Byron some *mal-du-siècle* of the eighteenth-century melancholia still filtered through Romanticism. In the wake of this, particularly artists and eccentric society figures cultivated a new clinical picture: tuberculosis. The pale, wasted consumptive radiated something heroic. This morbid aesthetics considered illness to be a source of female beauty, where in fact fashionable beauty was the source of illness.[512]

The picture of the pale fragile woman became in the hands of Victorian artists, especially the Pre-Raphaelite painters, the representation of the *femme fatale* (see also Chapter 11). By the end of the nineteenth century the 'new woman' had become in the eyes of middle-class men a dreaded *femme fatale*.[491] According to physicians they were 'neurotic' women, who should be treated in a firm manner. The anorexic girls belonged to the new generation of these 'hysterical shrews'. Yet, in those days the anorexic patient still continued to be a small footnote in learned medical treatises, though in 1893 the illness made its first public appearance in the short novel *The Heavenly Twins* by Sarah Grand.[529] Sisi and the anorexic patient were such 'twins', suggesting a close link between the ideal of slenderness and the anorexia nervosa picture, both incited by late-nineteenth-century culture. The real 'breakthrough' on a large scale and in a wide circle was still late, but what had been sown in Victorian soil would appear a century later almost ineradicable!

11
Morbid Miracle or Miraculous Morbidity?

In the previous chapter we have suggested a series of coherent hypotheses to explain the emergence of anorexia nervosa as a 'modern' illness in the last quarter of the nineteenth century. This implies that in our view the diagnosis had no right to exist in earlier periods because there was no such disorder as anorexia nervosa. Indeed, this study uncovered the occurrence of a wide variety of patterns of food refusal and self-starvation throughout history. Particularly in Chapter 7 we have discussed medical descriptions from earlier centuries, of which some are strongly suggestive of anorexia nervosa. But before the nineteenth century the picture of food refusal as a morbid phenomenon was at most a rare curiosity or a minor symptom of some well-known afflictions. Former physicians had to base their diagnoses almost exclusively on clinical examinations, i.e. on an accurate visual inspection of patients. Hence, their medical 'eye' had been well-trained. If a 'striking' phenomenon such as unexplained food abstinence did not 'strike' them and if even fairly adequate descriptions like Morton's met hardly any answering response, then we may conclude that self-starvation as a morbid phenomenon was rare or non-existent before the mid-nineteenth century.

This brings us back to our fundamental thesis (as discussed in Chapter 1): the interpretation of a phenomenon like food abstinence cannot be disconnected from its sociocultural context. From the fact that throughout history various forms of self-starvation have had certain outward characteristics in common, it cannot be concluded that there was a common explanation in whatever terms (medical or other). A superficial resemblance or analogy between behavioural characteristics all too easily leads to an equation between phenomena which widely differ as far as cause, function and meaning are concerned. To avoid this pitfall, in our chronicle of self-starvation (Chapters 2 to 9) we have tried to remain as faithful as possible to the description of contemporaries. Within this approach it has not been our frame of interpretation, but theirs that was the point of departure.

In that sense we have merely recounted the history of self-starvation and not the past of anorexia nervosa. The latter is only a century old and seems at present to be entering a new phase as a modern 'epidemic', crossing the border between illness and fashion. Formerly, excessive fasting was a spectacle, which partially through the intervention of physicians attempting to expose the 'deceit' gradually lost its attraction. In turn the 'miraculous maidens' had replaced the mediaeval fasting saints at a time when excessive asceticism was no longer an acknowledged attribute of sanctity. Of course, between these three great episodes of self-starvation — wonder, spectacle, illness — transitional periods are recognizable in which old and new forms exist alongside each other.

The shift from the religious context to the medical frame of mind has taken a few centuries. Particularly in the nineteenth century archaic forms of self-starvation — in the shape of fasting women, demoniacs and miraculous maids — occurred simultaneously alongside the new form, anorexic patients. But even today some anorexics may explain their self-starvation through religious concepts quite different from those held by psychiatrists and psychologists. In earlier days self-starvation as religious phenomenon or natural wonder was a meaningful figure against the background of historical periods in which the medical frame of mind played a minor or marginal role. Using present-day concepts for the construction of a historical bridge between fasting saints and anorexic patients looks to us like planning a transatlantic footbridge in the void . . .

Saints or patients?

When anorexia nervosa had developed into a well-known phenomenon and people started to be interested in its history, several authors linked the illness to the severe ascetic fasting in Christians of yore. Several clinicians recognized ascetic features in anorexia nervosa. The food abstinence of anorexics is also based on a far-reaching denial of physical needs, proceeding from the desire to achieve a certain ideal.[570] Other interpreters have made the trip through history in a reverse direction and put the excessive practices of fasting of late mediaeval religious women on a par with anorexia nervosa. For extended fasts, peculiar eating habits and resistance against every form of 'treatment' are some elements of hagiographies, which are also to be found in recent descriptions of anorexia nervosa. Therefore, according to some current clinicians, saints like Catharine of Siena, Catherine of Genoa, Margaret of Hungary, Joan of Arc, Lidwina of Schiedam and Wilgefortis resemble modern anorexics in many respects.

At first sight this hypothesis seems plausible: hagiographies about late mediaeval fasting saints contain numerous data which seem to support this interpretation. These saints were often high-born girls or women, who – in sharp contrast to the majority of their contemporaries – were seldom in want of food. A perfectionistic attitude and considerable lack of self-esteem were accompanied by peculiar eating habits. Frequently their incapacity or unwillingness to eat began at an early age and developed into a fixed pattern. Their self-starvation was met with fierce opposition from both their immediate entourage as well as the clergy, though efforts to persuade them to change their minds mostly failed. Generally, the consecrated host was the only 'food' whose intake was permitted according to their religious conviction. It is remarkable that some fasting saints showed an inclination to vomit just at the sight of earthly food. However, they had no difficulty at all in taking the Host; this was even the high point in their wretched existences.

These behavioural features might indicate that food abstinence in fasting saints was psychogenic in character, i.e caused by psychological factors. Although these holy women hardly took anything, they did not expect others to do the same. Several saints liked to prepare a meal for others without taking a mouthful of it themselves. Beyond this, their food intake was not confined to the consecrated Host. In some this was quite obvious; here we think of the fraudulent religious fasters and of the accounts about devils who tempted the saints to eating. In others, the extreme length of the food abstinence (to twenty years and beyond) suggests they were eating on the sly.

According to many hagiographies the holy fasts were frequently accompanied by constipation, absence of menses (amen-orrhoea) and sleeplessness. The need for rest was not given in to: numerous saints threw themselves fanatically into an overactive life. Sexual drives were defied. Many saints made the vow of virginity at an early age and/or made themselves physically unattractive (among other methods by means of emaciation). Others mortified their body to punish it because of sexual joys in the past or because they considered sexuality a vexation to which they had been subjected against their will (in marriage for instance). Often a deeply-rooted fear of sexuality seems to have played a part in persuading saints to fast.

The reader who is familiar with modern literature on anorexia nervosa will readily recognize many characteristics in this enu-meration. Yet the conclusion that fasting saints were in fact undiagnosed anorexics has to be rejected on the basis of several arguments. Let us first look at the observable behavioural charac-teristics: the peculiar eating behaviour, the obsession with food, eating on the sly or hoarding of food; the constipation, amenor-rhoea and sleeplessness; hyperactivity and decreased sexual drive. Although often interpreted as such, these are not to be considered 'typical symptoms' of anorexia nervosa. They are epiphenomena of prolonged fasting which have been observed in diverse experi-ments with voluntary fasters. So they are to be explained psychophysiologically as behavioural characteristics and physical side effects in voluntary starvation of whatever origin.[42] Further-more, when the saints suffered from other illnesses, it is difficult to establish whether the food refusal was the cause or the consequence of these afflictions.

Modern diagnostic criteria of anorexia nervosa (see Chapter 1) can only be applied if sufficient information on the psychoso-cial functioning of the faster is available. However, modern notions like psychological and social characteristics are totally absent in mediaeval hagiographies, unless the imagination of the interpreter reads too much into it (*Hineininterpretierung*). Further-more, major methodological problems impede a reliable interpre-tation. It is a highly questionable practice to retrospectively make a psychiatric diagnosis of a person from another culture and a different historical period, the more so if it is based on limited sources never meant for such purposes. Apart from the fact that information from hagiographies is polyinterpretable

and fragmentary, current interpreters are particularly confronted
with the deficient historical reliability of this material. Often the
difference between description and interpretation is far from
obvious in the available sources. Mediaeval hagiographers did
not write historically reliable biographies, but cultivated a literary genre.[79] They showed more zeal in demonstrating the
holiness of the candidate saint than in providing reliable historical
facts and medical-psychological data. What really happened was
subordinated to what should happen to the candidate saint
according to the contemporary ideal of sanctity.[117] Hence we
should not underestimate the risk of over- or misinterpretation
in using hagiographical material.

But it is not only methodological problems that seriously
impede reliable retrospective diagnostics. A more fundamental
objection against the equation of fasting saints to anorexics is the
neglect of the totally different contexts of both phenomena.
Both in the evolution of interpretations of the phenomenon as
well as in the changing motivations the process of secularization
is clearly reflected. Prolonged fasters were always seeking perfection in the value system of their culture, but the definition of
perfection altered as society became increasingly secularized. In
mediaeval hagiographies we vainly look for the relentless pursuit
of thinness which is currently considered to be an essential
characteristic of anorexia nervosa. There is no trace of saints
'dieting' from a fear of becoming fat. The highly valued ideals in
which both saints and anorexics are completely absorbed are
time-bound and widely divergent in content. Fasting saints were
not obsessed by the exterior, outward appearance. By contrast,
they strove for an inner, spiritual fusion with Christ's sufferings.
It was not a cult of slenderness but a religious-mystical cult that
dominated their life. In religiously fundamentalist circles the
latter may also occur in present-day anorexics. Although often
an expression of 'pathological pseudo-asceticism', even these rare
modern cases of holy fasting underline the interplay between the
cultural and motivational components of the disorder.[492]

Even if 'holy' fasting and 'morbid' pursuit of thinness share
common ground, they are widely divergent as far as origin and
meaning are concerned. Even in cases where people considered
the fasting saint to be ill, a comparison with anorexia nervosa is
not helpful. Occasionally also in the Middle Ages people noticed

the pathological side of prolonged fasting. Precisely for this reason several saints took great pains to demonstrate that their fasting was under control of their own will-power – a true form of asceticism – and did not proceed from any illness or demonic possession. In others, illness fulfilled a special function within their pattern of piety. To them it was not so much a condition which had to be cured, but primarily a means of increasing their suffering to bring their primary aim of uniting with Christ nearer. In particular women were praised because of their courageous and patient enduring of ill-health by which they were more likely to acquire the status of saint. So, even if people labelled fasting as 'sick', it was a theological model and not a medical-psychiatric one that remained the norm. Hence, holy fasting cannot possibly be divorced from its undeniably religious dimension. We cannot put fasting of saints on a par with anorexia nervosa without violating its essential meaning, both in the experience of the saints as well as of their social environment. At first sight fasting saints and anorexic patients may have much in common; on closer investigation, however, there are worlds of differences between them.

Two American historians made a thorough study of the fasting of saints. The first, Rudolph M. Bell, explicitly took as his point of departure a comparison between modern anorexics and a great number of Italian female saints, from the eleventh century on.[64] Finding both similarities and differences Bell is careful not to equate these fasting saints with anorexic patients. Instead he labels them 'holy anorexics', a circumscription which expresses both the religious and pathological dimension. Whether the latent problem manifests itself as anorexia nervosa or as 'holy anorexia' is determined, according to Bell, by cultural conditions. Both forms of fasting are put on a psychological continuum, as they are rooted in similar psychological motives, namely a search for self-identity and a pursuit of autonomy. But ultimately fasters derive their only identity from their self-starvation, over which they totally lose control.

Bell's interpretation corresponds to feminist views of anorexia nervosa. In these social-critical theories, anorexia nervosa is seen to be the primary symbol of women's oppression. Societal developments make women responsible for the upbringing of children. This particular situation creates a symbiotic relation between mother and daughter, which lies at the basis of the lack of autonomy characteristically found in girls. Mothers project their own needs onto their daughters, instead of 'listening' to their daughters' real needs and personal desires. Maturing girls are offered insufficient opportunities to experience and express their own emotions. In a patriarchal society, requiring of women subordination and bondage instead of assertive behaviour, daughters are then too frightened to fight effectively for their self-esteem and self-interest and to own their own existence by real means. Conflicts are therefore interiorized and fought out in battles with the body, the only domain they possess completely and without interference. These girls and women attempt to derive self-esteem and autonomy from self-starvation and emaciation.[47]

According to Bell 'holy anorexia' is closely linked with the patriarchal, hierarchic power structure of the mediaeval Roman Catholic Church, which assigned to the faithful (and certainly to women) a passive, dependent role. The behaviour of fasting saints is in Bell's view a form of opposition from women striving for more autonomy in a patriarchal society. By giving herself up to severe ascetic fasting, the 'holy anorexic' obeyed only God and withdrew from the male-dominated Church. The mediaeval fasting saint, like the modern anorexic, was driven by a time-bound ideal: the former by striving for sanctity, the latter by the pursuit of fashionable thinness. Both are driven by a profound need for identification: the saint desires to become one with Christ, the patient identifies with her ideal of slenderness. Both are perfectionistic in their aspirations: they are never satisfied with the results of their efforts to be truly holy or truly thin. They are continuously tortured by the fear of losing control over their pursuit of holiness or thinness.[64]

Unlike Bell's, the studies of holy fast by Caroline Walker Bynum primarily focus on the late mediaeval period and include saints from countries other than Italy.[73] But the major difference with Bell's work is that Bynum pays considerably more attention to the (late-) mediaeval context of fasting:

> Whereas Bell has been interested in women's fasting behaviour, putting it into a psychological context, I have concentrated on women's use of food as symbol, putting it into a cultural context.

Bynum categorically rejects the equation between anorexia nervosa and ascetic fasting. She tries to discover the meaning of food and fasting for women of those days and precisely why women's lives were characterized by self-starvation (and the feeding of others). Bynum's analysis is many sided and profound. She points out that both sexes on the basis of their religious conviction, renounced what was most controlled: men gave up money and property; women abstained from food. Furthermore, for women self-starvation and the feeding of others were from a cultural point of view the most acceptable forms of asceticism: preparing and distributing foods were traditionally considered women's tasks. The specific food practices of fasting saints were in fact religious expressions of social facts.

Apart from the fact that food was for women a self-evident and available means, Bynum calls attention to its special function for them. By their specific relationship to food they were able to control themselves as well as their social environment. In this way they succeeded in manipulating not only their own bodily functions, emotions, fertility and sexuality, but also their husbands, parents, ecclesiastic authorities and even their relationship with God. For women fasting and distribution of food to the poor were 'weapons' in a conflictual home environment. Hence, fasting was an effective method of escaping from marriage. Additionally, by the rejection of the communal meal, symbol of the family bond, and the renunciation of family property, an individual was able to criticize the values of family members in a non-overtly aggressive manner. By their food and fasting practices these women also managed to exert influence on ecclesiastic authorities. By means of 'visions' they were able to advise and criticize the clergy. By fasting they sought a direct encounter with God and bypassed the Church, which had reserved this privilege for itself. By means of their food practices these women acquired a place of their own within the patriarchal Church and were able to shape their lives in a constructive and acceptable way. It enabled them to serve a world with a wider perspective than kitchen or nursery.

To be sure, the writings of both historians are open to criticism. In our view, Bynum's efforts to study the meaning of food (abstinence) within the late mediaeval cultural-historical context seem to be the most fruitful. Yet her analysis of mediaeval piety appears to proceed one-sidedly from a selective, feminist-inspired interest in the cultural-symbolic significance of female mysticism. Bell is even more caught up in the coloured view of a current observer who psychologically analyses the distant past in the light of a modern, if not fashionable, hypothesis. None the less he also throws some light on the question of why it was predominantly women who gave themselves up to prolonged fasting. For women fasting appeared to be not only a religious act, but also a means of self-assertion in a world which offered them little scope for self-fulfilment. Precisely by abstaining from that of which they could freely dispose – food – they were able to acquire a certain degree of autonomy. This food abstinence increased their control over their own bodies as well as their social environment. Although fasting saints, miraculous maidens, hunger strikers and anorexics differ in many respects they have one thing in common: all have relatively little power. Self-starvation is one means of acquiring it. But however influential a 'weapon' it may be, it should also be seen as a double-edged sword: the psychological and physical self-injuries it may cause are no small price to pay for self-assertion!

On the basis of this argument we consider the question of whether or not fasting saints were anorexic to be irrelevant. In essence the irrelevance proceeds from the incompatibility of two worldviews: religious giving of meaning and medical-scientific explanation.[77] The important medical progress and the flourishing of psychiatry in particular are themselves source and epiphenomenon of a drastic secularization, which especially caught on in the nineteenth century and has reached an unprecedented climax in our own time. The vicissitudes of man in illness and health, or the order of the universe with its natural laws and mysteries, have been decreasingly attributed to magic or supernatural forces. Religious interpretations have been largely replaced by scientific explanations. The last century in particular witnessed to the growing tension between Church and Science. In disputes about the true nature of so-called 'miraculous' phenomena the notion of hysteria was central as an object of controversy: is a peculiar phenomenon such as prolonged food abstinence a sign of miraculous origin or a symptom of psychopathology? Or in other words: is it demonic possession or hysteria?

In the second half of the nineteenth century some striking

polemics were written around this theme. Between 1870 and 1875 theologians and physicians – including the Belgian Royal Academy of Medicine – were involved in a fierce paper war regarding Louise Lateau, the Walloon girl who displayed stigmata, had 'visions' and allegedly survived without food.[510] A similar polemic occurred, around the same time (1857–83), on account of a 'demonic possession' in a great number of girls and young women in the French town of Morzine, near the Swiss border. Like their former counterparts (see Chapter 3) the demoniac was no longer able to take common food without disgust and frequently threw it up. The meaning of this epidemic was strikingly summarized by a contemporary and pupil of the famous neurologist Charcot: 'Between the demonic possession of former days and the great hysteria of today the epidemic of Morzine forms an intermediate stage which makes a far-reaching comparison possible.'[382] In short, already a hundred years ago 'psychiatrization' of the past began. Although the professional jargon – formerly hysteria, nowadays anorexia – has changed, the current discussion is not essentially different and is certainly no 'novelty'.

Anorexic artists

The warning above against 'psychiatrization' of religious figures and phenomena has in essence to do with the risk of medicalization of whatever form of exceptional or unusual behaviour, considered 'abnormal' due to deviation from current norms. Artists often belong to a group of 'dissidents' or 'marginals' whose attitude or behaviour is often interpreted in psychiatric terms. The more eccentric they are, the more tempting it is to subject artistic creations or their creators to psychological and, in particular, psychoanalytical interpretations. No doubt, new and surprising insights may proceed from this and such interpretations present no difficulties as long as their limitations are recognized.

Parallel to the emergence of anorexia nervosa as a popular diagnosis, a wide variety of prominent figures have been identified retrospectively as being anorexic: from the nineteenth-century poets Emily Brontë[518] and Emily Dickinson[598] to the French 'modern mystic' Simone Weil,[78] from the late mediaeval monarchs Richard II and Mary Queen of Scots[557] to the

modern fairytale Princess Diana. Within the limited framework
of this book the discussion about the diagnostics of anorexia
nervosa will be confined to a few coryphaei from *belles lettres*.
We will discuss two figures from the start of the nineteenth
century (Byron and Barrett Browning), one example of High-
Victorian art (Rossetti), and two authors who witnessed the
turn of the century (Barrie and Kafka).

The English poet George Gordon Byron (1788–1824) has
been mentioned before in relation to nineteenth-century ideals
of beauty. By the end of his life Byron was already a myth,
which exerted far more influence than the literary impact of his
oeuvre.[609] Historically he is remembered as an aristocratic rebel,
an apostle of Romanticism, a reviled hero. Even during his life
his tumultuous and eccentric lifestyle made him a controversial
but simultaneously almost idolized figure. As a prototype of the
romantic melancholic he surely was 'a child of his time'. However, his exciting private life, and the scandalous reputation of
'lady-killer' rendered him a favourite subject of the yellow press
and gossip at parties. In this mystification, to which he himself
contributed to a considerable extent, his personal appearance
played a major part.

Born with a club foot and being 'a fat bashful boy', he
suffered on account of his outward appearance. His notorious
sexual escapades during his adolescence, however, seem to indicate that women found him attractive. In 1806, at the age of 18,
he was 14 stone 6 lb with a height of only 5 feet 8 1/2 inches. He
was obviously upset about his fatness and decided to drastically
reduce weight.[567] About this endeavour he made a bet with an
acquaintance, which he won by a fanatic regime of strict dieting
and violent exercise. Within a few months he reduced his
weight to 12 stone 7 lb; acquaintances found, according to his
own saying, 'great difficulty in acknowledging me to be the
same person'. The weight reduction did not satisfy him. Like a
'leguminous-eating ascetic', as he called himself, he persevered
anxiously to remain so. In 1811 he was only 9 stone 11 1/2 lb.
Numerous passages from his letters (especially to his plump
mother!) attest to his pride in his thin appearance. For the rest of
his life he remained obsessed by fear of fatness and preoccupied
with food. Apart from relentless exercise, in particular amazing
swimming marathons – perhaps partially to compensate for his

innate handicap – he put several methods of reducing weight to a test. Initially his diet consisted of biscuits and soda water, later of purely vegetarian meals or potatoes mashed in vinegar. To appease his hunger he chewed tobacco or smoked cigars, but occasionally he gave himself up to an abundant meal (then 'I gorge like an Arab or a Boa snake', he wrote). For this reason Byron took refuge in vomiting and purgative pills or consumed quantities of vinegar. Until the end of his days Lord Byron was in the habit of dining alone and even shortly before his death people were amazed by his physical endurance.

Initially Byron justified his severe dieting by arguing that walking hurt his club foot more when he was fat. Gradually it became an expression of his ascetic way of life, from which, according to his own saying, he drew the strength to exercise his mind. At the end of his life, when he was described as 'unnaturally thin', his way of life had become part of a body culture cultivated by himself.[567] This cultivation of outward appearance soon became part of the mystification around Byron. Initially the pining Romanticist was an eccentric figure whose fashionable nature did not lie so much in his thinness as in his pale but sensual appearance. 'Byronism' was imitated by young men from bourgeois circles in the first half of the nineteenth century, but in subsequent decades the picture of the frail, consumptive figure pining in romantic tragedy was particularly adopted by women: it became the prototype of the *femme fatale*.[493] On the one hand this is peculiar because Byron himself abhorred fragile women and preferred 'curvaceous forms'. On the other hand his cynicism and ambivalence towards women was expressed in the famous and frequently quoted sally: 'Women should never be seen eating or drinking, unless it be lobster salad and Champagne'. It is perhaps Byron's unpredictability, along with the sensuality and passion in his appearance and oeuvre, which transformed him into a legendary *homme fatal*, a Don Juan figure tempting women by a glance and plunging them into misery. That is the myth he created himself. The anorexia nervosa, from which he undoubtedly suffered, was one *avant la lettre* – a nice title for a melancholic poet. Apparently the time was not yet ripe for such an extreme body cult. He was born a century too early and belonged to the wrong sex.

Of Elizabeth Barrett Browning (1806–61), though famous in

her day, there only remains the mere shadow of a romantic legend.[609] Perhaps partially because of the strict isolation from the outside world father Barrett imposed upon his favourite daughter 'Ba' (her petname, abbreviated from 'baby'), Elizabeth's talents – and father's highly intellectual expectations of her – manifested themselves early. At the age of 8 she had already learnt Latin and Greek, and at 12 she wrote her first poem, which her father had published anonymously in 1820. In the same year she fell from her horse, suffering a grave back injury which made her bedridden. She grew up as a weak 'handicapped' girl whose health greatly worried her family.[505] The compulsory bedrest stimulated her even more to daydreaming, reading and writing. The strong bond with her exacting and overprotective father became even more intense after the death in 1829 of her mother, an inconspicuous figure in the background of this intellectual bourgeois family. In 1835 the family moved to London where the father arranged that his showpiece Elizabeth should soon become known as a 'literary genius'. However, her fragile health seemed to doom her to pass her life as an old maid. When she began spitting and coughing blood, she was sent to a seaside resort for a rest-cure, but during her stay there her favourite brother drowned. Disabled by a 'moral' shock, she had to be taken back to London.

For three years, between 1841 and 1845, Elizabeth lay on her bed in a darkened room, accompanied only by her little dog. Dejection and weakness impeded her walking. During that period she started to take morphine for the constant pains and sleeplessness. Through correspondence she came into contact with the poet Robert Browning (1812–89). Of course her father did not object to the 'intellectual' visits of this well-known poet, who appeared to favourably influence Elizabeth's health. However, from conversations at the sick-bed a secret passion arose. In 1846, at a time when Elizabeth had to make a decision about a possible new rest-cure in the south, she decided to marry Robert. The ceremony took place in secret, for she knew that her father would never approve of it. And indeed, what he had done to another sister he also did to her: from that day on he refused all contact with her, a cause he persisted in until his death. The Brownings left for Italy where they remained to live. Elizabeth cheered up in the first years of her marriage, although she continued to be frail, pale and dependent on morphine. In 1849 she gave birth to a healthy son and in subsequent years her fame increased in literary circles. However, gradually her health failed and it deteriorated markedly after the decease of her father in 1857. Four years later she had become a miserable wreck: she spewed blood abundantly, totally lost her appetite and had the appearance of a living skeleton. Her poignant death was a climax of romantic tragedy; when she coughed painfully that night in June 1861, Robert came to sit on her sick-bed. Bending over her, he asked: 'How do you feel?'. 'Beautiful', was her last word and she died in his arms, 'smilingly, happily, and with a face like a girl's'.[505]

Elizabeth Barrett Browning embodied the myth of the 'angelic invalid' and her life passed according to the melodramatic script of romantic love. According to the American psychologist Carol R. Lewis, her story also fits the life scenario of an anorexic patient.[553] Lewis interprets the biographical information about the Barretts in the light of modern systems theory of 'typical' relationships within anorexic families.[474] Through her chronic invalidism Elizabeth would have fulfilled the role of victim, enabling the other children to escape from the oppressive family bonds. She was not able to disentangle herself from the strong bond with her father, who wanted to protect her from all evil at home as in an isolated sanatorium. The only personal life which was left to her was the escape into daydreaming and poetry, until she was liberated from the 'cage' of her sick-bed by the affectionate Robert. However, Lewis' argumentation is lacking a solid base and specificity: it offers a far-reaching interpretation on the basis of fragmentary family characteristics which have additionally not been proven to be typical of an anorexia nervosa family. Other theoreticians might find an argument for an anorexia-like problem in the fact that Elizabeth had withdrawn into an intellectual, childish asexual world. We might speak, for instance, of an identity conflict or fear of adulthood. When Elizabeth at the age of 12 read one of the first feminist books, it made such an impression upon her that 'through the whole course of my childhood, I had a steady indignation against Nature who made me a woman.' [506] But how many Victorian women would not have judged their sex likewise? We can hardly judge this a closely reasoned argument for the existence of anorexia nervosa.

The London psychiatrist and expert in anorexia nervosa, Peter Dally, wrote a 'psychological portray' of Elizabeth Barrett Browning.[505] He states that she suffered from anxiety states which, in 1821–23, turned into the clinical picture of anorexia nervosa. She knew a girl in the neighbourhood 'wearing away like a snow wreath' and becoming at last unable to take food. Elizabeth herself 'lost weight steadily until she was so thin that her family feared for her life. At one time the only nourishment she would agree to take was highly seasoned food.' The doctors could not find any physical explanation for her emaciated state (there was nothing wrong with her stomach and bowels, no sign of tuberculosis). Finally, a physician proposed 'an entire change of air', advice which suggests that a psychological origin was suspected. She stayed almost a year at the Spa Hotel in Gloucester, gradually improved and resumed writing poetry. She remained in a thin frail condition and from 1837 her medical condition became rather complex.

> There is little doubt that tuberculosis gained a permanent foothold in Elizabeth at this time. Its virulence was limited, but it was able to manifest itself openly in the future whenever she became thin and run down.

According to Dally, in the following years she displayed a combination of tuberculosis and anorexia nervosa. A clear episode of the latter developed again during the period she was bedridden (1841–45). Being very thin, she avoided fattening foods and ate only small amounts, while her lapdog Flush grew fat on the rests of her scanty meals. Her worried father repeatedly warned her that she would never recover by eating dry toast! But, probably through Robert Browning's influence, Elizabeth's health slowly but steadily improved again. At that time, however, she was taking so much morphine that she became dependent on it. This could also explain why she continued to eat little since morphine reduces the hunger.

In short, the medical condition of Elizabeth Barrett Browning is difficult to diagnose. Most interesting in her case is the combination of tuberculosis and anorexia nervosa within a sphere of mystery and secrecy, which soon tempted numerous contemporaries to all kinds of speculations about the true nature of her affliction. It was part of the myth around her person, which she had herself created in silent alliance with her father. Thus, she became entangled in her own legend of 'angelic invalid' and literary child prodigy. We may add to her tragic romantic life story a suitably melodramatic epilogue: for people with some interest in literature she is often remembered only as the wife of the well-known romantic poet Robert Browning, the man who for a decade succeeded in liberating her from a morbid myth.

The passage of time has also eroded the reminiscence of another Victorian author. For art connoisseurs the name Rossetti evokes images of 'Pre-Raphaelite' painting. Indeed, Dante Gabriël Rossetti (1828–82) was one of the major initiators and representatives of this influential school of art, which expressed the romantic Victorian nostalgia for the Middle Ages.[487] These artists wanted to associate themselves with the noble symbolism and natural simplicity of 'true' art, which had declined in the sixteenth century after the masterpieces of the Italian painter Raphael. They owed their fame to portraits of mysterious looking women whose appearance – ranging from ecstatic angelic figures to pitiful melancholics – is a fascinating mixture of mysticism and sensuality. The typical 'Pre-Raphaelite woman' was the opposite of the Rubens' ideal of beauty: the fixed look of her pale face and the frail slenderness of her figure became the hall mark of this 'new woman', at one time prototype of the romantic consumptive, at another symbol of the *femme fatale*. One of Rossetti's favourite models was his youngest sister Christina Georgina Rossetti (1830–94).

Christina led a retiring life, utterly pious and contemplative, almost as a *religieuse* – she often thought of entering a nunnery. Her rigid Anglican faith led her to reject two offers of marriage and she refused to read any book containing the least irreligious or immoral passage. Religious themes dominated her poetry and prose, and especially at the end of her life she expressed her concern about the moral decline of society and social problems like prostitution, unemployment and poverty. In her life there was no room for sentiment and romance. Her collections of poems were often melancholic but without a semblance of melodrama. She was obsessed by death and the fear of being eternally doomed by God. Her poetry seemed to be a form of meditation, an effort to flee from the worldly existence.[609] At the age of 29 Christina wrote *Goblin Market*, an allegorical poem about the temptations of sin. While Laura could not resist the alluring food offered by goblins – 'I ate and ate my fill, Yet my mouth waters still' – her sister Lizzie 'Would not open lip from lip, Lest they should cram a mouthful in'.[572]

An analysis of *Goblin Market* in a literary magazine by Paula Marantz Cohen concludes that the poem betrays a pattern of anorexia nervosa.[502] In fact this conclusion is based on a far-reaching psychological interpretation, particularly regarding the theme of self-denial: the tension between temptation (sexuality, nourishment) and renunciation (asceticism, fasting). Cohen points out all kinds of symbolic meanings that would be characteristic of anorexic nervosa, while Christina's biography also contains references that point to the same diagnosis. The interpreter also refers to Rossetti's family entanglements in an analysis that displays great resemblance to Lewis's discussion of the case of Elizabeth Barrett Browning. The facts on which to base a diagnosis, however, are fairly scarce. We know that Christina Rossetti's life took a strange turn between 12 and 16 years of age: during that period an attractive, open-hearted child became silent and depressed as a result of a mysterious illness. She would have been thin in her youth, whereas she was 'over-plump' at a more advanced age; Christina called herself in letters a 'fat poetess'. These brief data, within the context of a life of spirituality and renunciation of worldly existence, leave little doubt regarding the conclusion of anorexia nervosa, according to Cohen. We, in contrast, are not convinced by this argument because essential information on Christina's alleged anorexic behaviour is lacking. The cornerstone of Cohen's reasoning is the interpretation of Christina's scrupulosity and religious devotion as a 'flight' from a world of sensual enjoyment and sexuality. But how many girls and women seeking the isolation of a nunnery should then be 'suspected'? And is the prudishness of a Victorian woman not more a sign of the times than a sign of pathology?

Two years before the publication of *Goblin Market* and a year before the decease of Elizabeth Barrett Browning, the Scottish writer Sir James Matthew Barrie (1860–1937) was born. His most famous creation is *Peter Pan, the boy who would not grow up*, a play which had its premiere on 24 December 1904.

The characterization of anorexia nervosa as the 'Peter Pan syndrome' refers to the central theme of eternal childhood, the wish not to grow up.[520] This intriguing theme may be found in the life of Barrie himself. For the first six years of his life, he seems to have been an ordinary little boy who stood in the shadow of his brilliant older brother David. Being mother's favourite, David's sudden death in a skating accident the day before his fourteenth birthday caused extreme mourning: at first she refused to speak or eat, and she stayed in bed for over a year. During these months James spent most of his time in his mother's room, trying to comfort and cheer her. He conceived an intense desire to replace his dead brother and promised his mother that one day he too would be a famous man and make her as proud as David would have done.

> Barrie got his desire, and kept his promise to his mother, but at a great cost. He became a famous man, and – in a peculiar, awful way – he became David: David exactly as he had been on the day he died. He became, and remained for the rest of his long life, a brilliant boy just short of puberty whose deepest attachment was to his mother. The resemblance was more than psychological: Barrie never grew to be more than five feet tall, and he was always extremely slight and youthful in appearance ... And though given to romantic crushes on pretty women, he was apparently incapable of physical love. His marriage at thirty-four to an actress in his first hit play was never consummated.[520]

It is possible that Barrie's inability to mature was physical rather than psychological; the result of incomplete puberty caused by a glandular deficiency. On the other hand, given his life-history a psychophysiological interpretation is quite tempting. Like Peter Pan, unconsciously he may have chosen not to grow up. Pediatricians are familiar with psychosocial growth retardation without organic aetiology. In the majority of cases it is found in pre-school children who are emotionally neglected or victims of malnutrition in the context of a disturbed parent–child interaction. In adolescents it may be a 'disguised' form of anorexia nervosa. Indeed, inadequate food intake in pre-puberty may lead to developmental retardation, which can be mostly restored after refeeding. Yet some cases of anorexia nervosa have been described, both in boys and girls, which appeared to be partially or totally irreversible.

Was James Barrie an example of such an undetected anorexia nervosa? We cannot demonstrate this conclusively, as information on Barrie's medical history and accounts of his eating habits are lacking. In venturing this guess, the best evidence available comes from his completely forgotten drama *Little Mary*. This play already foreshadows the themes that Barrie was to develop in *Peter Pan*. The leading character in *Little Mary* is Moira, a name which means 'fate' in Greek mythology. At the age of 12, Moira's grandfather, an old apothecary who did not really believe in his profession, had initiated her into his secret life work: a voluminous work which contained his explanation and cure for the world's ills. After her grandfather's death Moira, now 18 years old, puts his wisdom into effect and becomes a miraculous healer. Her presence within a noble family called the Millicents – depicted by Barrie as indolent and overfed – brings about drastic changes: everybody gets up earlier, eats smaller meals, and becomes very active. She also succeeds in curing Lady Millicent, who had been depressed and unable to walk after the loss of a lover (note the resemblance to Barrie's mother). At the insistence of the uncle, who had known her as a child in her grandfather's apothecary, she reveals the secret of her cure: 'People suffer from eating too much.' They have pampered the 'organ', which should not be mentioned by name and which she refers to euphemistically as 'Little Mary': the stomach! And she told the recovered lady: 'The moment the weight was taken off your organ you began to think healthily again.' But the family finds this explanation so disgusting that they renounce her. Only her uncle remains true to her and asks her to marry him in order to witness the miracle of rejuvenation. Moira consents and so the play ends.

Interpreting Barrie's play psychologically, we note that weight in *Little Mary* has a double significance involving the related but not identical (body) weight brought about by eating and the symbolic weight one has to shoulder as a burden of life. Moira rescues her patients from the physical (and emotionally depleting) burden by having them eat less and become hyperactive, a typical anorexic behaviour. The play in effect extols self-starvation as a way of life, a cure for the ills of the body and society, but one that must be kept secret. Perhaps this anorexic-like stance was Barrie's personal secret too; his way of taking onto himself the burden of his mother's depression, of her refusal to eat or get out of bed after his brother David's death, while at the same time preventing himself from 'growing up' and eventually becoming a man. The message of not eating as a way to health and longevity is repeated in *Peter Pan* in a literally fantastic form: Peter is such a lightweight that he is even able to fly. Which anorexic ballet dancer did not once indulge in fancies about such a 'feather'-light existence?[57] Barrie identified with children who did not want or could not grow up. It is the fantasy of eternal childhood that need never confront the burden of adulthood: the conflicts of sexuality, loss and mourning, death and depression. Admittedly, these are psychological interpretations driven by analogy. We cannot prove conclusively that James Barrie was anorexic. But from a cultural-historical point of view his 'Peter Pan' figure has an intriguing significance: it can be seen as the embodiment of society's ambivalence towards the ever-enlarging gap between childhood and adulthood, that 'moratorium' of adolescence that – as we have described in Chapter 10 – started to concern turn of the century psychologists, psychiatrists and pedagogues.

By the time *Peter Pan* was first performed in 1904, Franz Kafka had reached adulthood. In the remaining twenty years of his life he wrote a masterly oeuvre, wherein among others the theme of ascetic fasting is explicitly interwoven. '*A Fasting-Artist*' is a moving example of this, as we discussed in Chapter 5. This short story aroused a great number of interpretations, among them numerous efforts to interpret it allegorically.[234] It was interpreted as a cultural-critical treatise: symbolically Kafka would have represented the position of religion, but particularly of art and artist within the current society. Another important theme would be the contrast between asceticism and vitality. The fasting-artist would refer to a 'free spiritual life based on asceticism', 'the grotesque metaphor for the isolated breakthrough to the Spirit in an alienated world'. Starvation as victory over the vital body in space and time contrasts with the panther as embodiment of pure, spiritless vitality. Apart from such reflections about its 'deeper' allegorical significance, we pointed out before that Kafka's tale provides a historically reliable account of the phenomenon of the hunger artist. However, there is more: Kafka's characterization of the fasting-artist's inner life attests to a psychological insight, which he cannot have derived only from publications about the phenomenon. His analysis indicates a personally lived through involvement and introspection, as is also to be found in the rest of his oeuvre.

Apparently Kafka himself was familiar with the art of fasting. His way of life can certainly be characterized as ascetic: sexuality was frightening to him and he took neither alcohol nor meat in order to retain a feeling of physical purity and commitment to nature. Choice of food had been a lifelong problem. From his youth he had suffered from eating problems. Although he himself restricted his food intake, he liked to see other people eating and he frequently fantasized about gorging. He was unhappy and unsatisfied with his body. In letters he repeatedly lamented about his thinness. 'I am the thinnest human being I know', he once wrote about his appearance. Nevertheless, with some kind of happiness he plunged himself into physical activities such as swimming, gymnastics and running.[237] His novels, short stories and letters reflect a great preoccupation with food: no less than over 500 passages from his work would substantiate this. These facts, added to the climate of upbringing in Kafka's family, his perfectionistic attitude towards his literary work, his depressive-compulsive personality, his loneliness, his disturbed psychosexual development and his deeply rooted problems regarding his striving for autonomy; all these make some clinicians conclude that Kafka suffered from anorexia nervosa.

Kafka's story about the hunger artist would be the literary acting out of his own anorexic problem. According to the German psychiatrist Gerd Schütze, Kafka represents in his story 'the essence, tragedy and desire of anorexics in a way only an insider is able to'.[577] This is significantly illustrated by Kafka's description of the involuntary-voluntary food abstinence; his urge to fasting, quenching the desire of food, none the less does not bring self-satisfaction. Besides, according to Schütze, another problem with which Kafka struggled all his life, manifests itself in the story: the choice between 'literature' and 'life'. Kafka did not succeed in finding a satisfying solution for this. In the story this is symbolized by the panther, paragon of vitality, which replaces the deceased fasting-artist, culminating point of spiritualization. In anorexia nervosa, too, the central problem is to integrate bodiliness into the total personality, according to Schütze:

Just like the hunger artist anorexics, despite searching intensively, do
not succeed in finding the food they like; they do not succeed in
keeping stable the mental and physical unity under the burden of
puberty and adolescence.

Ernst Verbeek, former professor of psychiatry at the University
of Ghent in Belgium and an anorexia nervosa specialist who has
thoroughly studied Kafka's life and work, mainly agrees with
Schütze's view.[266] Verbeek points to the megalomania, the
narcissism of fasting-artist and anorexic, and of Kafka himself, in
whom he recognizes apart from an anorexia syndrome, a narcissis-
tic neurosis as a developmental disturbance. In the story of the
hunger artist Kafka on the one hand puts fasting on a par with
life, on the other he gives it the more tragic meaning of 'hunger
for life, which will never be quenched'. Here hunger and life are
assigned the two-sided meaning in the split between the spiritual
and the physical, between helplessness and vitality. According to
Verbeek the subtlety of Kafka's short story lies in 'the combination of his eating disorder, called anorexia nervosa, with the
simulated asceticism in the form of an aversion to filth, and with
writing, which implies denial of life.'

Similar parallels between Kafka's art of fasting and anorexia
nervosa were noticed by another eating disorders expert, the
psychiatrist Manfred Fichter from Munich. He also stresses the
repeated references to fasting and asceticism in Kafka's life and
work.[237] Additionally he points to Kafka's sadomasochistic fantasies and his self-destructive attitude towards his own health.
Fichter recognizes in Kafka a psychological problem which
would be typical of anorexics: an achievement-oriented stance
and perfectionism with an unsatisfying striving for acknowledgement by others; the conflicting process of disengagement from
the dependency towards his parents; the problematic development of his sexual identity; the unfulfilled desires, the absence of
self-assertion and finally his loneliness. We leave it undecided,
whether all these interpretations proceed from Kafka's inspiring
person and work rather than from the imagination of psychiatrists.

Whereas a possible diagnosis of anorexia nervosa in Rossetti
and Barrie is merely based on speculative explanations, this does
not hold for Barrett Browning, Byron and Kafka. Their thinking

and behaviour more clearly attest to an anorexic way of life. However, it remains a diagnosis *post factum*. In the case of Lord Byron this is understandable as he came a century too early. When Elizabeth Barrett Browning became bed-ridden, anorexia nervosa had not yet acquired a place in the pantheon of medicine. Moreover wasting away from tuberculosis, being horrible and romantic at the same time, was a far more acceptable medical explanation in those days. For the same reason a superimposed anorexia nervosa was not considered in Kafka's case. Additionally we may assume that the diagnosis was more likely to be over-looked in males, as it probably still is today since male anorexia nervosa remains a relative rarity.[56] In striking contrast, in females an 'anorexic' way of life has reached fashionable proportions, especially in the last decades. We started this book with the notion that it partially deals here with a mysterious 'epidemic', and we will conclude it likewise.

The mysterious epidemic

Apart from fitness training, laxatives, appetite suppressants and questionable slimming pills, numerous women use diets to achieve their 'ideal weight'. The enormous proportions of this longing for thinness are a modern phenomenon. In the not so distant past a majority of the population could not even afford the luxury of dieting. Most people could only dream of fatness, not to mention control of food intake. Daily life was one of real survival: every day gathering enough food to stay alive. In such an uncertain existence, which was infested by famines until well into the nineteenth century, striving for thinness was a far from obvious goal. As everyone could perceive with their own eyes, thinness and fasting went hand in hand with death. In times of continuously recurrent famines it was by no means advisable to strive for slimness, least of all for women who had to meet the nutritional demands of pregnancy and lactation. That is why popular medicine had numerous medicines to counter thinness: for centuries 'gaining' instead of 'losing' was the goal for many.[37]

Not everyone laboured under the yoke of hunger. While the mass dined miserably, a tiny privileged elite was able to eat copiously. Take for instance the carouses in ancient Rome or the impressive banquets at mediaeval courts. The happy few taking part in such occasions would also be able to afford the luxury of lamenting corpulence and the necessity of slimming. However, indications that life in these circles was dominated by this concern are lacking. Yet, some well to do people did experience their fatness as a problem. Reflections on *polysarcia* (literally: 'much flesh') with corresponding therapies like physical exercise and diets are to be found in works from Classical times.[275] This interest did not so much proceed from aesthetic considerations but rather from the awareness that an exceptional body size might bring about troubles and medical risks. None the less, for centuries the attitude towards corpulence was rather positive. As thinness was allied with poverty, illness and misery, people associated a certain extent of *embonpoint* with wealth, health and prosperity. For a long time moderate stoutness was status-raising for males and thus for many desirable. This fact explains the publication, until well into the nineteenth century, of books and advertisements recommending cures for thinness.

At present women are the 'privileged' objects of diet campaigns and the most important consumers of the slimming industry. Yet, for ages a body image was idealized which by today's standards may be called rather 'fleshy'. A typical example of this is the female figures which the early-seventeenth-century Flemish painter Peter Paul Rubens immortalized on his baroque canvases. Such an ideal of beauty was not merely a matter of aesthetics. As wife or mother, fat women also offered the practical advantages that they were likely to be healthy and strong. Symbolized by the prehistoric statue of the obese Venus of Willendorf, an ample supply of body fat implied the promise of fertility. It was the visible guarantee of offspring, a not unimportant fact in a time where many did not reach their fortieth year and infant mortality occurred in almost every family.

Only from the eighteenth century on, when more of society gradually had access to more food, were the first signs of a shift noticeable. The improved food supply reduced the possibility of upper classes distinguishing themselves from the emerging bourgeoisie through the quantity of food to be eaten. Careful preparation of a more limited quantity of food, expressing a 'refined' taste, was a better way of keeping up one's standing. Parallel to this 'civilizing of appetite' the ideal body image was gradually changing. Instead of a plump body, slenderness began to appeal to the upper classes (especially females). Slenderness not only fitted the changed gastronomy, but became a new means of distinguishing oneself from the lower classes.

In the second half of the eighteenth century women first began to model their body after contemporary fashion for aesthetic reasons. In earlier days they had tried to achieve the for 'beauties' indispensable pale complexion through special eating habits (see Chapter 7). Now a certain bodily figure became a special object of concern. Women's fashion of those days prescribed an 'hour-glass figure' (large hips and big breasts) and so it was their task to maintain a wasp-waist. Young women were laced in tight corsets, while some took refuge in diets. That this could already lead to excesses in the eighteenth century is illustrated by an example from the work of Erasmus Darwin (see Chapter 7). Another exceptional example is to be found in a treatise from 1768 by the Swiss physician Francis de Valangin (1725–1805):

> A young Lady who was inclined to be fat, was advised to make use of Vinegar, to reduce her Fat; she lived accordingly upon pickled Mangoes and other Pickles, which in a short Time brought on a Train of Hysteric Disorders; these she increased much by too spare a Diet; for though she had left off the Pickles, yet she lived only upon Tea, with the smallest Quantity of Bread and Butter, till she had brought herself almost to Death's Door; but being at last prevailed upon by her Physician to take more nourishing Food, to increase the Quantity daily, without too much distending her contracted Stomach at first, and to drink a little generous wine; she soon recovered a perfect State of Health.[279]

This description is an early example of a girl who, in a relentless pursuit of the desired slimness, drove herself almost to death. Yet, it would take a substantial period of time before the virus of the cult of slenderness induced girls to imitate this young lady on a large scale.

Meanwhile it will be apparent to the reader that we seek historically demonstrable connections between the spread of the ideal of slenderness and anorexia nervosa in affluent societies. By labelling anorexia nervosa a culture-bound syndrome, we already suggested in Chapter 1 that the 'epidemic' is not as mysterious as it looks. The essence of the explanation lies in the association: female beauty – body culture – self-control. [519] In the previous chapter we have analysed the sociocultural background of the emergence of anorexia nervosa in the last quarter of the nineteenth century. In our view the bourgeois life of our Victorian ancestors seems to contain enough elements to explain the occurrence of this 'new' syndrome. Yet, at first glance there are some differences between turn-of-the-century anorexia nervosa and the current phenomenon. Today the latter is fairly well-known, occurs relatively frequently and is considered to be a morbid desire for thinness. Hence, we will discuss and try to explain whether anorexia nervosa indeed occurred so rarely in the previous century and whether an obsession for slimness was involved.

Research into the prevalence of a certain affliction in earlier centuries is a hazardous undertaking for at least two reasons. Lacking a systematic registration of illnesses in a population, we often have to make a rough estimation based on partial and/or less reliable data. Beyond this, former medical terminology is difficult to interpret due to a lack of unequivocality and comparability to current pathology. We are familiar with only one study of the prevalence of anorexia nervosa in the nineteenth century. The British psychiatrist William L. Parry-Jones explored the archives of four asylums and two general infirmaries from the period of *grosso modo* 1820 to 1890.[21] This extensive exploration incorporates over 36,000 admissions. Numerous cases concerned food refusal and emaciation associated with striking forms of mental disorders (melancholia, mania and dementia) for which they were treated at the asylums. In the latter only thirteen cases appeared suggestive of anorexia nervosa, without being diagnosed as such at the time. Interesting are the data concerning the general infirmaries in the period 1870–1917: besides twenty-seven cases suggestive of anorexia nervosa, nine patients between the ages of 16 and 43 (among them seven women and two men) were explicitly diagnosed as such. Another remarkable finding is the rare diagnosis of chlorosis in these general infirmaries before 1870 (only two cases against 123 cases of amenorrhoea), while in the period 1870–71 and 1890–1912 respectively sixty and fourteen cases of chlorosis (thirteen of them in 1903) were diagnosed.

Parry-Jones' research demonstrates that, except for one case in 1876, the diagnosis of anorexia nervosa was only recorded after 1890 and this merely in general infirmaries. Thus the illness was considered primarily – if not exclusively – a somatic rather than a psychiatric affliction. Another interesting conclusion is the frequent occurrence of amenorrhoea and, even more intriguing, of chlorosis. This brings us to the first possible explanation of the only small familiarity with anorexia nervosa in medical circles by the end of the previous century. Was chlorosis perhaps a variant of anorexia nervosa? As we described in Chapter 7 chlorosis or 'green sickness' had a prominent place within eighteenth- and nineteenth-century pathology and disappeared rapidly in the 1920s. This may be explained by its resemblance to anorexia nervosa, which in our century has become better known and is diagnosed more frequently.

Various hypotheses have been suggested for the decline of chlorosis, in which changes in the pattern of life are particularly stressed. It has been hypothesized that the emergence of chlorosis was facilitated by the wearing of a corset, a fashion which reached its climax in the nineteenth century and fell into disuse by the beginning of this century.[344] Thus the disappearance of chlorosis would reflect the increasing emancipation of women. Others attribute the decline to the emerging welfare society and specifically point to improved nutrition.[378] In fact the latter theory is connected with the major explanation of the rise and fall of chlorosis, namely that it was actually a form of anaemia. This may have been caused particularly by nutritional deficits (lack of iron, avoidance of meat) and loss of blood (by internal bleedings due to ulcers or because of frequent blood-lettings). The disappearance of blood-letting as a treatment, the spread of iron therapy and in particular more accurate medical diagnostics and corresponding treatments were responsible for the decline of chlorosis as a medical entity.[373;583]

When a new obscure illness emerged, chlorosis had also lost its sociocultural significance as a mysterious affliction of girls and young women. In the same period in which physicians related chlorosis to anaemia and no longer considered absence of menses and eating disorders to be chlorotic symptoms, anorexia nervosa acquired a permanent place within medicine. The 'banished' symptoms of classical green sickness were easily absorbed by this new syndrome. The connection between anorexia nervosa and chlorosis is particularly addressed by the British medical historian Irvine S.L. Loudon.[351;352] He distinguishes two kinds of chlorosis. The first form ('chloro-anaemia') indeed concerned anaemia. The second form ('chloro-anorexia') primarily occurred in girls between 14 and 21 years and was mostly accompanied by eating disorders, occasionally also with emaciation. This resemblance, however, does not justify an equation, according to Loudon. Although he denies that 'chloro-anorexia' and anorexia nervosa are different labels for the same phenomenon, he does put forward the idea that both are manifestations of similar psychological reactions to pubertal problems.

A possible overlap or confusion with chlorosis may partially explain why it took some time for anorexia nervosa to become known and widespread. None the less, the clinical pictures show striking differences. Although digestive and eating disturbances frequently occurred in chlorosis, it was rarely expressed in excessive food refusal. Emaciation was also rather exceptional and was certainly not a striking feature of chlorosis. Moreover, the special attractiveness imputed to these patients undoubtedly distinguished them from the occasionally horrible wasting of anorexics. The chlorotic patient probably personified an aristocratic ideal of beauty, specifically with the pale complexion. Finally, in the first descriptions of anorexia nervosa striking characteristics were observed which were lacking in chlorotic patients: conflicting interactions between parents and patient, wherein the latter also stubbornly resisted medical intervention. Thus, anorexia nervosa is in part closely connected to the greensickness – as typical afflictions associated with female puberty – but there are enough indications to characterize anorexia nervosa as a new syndrome.

In addition, it was not only distinct from chlorosis, but from various other illnesses in which a disturbed food intake was part of the clinical picture. In the nineteenth century a number of possible 'clinical analogues' of anorexia nervosa are recognizable as well as chlorosis.[10] Doctors at the time had several clinical entities to account for a wide range of deranged eating behaviour. Particularly for pubertal girls with symptoms like food refusal, loss of appetite, difficult deglutition, persistent vomiting or vague epigastric malaise a wide spectrum of diagnoses was available: sitophobia, spasmodic dysphagia, globus hystericus, gastralgia, gastric neurasthenia or nervous dyspepsia, etc. One of the most intriguing late-nineteenth-century clinical analogues is the frequently observed hysterical or nervous vomiting, a kind of psychogenic vomiting not seldom associated with persistent food abstinence or overeating.

Nevertheless, in contrast to all these afflictions, anorexia nervosa seems to be closely connected with a changed body culture: it became the morbid caricature of the fear of becoming fat. This leads us to an earlier question: to what extent did nineteenth-century anorexics suffer from 'real' anorexia nervosa? The reports of Gull and Lasègue, which we discussed in Chapter 8, were silent about the pursuit of thinness or a fear of fatness. However, it is known that certain anorexics keep their desire to slim in secret or even categorically deny it by arguing that 'against their will' they are unable to eat normally. Sometimes they account for their reduced food intake by referring to painful digestion. Nowadays clinicians are quite familiar with such 'rationalizations' and the same holds for example for the intake of laxatives because of 'constipation' (in fact caused by dieting itself). Thus, it seems very likely that the first anorexics may have misled their physicians by such rationalizations.[460] Lasègue, for instance, apparently gave credence to his anorexic patients who argued that their fast was caused by a 'painfully inflamed stomach'. At that time such an explanation appeared to be quite reasonable: 'gastric hysteria' and different forms of dyspepsia were popular medical terms. Nevertheless, it would not take long before the quest for slimness was exposed as the driving force behind anorexia nervosa.[430] This weight phobia was initially acknowledged in French-language sources.

As far as we know, the Swiss physician Rist was the first to suggest in 1878 that these patients did not suffer from a hysterical affliction, but from a specific syndrome which made their fasting undeniably different from the food refusal in the insane, melancholics and hypochondriacs.[457] His anorexic patient (Mlle X.) did not have the typical stomach ache according to Lasègue. At the age of 16, shortly before her emaciation set in, she was very plump and so Rist wondered 'whether Mlle X., feeling too fat, did not refuse to eat in order to emaciate in the end'. Such a supposition might appear unlikely, Rist admitted, considering her current state of horrible wasting. That girls could go too far in their pursuit of thinness, had been described by Worthington one year before in his thesis on obesity, without mentioning anorexia nervosa.[483] In his influential handbook on neuroses from 1883, Huchard considered the cause of *anorexie hystérique* to be, apart from painful digestion, 'a special psychic condition, which is important to emphasize: some hysterics fear having an embonpoint'.[397] But it was particularly Charcot who focused attention on the fear of gaining weight, as we know from the earlier quoted commentaries of Janet.[440] After Charcot had observed a patient wearing a ribbon around her waist as a measure that the waist was not to exceed, the great professor became so obsessed by the notion of obesity, Janet ironically remarked, that in every anorexic he used to look for a similar ribbon. To Janet, however, such an *idée fixe* was too simple an explanation, though he had to admit that 'coquetries' with regard to slenderness had become very frequent in his day.

The turn of the century had already arrived when Janet wrote his commentaries. At that time it was widely viewed as medically and aesthetically reprehensible to be overweight and both beauty and health had become 'weighty' matters, not least of all for young women. In contrast to 'miraculous maidens' and fasting-artists, anorexics showed a wholly different aspect – sickly to be sure – of an ever increasing and more general concern about their body size. In 1905 Sir Thomas Clifford Allbutt (1836–1925), Professor of Medicine at the University of Cambridge, established that girls were obsessed by slimness: 'Many young women, as their frames develop, fall into a panic fear of obesity, and not only cut down on their food, but swallow vinegar and other alleged antidotes to fatness.'[319] The praised moderation of Victorian bourgeoisie was not merely translated into 'self-control' of food intake, but also into 'self-discipline' of physical training. Equalling an aesthetic or sporting top model, achieving ideal sizes, competing at professional and intellectual level; it was all comprised in a sphere of achievement, measurableness and comparison. Women too fell under the spell of the competitive fever of 'faster, higher, stronger' and also slimmer.

The turn-of-the-century popular press exhorted: lack of exercise induces fatness, which in turn leads to lack of exercise; or fat persons are lazy and lazy people are fat![580] This continued into the 1920s before the mass media began to pay attention to the fashion of slenderness and its possible excesses. Around 1912 a journalist remarked in this context that he could divide the world into two kinds of people: fat persons trying to lose weight and skinny persons attempting to gain weight. When he reconsidered the problem in 1927, he observed a drastic change: fatness is completely out of fashion; we are in the age of emaciation, especially in women.[586] An analysis of women's photographs and fashion pictures in American women's magazines at the time demonstrates a significant increase of slender figures and also an increase in the number of articles about fatness. In the 1920s the ideal of a tight rectilinear silhouette in women replaced the formerly favourite 'hour-glass figure'. Statistics of American universities showed the consequence of the new fashion among contemporary female students: their average weight decreased.[586]

However, the following criticism of the 'new aesthetic' found little response in 1924, although it sounds quite familiar to us:

> The persistent fashion of slenderness reduced their fondness for sweets, made them more moderate, sober, only inclined to drinking water and tea. This fashion incited the fair sex towards physical activities which are indispensable to keep the slender silhouette, the latter also being impossible for a woman lying in bed all day. But (the reverse of the medal) this fashion also incited: laxatives causing enteritis, hunger diets making city-dwellers susceptible to anaemia, tuberculosis and disturbances of the nervous system. And then I say nothing about women who, in order to remain slim, poison themselves with preparations of the thyroid gland.[568]

Yet the 1920s are fairly exceptional compared to what manifested itself some decades later: the ideal body model was predominantly moulded by clothes, tight as a tube with crushing of the bosom; there was no question of diets to 'shape' a slender figure in women's magazines from the 1920s. [592] Afterwards – possibly in response to the great economic depression – more curvaceous figures became the vogue again.

If we explore the popular American women's magazines in recent years, a gradual increase in the number of articles on diets and slenderness is noticeable: on a limited scale in the period 1930–40, more widely after 1950, more strikingly in the 1970s,

and drastically from 1980 on.[484;522] The changes in medical
interest in eating disorders closely correspond to these periods:
after an obscure period due to confusion with a pituitary disturbance, anorexia nervosa is gradually rediscovered in the 1930s,
goes through a flourishing of psychological theories after 1950
and is fiercely disputed from 1970 on. In the 1980s, with their
explosively growing interest in the rage for slenderness, a 'new'
variant of anorexia nervosa is spreading: bulimia or bulimia
nervosa. In the two decades between 1960 and 1980 the 'ideal'
woman has become taller and slimmer, though the 'normal'
woman below the age of 30 has gained a few pounds in weight
compared to her peers from the 1950s.[522] This growing area of
tension between reality and ideal, fuelled by the power of
publicity and mass media, has been cleverly exploited by the
diet industry. Meanwhile questionnaires and other large-scale
investigations have demonstrated the extent of this obsession
with slimness and its excesses, so that there is talk of an
epidemic-like and culture-bound spreading of eating disorders.[528]

Yet, all these findings do not answer the question of why it
was particularly women who took refuge or sought for a
solution in extreme fasting.[543] Our cultural-historical analysis of
anorexia nervosa has tried to put this question in a wider
context. Feminist interpretations suggest interesting hypotheses,
but often seem too one-sided or too generalizing as if *the*
woman is a uniform specimen and *the* anorexic one commonly
recognizable type. The awakening of emancipatory notions is
just one important piece in our historical puzzle. The emergence
of the 'new woman' – and her 'new' afflictions – occurred
within a sociocultural climate in which numerous (problematic)
developments were seething or reached their climax: the fight
between Church and science, the ideals of the bourgeois family,
forbidden sexuality, awakening adolescence. Meanwhile much
seems to have changed in our culture – or is this merely
outward appearance? At present the corset of Victorian women
has been replaced by the corset of self-control. Formerly external
coercion – literally being laced by others – has been replaced by
inner coercion: control your body, keep it under restraint. But
have women become more liberated by that means?

Anorexia nervosa has been described as 'a glamorous cross

between two Victorian favourites, consumption and hysteria, but updated for a modern audience'.[501] But who is writing the script, who is choosing the actors, and who is the director? In the case of nineteenth-century hysteria this seems obvious. Charcot's hysterical patients were so attuned to him that after his death they stopped being hysterical. The *grande hystérie* has been in decay for as long as Charcot himself. Indeed, the 'Napoleon of the neuroses' was not aware of the communicative significance of hysteria. The behavioural pattern he has catalogued so diligently can be seen as a kind of *folie à deux* proceeding from the collusion between the professor and his patients. Are present-day psychologists and psychiatrists the 'Charcots' of anorexia nervosa?

Anyone not familiar with history is doomed to repeat it. We do not know whether this book has made the reader any wiser. Even if man is a question without an answer, the knack is still to put the right questions. But we realize that in certain respects it is easier to question the past than to find answers for current problems. In our exploration of that past we have not clarified mysteries – perhaps we have even produced more of them. History does not always 'work' as we might expect. What it does produce is a feeling of nostalgia. We are now 'stranded in the present',[544] where yesterday's reality has already become part of recent history. Through this book we are joining in the endless dialogue between past and present. Our chronicle of self-starvation has come to an end, all be it an open end, for the past is by definition incomplete.

References

For ease of reference, we present a structured bibliography. First we give some general sources specifically dealing with the history of anorexia nervosa. Then references are listed by chapter, alphabetically ordered but numbered continuously as some references are used in different chapters and others have served as background reading for the chapter concerned without being specifically mentioned in the text.

Publications pre-1900 (mostly primary sources) are indicated with an asterisk (★). Whenever possible we have given sources in the English language. Where we were not able to refer to an English version, the translation of a quotation is ours. The reader interested in more detailed documentation will find it useful to consult the second and separately published volume of the original Dutch edition of this book (*Van vastenwonder tot magerzucht: annotatie.* Amsterdam, Boom, 1988), containing 147 pages of notes, comments and references.

A. General publications on the history of anorexia nervosa

1 Beumont, P.J.V. (1991), 'The history of eating and dieting disorders', *Clinics in Applied Nutrition* 1(2), 9–20.
2 Beumont, P.J.V., M.S. Al-Alami and S.W. Touyz (1987), 'The evolution of the concept of anorexia nervosa'. P.J.V. Beumont, G.D. Burrows and R.C. Casper (eds), *Handbook of Eating Disorders. Part 1: Anorexia and Bulimia Nervosa*, Amsterdam – New York, Elsevier Science, 105–16.
3 Bliss, E.L. and C.H.H. Branch (1960), *Anorexia Nervosa: Its History, Psychology and Biology*, New York, Paul B. Hoeber, 1–22 (history of anorexia nervosa).
4 Borghi, A. (1973), 'Evoluzione storica delle conoscenze sul problema della cosidetta anoressia psicogena', *Episteme* (Milan), 7, 243–71.
5 Bruch, H. (1973), *Eating Disorders: Obesity, Anorexia Nervosa, and the Person Within*, New York, Basic Books, 211–26 (history of the concept of anorexia nervosa).
6 Brumberg, J.J. (1985), ' "Fasting girls": reflections on writing the history of anorexia nervosa'. A. Boardman Smits and J.W. Hagen (eds), *History and Research in Child Development*,

Monographs of the Society for Research in Child Development, Serial 211, 50 (4–5). Chicago: University of Chicago Press, 93–104.

7 Brumberg, J.J. (1988), *Fasting Girls: The Emergence of Anorexia Nervosa as a Modern Disease*, Cambridge, Harvard University Press.

8 Carrier, J. (1939), *L'anorexie mentale: trouble instinctivo-affectif*, Paris, Editions Le François, 7–37 (historical).

9 Crémieux, A. (1954), *Les difficultés alimentaires de l'enfant: les anorexies mentales infantiles et juvéniles*, Paris, Presses Universitaires de France, 21–35 (some historical notes).

10 DiNicola, V.F. (1990), 'Anorexia multiforme: self-starvation in historical and cultural context', *Transcultural Psychiatric Research Review*, 27, 165–96, 245–86.

11 Eckart, W. (1981), 'Anorexia nervosa historica? Theoretisch-historische Anmerkungen zu einem Forschungsproblem', R. Meermann (ed.), *Anorexia Nervosa: Ursachen und Behandlung*, Stuttgart, Ferdinand Enke, 74–83.

12 Ferro, F.M. (1988), 'Un confronto storico sull' anoressia mentale', *Giornale storico della psicologia dinamice*, 12, 19–48.

13 Habermas, T. (1990), *Heisshunger: Historische Bedingungen der Bulimia nervosa*, Frankfurt, Fischer.

14 Kaufman, M.R. and M. Heiman (eds), (1964), *Evolution of Psychosomatic Concepts. Anorexia Nervosa: A Paradigm*, New York, International Universities Press.

15 Kestemberg, E., J. Kestemberg and S. Decobert (1972), *La faim et le corps: une étude psychanalytique de l'anorexie mentale*, Paris, Presses Universitaires de France, 13–41 (Historical).

16 Lasserre, P. (1971), 'Le concept d'anorexie mentale et l'histoire de la pensée psychiatrique', *Psychologie médicale*, 3, 607–40.

17 Lucas, A.R. (1981), 'Toward the understanding of anorexia nervosa as a disease entity', *Mayo Clinic Proceedings*, 56, 254–64.

18 Morgan, H.G. (1977), 'Fasting girls and our attitudes to them', *British Medical Journal*, 2, 1652–55.

19 Morgan, H.G. (1979), 'Fasting girls: past, present and future', R.N. Gaind and B.L. Hudson (eds), *Current Themes in Psychiatry*, vol 2, London, Macmillan, 300–14.

20 Noguès, G. (1913), *L'Anorexie mentale: ses rapports avec la psychophysiologie de la faim*, Toulouse, Ch. Dirion, 57–69 (historical).

21 Parry-Jones, W.L. (1985), 'Archival exploration of anorexia nervosa', *Journal of Psychiatric Research*, 19, 95–100.

22 Raimbault, G. and C. Eliacheff (1989), *Les indomptables: figures de l'anorexie*, Paris, Odile Jacob.

23 Russell, G.F.M. (1985), 'The changing nature of anorexia nervosa', *Journal of Psychiatric Research*, 19, 101–9. Reprinted in G.I. Szmukler, P.D. Slade, P. Harris, D. Benton and G.F.M. Russell (eds), (1986), *Anorexia Nervosa and Bulimic Disorders*, Oxford, Pergamon Press, 101–9.

24 Russell G.F.M. and J. Treasure (1989), 'The modern history of anorexia nervosa: an interpretation of why the illness has changed', *Annals of the New York Academy of Sciences*, 575, 13–30.

25 Schadewaldt, H. (1965), 'Medizingeschichtliche Betrachtungen zum Anorexie-Problem'. J.E. Meyer and H. Feldmann (eds), *Anorexia Nervosa*, Stuttgart, Georg Thieme, 1–14.

26 Selvini Palazzoli, M. (1974), *Self-Starvation: from the Intrapsychic to the Transpersonal Approach to Anorexia Nervosa*, London, Chaucer/Human Context Books, 3–11 (historical survey).

27 Shorter, E. (1993), *From Biology to Society: A History of Psychosomatic Illness in the Modern Era*, New York, Free Press (Chapter 6: 'Self-starvation').

28 Skrabanek, P. (1983), 'Notes towards the history of anorexia nervosa', *Janus*, 70 (1–2), 109–28.

29 Sours, J.A. (1980), *Starving to Death in a Sea of Objects: The Anorexia Nervosa Syndrome*, New York, Jason Aronson, 203–18 (a history of the anorexia nervosa syndrome).

30 Thomä, H. (1961), *Anorexia nervosa: Geschichte, Klinik und Theorien der Pubertätsmagersucht*, Bern-Stuttgart, Hans Huber/Ernst Klett, 11–30 (historic overview). Translation: *Anorexia Nervosa*, New York, International Universities Press, 1967.

31 Van Deth, R. and W. Vandereycken (1994), 'The eating disorders'. G. Berrios and R. Porter (eds), *A History of Clinical Psychiatry*, London, Athlone.

B. Literature for Chapter 1

32 Ackerknecht, E.H. (1982), 'The history of psychosomatic medicine', *Psychological Medicine*, 12, 17–24.

33 Appels, A. (1986), 'Culture and disease', *Social Science and Medicine*, 23, 477–83.

34 Bordo, S. (1985), 'Anorexia nervosa: psychopathology as the crystallization of culture', *Philosophical Forum*, 17, 73–104.

35 Bordo, S. (1990), 'Reading the slender body'. M. Jacobus, E. Fox Keller and S. Shuttleworth (eds), *Body/Politics: Women and the Discourses of Science*, London, Routledge, 83–112.

36 Bull, M. (1990), 'Secularization and medicalization', *British Journal of Sociology*, 41, 245–61.

37 Clauser, G. and J. Spranger (1957), 'Hinweise auf die Ätiologie der Fett- und Magersucht aus Volkstum, Kunst, Medizinge- schichte und Wissenschaft', *Münchener medizinische Wochenschrift* 99, 53–8.

38 De Mause, L. (1975), *The New Psychohistory*, New York, Psycho- history Press.

39 De Swaan, A. (1982), 'Historische psychopathologie en socioge- nese van het moderne karakter'. M. Damen (ed.), *Geschiedenis, psychologie, mentaliteit*, Amsterdam, Uitgeverij Skript, 63–76.

40 Elias, N. (1969), *Über den Prozess der Zivilisation: soziogenetische und psychogenetische Untersuchungen*, Bern-München, Francke. Translation: *The Civilising Process*, Oxford, Basil Blackwell, 1978.

41 Ellenberger, H. (1970), *The Discovery of the Unconscious: The History and Evolution of Dynamic Psychiatry*, New York, Basic Books.

42 Garfinkel, P.E. and D.M. Garner (1982), *Anorexia Nervosa: A Multidimensional Perspective*, New York, Brunner/Mazel.

43 Glatzel, J., (ed.) (1973), *Gestaltwandel psychiatrischer Krankheits- bilder*, Stuttgart, Schattauer.

44 Haffter, C. (1979), 'Die Entstehung des Begriffs der Zivilisations- krankheiten', *Gesnerus*, 36, 228–37.

45 Jaspers, K. (1973), *Allgemeine Psychopathologie* (9th ed.), Berlin- Heidelberg, Springer-Verlag. Translation: *General psychopathol- ogy*, Manchester, University of Manchester Press, 1962.

46 Jones, D. (1981), Structural discontinuity and the development of anorexia nervosa, *Sociological Forum* 14, p. 233–45.

47 Lawrence, M. (1979), 'Anorexia nervosa: the control paradox', *Women's Studies International Quarterly*, 2, 93–101.

48 Meyer, J.E. and H. Feldmann, (eds) (1965), *Anorexia nervosa*, Stuttgart, Georg Thieme.

49 Prince, R. (1985), 'The concept of culture-bound syndromes: anorexia nervosa and brain-fag', *Social Science and Medicine*, 21, 197–203.

50 Ritenbaugh, C. (1982), 'Obesity as a culture-bound syndrome', *Culture, Medicine and Psychiatry*, 6, 347–61.

51 Selvini Palazzoli, M. (1985), 'Anorexia nervosa: a syndrome of the affluent society', *Transcultural Psychiatric Research Review*, 22, 199–205.

52 Sontag, S. (1978), *Illness as Metaphor*, New York, Farrar-Straus- Giroux.

53 Swartz, L. (1985), 'Anorexia nervosa as a culture-bound syn- drome', *Social Science and Medicine*, 20, 725–30.

54 Van den Berg, J.H. (1956), *Metabletica of leer der veranderingen:*

beginselen van een historische psychologie, Nijkerk, Callenbach. Translation: *The Changing Nature of Man: Introduction to a Historical Psychology*, New York, Norton, 1961.

55 Vandereycken, W. and H.W. Hoek, (1993), 'Are eating disorders culture-bound syndromes?'. K.A. Halmi (ed.), *Psychobiology and Treatment of Anorexia Nervosa and Bulimia Nervosa*, Washington DC, American Psychiatric Press, 19–36.

56 Vandereycken, W. and R. Meermann, (1984), *Anorexia Nervosa: A Clinician's Guide to Treatment*, Berlin-New York, Walter de Gruyter.

57 Vincent, L.M. (1979), *Competing with the Sylph: Dancers and the Pursuit of Ideal Body Form*, New York, Andrews & McMeel.

58 Von Baeyer, W. (1959), '"Metabletica": Bemerkungen zum gleichnamigen Werke von J.H. van den Berg, zugleich zum Problem der Pubertätsmagersucht', *Nervenarzt*, 30, 81–5.

C. Literature for Chapter 2

59 Arbesmann, R. (1929), *Das Fasten bei den Griechen und Römern*, Giessen, A. Töpelmann.

60 Arbesmann, R. (1949–51), 'Fasting and prophecy in pagan and christian antiquity', *Traditio*, 7, 1–71.

61 Arbesmann, R. (1969), 'Fasten, Fastenspeisen, Fasttage', T. Klauser et al. (eds), *Reallexikon für Antike und Christentum*, vol 7, Stuttgart, A. Hiersemann, 447–524.

*62 Athanasius (4th century), *Vita Antonii*, German translation: *Leben des Heiligen Antonius*, Kempten-Munich, Kösel, 1917.

*63 Baumgarten, K. (1504), *Grosse Legenda der hailigsten Frawen Sandt Hedwigis*, Breslau (publisher not known).

64 Bell, R.M. (1985), *Holy Anorexia*, Chicago-London, University of Chicago Press.

65 Bell, R.M. (1988), 'Self-portraits of holy anorexia'. D. Hardoff and E. Chigier (eds), *Eating Disorders in Adolescents and Young Adults: An International Perspective*, London, Freund Publishing House, 35–46.

66 Bihlmeyer, K. (1932), 'Die Schwäbische Mystikerin Elsbeth Achler von Reute (+ 1420) und die Überlieferung ihrer Vita'. G. Baesecke and F.J. Schneider (eds), *Festgabe Philipp Strauch*, Halle, Max Niemeyer Verlag, 88–109.

67 Bouton, A. et al. (1967), 'Jeûne'. G. Jacquemet et al. (eds), *Catholicisme: hier, aujourd'hui, demain*, vol 6, Paris, Letouzey, 827–50.

68 Brown, J.C. (1986), *Immodest Acts: The Life of a Lesbian Nun in Renaissance Italy*, New York-Oxford, Oxford University Press.

69 Brown, P. (1981), *The Cult of the Saints: Its Rise and Function in Latin Christianity*, Chicago, Chicago University Press.

70 Budge, E.A.W. (1904), *The Book of Paradise, Being the Histories and Sayings of the Monks and Ascetics of the Egyptian Desert by Palladius, Hieronymus and others*, Leipzig-London, W. Drugulin.

71 Bynum, C.W. (1984), 'Women mystics and eucharistic devotion in the 13th century', *Women's Studies*, 11, 179–214.

72 Bynum, C.W. (1985), 'Fast, feast, and flesh: the religious significance of food to medieval women', *Representations*, 11, 1–25.

73 Bynum, C.W. (1987), *Holy Feast and Holy Fast: The Religious Significance of Food to Medieval Women*, Berkeley-London, University of California Press.

74 Bynum, C.W. (1988), 'Holy anorexia in modern Portugal', *Culture, Medicine and Psychiatry*, 12, 239–48.

75 Bynum, C.W. (1991), *Fragmentation and Redemption: Essays on Gender and the Human Body in Medieval Religion*, New York, Zone Books.

76 Cabrol, F. (1927), 'Jeûnes'. F. Cabrol and H. Leclercq (eds), *Dictionnaire d'archéologie chrétienne et de liturgie*, vol 7 (2), Paris, Letouzey, 2481–501.

77 Carmichael, A.C. (1989), 'Past fasts: medieval saints with the will to starve', *Journal of Interdisciplinary History*, 19, 635–44.

78 Coles, R. (1987), *Simone Weil: A Modern Pilgrimage*, Reading, Addison-Wesley.

79 Delehaye, H. (1906), *Les légendes hagiographiques*, Brussels, Vromant.

80 Delumeau, J. (1983), *Le péché et la peur: la culpabilisation en occident [XIIIe-XVIIIe siècles]*, Paris, Fayard.

*81 Dévilliers (1803), D'une mort volontairement causée par abstinence', *Journal de médecine, chirurgie, pharmacie* (Paris), 6, 517–25.

82 Farges, A. (1926), *Mystical Phenomena Compared with their Human and Diabolical Counterfeits*, London, Burns Oates & Washbourne.

83 Farmer, D.H. (1978), *The Oxford Dictionary of Saints*, Oxford, Clarendon Press.

84 Gerlich, F. (1929), *Die stigmatisierte Therese Neumann von Konnersreuth*, Munich, Kösel & Pustet.

85 Gerlitz, P. (1955), 'Das Fasten im religionsgeschichtlichen Vergleich', *Zeitschrift für Religions- und Geistesgeschichte*, 7, 116–26.

86 Gerlitz, P. et al. (1983), 'Fasten/Fasttage'. H.R. Balz et al. (eds), *Theologische Realenzyklopädie*, vol 11, Berlin-New York, Walter de Gruyter, 42–59.

87 Habermas, T. (1986), 'Friderada: a case of miraculous fasting', *International Journal of Eating Disorders*, 5, 555–62.

88 Halmi, K.A. (1982), 'The diagnosis and treatment of anorexia

nervosa'. M.R. Zales (ed.), *Eating, Sleeping and Sexuality*, New York, Brunner/Mazel, 43–58.

89 Hardman, O. (1924), *The Ideals of Ascetism: An Essay in the Comparative Study of Religion*, London, SPCK.

90 Henisch, B.A. (1976), *Fast and Feast: Food in Medieval Society*, University Park, Pennsylvania State University Press.

91 Heun, E. (1973), 'Askese und Fasten bei den alten Christen', *Medizinische Welt*, 24, 265–70.

92 Höcht, J.M. (1951–52), *Träger der Wundmale Christi: eine Geschichte der bedeutendsten Stigmatisierten von Franziskus bis zur Gegenwart*, Wiesbaden, Credo Verlag.

93 Hook, J. (1980), 'St Catherine of Siena', *History Today* (July), 28–32.

★94 Imbert-Gourbeyre, A. (1873), *Les stigmatisées*, Paris, V. Palmé.

95 Jacobi, W. (1923), *Die Stigmatisierten: Beiträge zur Psychologie der Mystik*, Munich, J.F. Bergmann.

96 Lacey, J.H. (1982), 'Anorexia nervosa and a bearded female saint', *British Medical Journal*, 285, 1816–17.

★97 Lambertini, P. (1734–38), *De servorum dei beatificatione et beatorum canonizatione*, Bologna, Formis Longhi Excusoris Archiepiscopalis.

98 MacCulloch, J.A. and A.J. Maclean (1912), 'Fasting'. J. Hastings (ed.), *Encyclopaedia of Religion and Ethics*, vol 5, Edinburgh, T. & T. Clark, 759–71.

99 Meier, J. (1923), *Das Leben der Schwestern zu Töss*, Erlenbach-Zürich, Rotapfel Verlag (first edn 1454).

100 Mugnier, F. (1937), 'Abstinence'. M. Viller (ed.), *Dictionnaire de spiritualité, ascétique et mystique. Doctrine et histoire*, vol 1, Paris, G. Beauchesne, 112–33.

101 Musurillo, H. (1956), 'The problem of ascetical fasting in the Greek patristic writers', *Traditio*, 12, 1–64.

102 Nigg, W. (1946), *Grosse Heilige*, Zürich, Artemis Verlag.

103 Pater, T. (1946), *Miraculous Abstinence: A Study of one of the Extraordinary Mystical Phenomena*, Washington, DC, Catholic University of America Press.

104 Rabino, A. (1965), 'Digiuni miracolosi', *Minerva medica*, 56, 887–90.

105 Schümmer, J. (1933), *Die altchristliche Fastenpraxis. Mit besonderer Berücksichtigung der Schriften Tertullians*, Münster, Aschendorff.

106 Sheils, W.J., (ed.), (1985), *Monks, Hermits and the Ascetic Tradition*, Oxford, Basil Blackwell.

107 Sieben, H.J. (1974), 'Dossier patristique sur le jeûne'. M. Viller et al. (eds), *Dictionnaire de la spiritualité, ascétique et mystique. Doctrine et histoire*, vol 8, Paris, G. Beauchesne, 1175–79.

108 Strathmann, H. and P. Keseling (1950), 'Askese'. T. Klauser et al. (eds), *Reallexikon für Antike und Christentum*, vol 1, Stuttgart, A. Hiersemann, 749–95.

109 Summers, M. (1950), *The Physical Phenomena of Mysticism, with Special Reference to the Stigmata, Divine and Diabolic*, New York-London, Rider.

110 Thomas, K.V. (1971), *Religion and the Decline of Magic: Studies in the Popular Beliefs in Sixteenth and Seventeenth Century England*, London, Weidenfeld & Nicolson.

111 Thurston, H. (1952), edited by J.H. Crehan, *The Physical Phenomena of Mysticism*, London, Burns & Oates.

112 Vauchez, A. (1981), *La sainteté en occident aux derniers siècles du moyen-âge d'après les proces de canonisation et les documents hagiographiques*, Palais Farnèse, École Française de Rome.

113 Villien, A. (1935), 'Abstinence'. R. Naz (ed.), *Dictionnaire de droit canonique*, vol 1, Paris, Letouzey, 129–35.

114 Waddell, H. (1936), *The Desert Fathers: Translations from the Latin*, London, Constable.

115 Warner, M. (1981), *Joan of Arc: The Image of Female Heroism*, New York, Alfred A. Knopf.

116 Weinstein, D. and R.M. Bell (1982), *Saints and Society: The Two Worlds of Western Christendom, 1000-1700*, Chicago-London, University of Chicago Press.

117 Wilson, S. (ed.), (1983), *Saints and Their Cults: Studies in Religious Sociology, Folklore and History*, Cambridge, Cambridge University Press.

★118 Zöckler, O. (1897), *Askese und Mönchtum*, Frankfurt, Heyder & Zimmer.

★119 Zwingli, U. (1522), *Von Freiheit der Speisen* (re-edited by O. Walther), Halle, Niemeyer, 1900.

D. Literature for Chapter 3

120 Anderson, R.D. (1970), 'The history of witchcraft: a review with some psychiatric comments', *American Journal of Psychiatry*, 126, 1727–35.

121 Barton, G.A. (1918), 'Possession'. J. Hastings (ed.), *Encyclopaedia of Religion and Ethics*, vol 10, Edinburgh/New York, Clark/Scribner', 133–9.

122 Baschwitz, K. (1963), *Hexen und Hexenprozesse: die Geschichte eines Massenwahns und seine Bekämpfung*, Munich, Rütten & Loening.

123 Debongnie, P. (1948), 'Les confessions d'une possédée, Jeanne Fery (1584–1585)', *Études Carmélitaines* (Paris), 27, 386–419.

124 Demos, J.P. (1982), *Entertaining Satan: Witchcraft and the Culture of Early New England*, Oxford-New York, Oxford University Press.

125 Den Boer, A.W. and J. Schouten (no date), *Oud-Oudewater*, Oudewater, Stichting Waaggebouw.

126 Ernst, C. (1979), 'Der Exorzismus', *Psychologie des 20. Jahrhunderts*, vol 15, Zürich, Kindler, 717–25.

127 Ewen, C.L. (1933), *Witchcraft and Demonianism: A Concise Account Derived from Sworn Depositions and Confessions Obtained in the Courts of England and Wales*, London, Heath Cranton.

128 Goodman, F.D. (1980), *The Exorcism of Anneliese Michel*, New York, Doubleday.

129 Kemp, S. (1990), *Medieval Psychology*, New York-London, Greenwood Press.

★130 Kerner, J. (1836), *Nachricht von dem Vorkommen des Besessenseyns eines dämonisch-magnetischen Leydens und seiner schon im Alterthume bekannten Heilung durch magisch-magnetisches Einwirken*, Augsburg-Stuttgart, Cotta.

131 Kirsch, I. (1978), 'Demonology and the rise of science', *Journal of the History of Behavioral Sciences*, 14, 149–57.

★132 Kramer, H. and Sprenger, J. (1486), *Malleus maleficarum* (English translation), London, Pushkin Press, 1948.

133 Mester, H. (1981), 'Besessenheit, psychodynamisch betrachtet', *Psychotherapie und medizinische Psychologie*, 31, 101–12.

★134 Migne, J.P., (ed.), (1861), *Sancti Prosperi Aquitani, opera omnia. Volume 1: Liber de promissionibus et praedictionibus, in Patrologiae cursus completus*, patrologia Latina, vol 51, Paris, d'Amboise.

135 Mischo, J. and U.J. Niemann (1983), 'Die Besessenheit der Anneliese Michel (Klingenberg) in interdisziplinärer Sicht', *Zeitschrift für Parapsychologie*, 25, 129–94.

★136 M.J. (1669), *The Hartfordshire Wonder or Strange News from Ware: Being an Exact and True Relation of one Jane Stretton*, London, J. Clark. Reprinted with an introduction by W.B. Gerish in *Hertfordshire Folklore Society*, 5, 908, 4–15.

137 Oesterreich, T.K. (1921), *Die Besessenheit*, Langensalza, Wendt & Klauwell. Translation: *Possession, Demoniacal and Other*, London/Chicago, Kegan Paul/de Laurence, 1930.

138 Robbins, R.H. (1959), *The Encyclopedia of Witchcraft and Demonology*, London, Peter Nevill.

139 Rosen, G. (1968), *Madness in Society: Chapters in the Historical Sociology of Mental Illness*, New York, Harper & Row.

140 Spanos, N.P. (1978), 'Witchcraft in histories of psychiatry: a critical analysis and an alternative conceptualization', *Psychological Medicine*, 8, 417–39.

141 Timerding, H. (1929), *Die christliche Frühzeit Deutschlands in den Berichten über die Bekehrer*, Jena, Diederichs.

142 Van Dam, W.C. (1970), *Dämonen und Besessene: die Dämonen in Geschichte und Gegenwart und ihre Austreibung*, Aschaffenburg, Pattloch.

*143 Von Görres, J.J. (1836–42), *Die christliche Mystik*, Regensburg-Munich, G.J. Manz.

144 Walker, D.P. (1981), *Unclean Spirits: Possession and Exorcism in France and England in the late Sixteenth and Early Seventeenth Centuries*, London, Scolar Press.

E. Literature for Chapter 4

145 Accornero, F. (1943), 'L'anoressia mentale. Una priorità italiana e l'osservazione di 4 casi', *Rivista sperimentale di Freniatria*, 67, 447–89.

*146 Alberdingk Thijm, J.A. (1871), 'Bessie van Meurs, gerehabiliteerd', *Dietsche warande*, 9, 469–72.

*147 Alberdingk Thijm, J.A. (1872), 'Eva Vliegen, bekend onder den naam 'Bessie van Meurs'. J.A. Alberdingk Thijm, *Volksalmanak voor Nederlandsche katholieken*, Amsterdam, C.L. van Langenhuysen, 247–51.

*148 Anonymous (1597), *Most True and More Admirable Newes, Expressing the Miraculous Preservation of a Young Maiden of the Towne of Glabbich in the Dukedome of Gulische*, London, Adam Islip & Thomas Stirrop.

*149 Anonymous (1607), *Warhafftige Beschreibung von einer Jungfrauen die jetzt vergangen Michaelis sechs gantzer Jahr keiner Speiss noch tranck genossen auch nicht arbeit oder schaffet*, Bern, (publisher not known).

*150 Anonymous (1611), *Pourtraict a vif d'Eva Vliegen de Meurs laquelle en 14 ans ny mangés ny beu, agée à present de 36 ans*, Zutphen, André Jansen. Translation: *The Protestants and Iesuites up in Armes in Gulicke-land. Also, A true and Wonderfull Relation of a Dutch Maiden [called Eve Fliegen of Meurs in the County of Meurs] who being Now [this Present Yeare] 36 Yeares of Age, hath Fasted for the Space of 14 yeares*, London, Nicholas Bourne, 1611.

*151 Anonymous (1614), *Een warachtige beschrijvinge van het groot mirakel en teecken des Heeren, het welcke gheschiedt is binnen de stad van Meurs*, Amsterdam, Breughel Jansz.

*152 Anonymous (1810), *An Account of the Extraordinary Abstinence of Ann Moor, of Tutbury, Staffordshire, who has, since June 1807, lived Entirely without Food; Giving the Particulars of her Life to the Present Time*, Uttoxeter, R. Richards (third edn).

*153 Binz, C. (1896), Doctor Johann Weyer, ein rheinischer Arzt, der erste Bekämpfer des Hexenwahns. Ein Beitrag zur Geschichte der Aufklärung und der Heilkunde, Berlin, A. Hirschwald.

*154 Blair, P. (1719–1733), 'Of a boy in Scotland that lived very long without food', Philosophical Transactions of the Royal Society of London, IV, 44–5.

*155 Bucoldianus, G. (1542), Von dem Meydlin welchs on essen unnd trincken lebt – Eyn kurtze erzelung, Speyer, H. Vogtherr & H. Schiesser.

*156 Campbell, J.A. (1878), 'Feeding versus fasting', British Medical Journal, 1, 254–55.

*157 Campbell, R. (1732–1744), 'Concerning a man who lived eighteen years on water', Philosophical Transactions of the Royal Society of London, IX, 238.

*158 Citois, F. (1603), A True and Admirable Historie, of a Mayden of Confolens, in the Province of Poitiers: that for the Space of Three Yeeres and More hath Lived, and yet Doth, without Receiving either Meate or Drinke, London, I. Roberts (first Latin and French edn in 1602).

159 Cule, J. (1967), Wreath on the Crown: The Story of Sarah Jacob the Welsh Fasting Girl, Llandysyl, Gomerian Press.

160 D.F. (1856), 'Eva Vlieghen nog eens herdacht', De Navorscher, 6, 132–33.

161 Diekmeier, L. (1959), 'Krankheitsbild und künstlerische Darstellungen des 'Wundermädchens von Speyer' Margaretha Weiss', Kinderärztliche Praxis, 27, 107–15.

*162 Döbeln, J.J. (1724), Historia inediae diuturnae Esthera Norre Obyensis Scanicae: vollständiger historischer Bericht von einem schwedischen Frauenzimmer namens Esther Johannen, gebürtig von Norre Oby, und ihrem langweiligen zehnjährigen Fasten, Halle, Hendel.

*163 Dougal, J. (1881), 'Report on the fasting girl at Chapelton', Lancet, 1, 755–6.

*164 Dougal, J. (1882), 'A fasting girl', British Medical Journal, 1, 631–2.

*165 Eccles, J. (1744), 'An extraordinary abstinence: first thirty four days, and soon after fifty four days accompanied with some remarkable symptoms', Medical Essays and Observations (Edinburgh), 5 (2), 471–7.

*166 Fowler, R. (1871), A Complete History of the Case of the Welsh Fasting-girl [Sarah Jacob] with Comments Thereon; and Observations on Death from Starvation, London, H. Renshaw.

*167 F.W.S. (1832), 'Eva Vliegen van Meurs', Almanak voor Blijgeestigen, 7, 50–61.

*168 Grant, F. (1878), 'The Market Harborough fasting girl', British Medical Journal, 1, 152.

169 Grünenwald, L. (1903), 'Margaretha Weyss, das Wundermädchen von Roth, 1542', *Pfälzisches Museum*, 20 (3), 39–41.

*170 Gruner, J. (1800), *Authentische aktenmässige Erzählung der Betrügerei eines angeblichen Wundermädchens im Hochstift Osnabrück, das seit zwei Jahren ohne Speisen und Getränke gelebt haben wollte*, Berlin, Vossische Buchhandlung.

*171 H.A. (1669), *Mirabile pecci: or the Non-such Wonder of the Peak in Darby-Shire. Discovered in a Full . . .Narrative of the . . . Piety and Preservation of Martha Taylor, one who hath been Supported . . . above a Year . . . without the Use of Meat and Drink*, London, T. Parkhurst.

*172 Hammond, W.A. (1879), *Fasting Girls: Their Physiology and Pathology*, New York, G.P. Putnam.

*173 Henderson, A. (1813), *An Examination of the Imposture of Ann Moore, Called the Fasting Woman of Tutbury, Illustrated with Remarks on Other Cases of Real and Pretended Abstinence*, London, Underwood & Blacks.

174 Holländer, E. (1921), *Wunder, Wundergeburt und Wundergestalt in Einblattdrucken des 15. bis 18. Jahrhunderts: Kulturhistorische Studie*, Stuttgart, Ferdinand Enke.

*175 Hössle, J.G. (1780), *Krankengeschichte der Anna Maria Zettlerin, welche 10 Jahre lang ohne Speis und Trank lebte*, Dillingen, publisher not known.

*176 Johnston, N. (1667–1671), 'Letter in Latin (dated 29 June 1669) to Dr Timothy Clarke concerning the young fasting woman in Derbyshire, named Martha Taylor, together with the apprehension of some imposture in the affair', *Journal Book of the Royal Society of London*, III, 389–92.

177 Klimm, F. (1952), 'Das Wundermädchen Margaretha Weiss aus Roth bei Speyer von Hans Baldung Grien mit dem Silberstift vierfach aufgenommen', *Pfälzer Heimat*, 3, 101–4.

*178 Kolb, C., A. Loelmannus, H. Smetius and J.J. Theodorus (1589), *A Notable and Prodigious Historie of a Mayden, who for Sundry Yeeres neither Eateth, Drinketh, nor Sleepeth, neyther Avoydeth any Excrements, and yet Liveth*, London, John Woolfe, translation from the German edition of 1585. Reprinted in W.E.A. Axon (ed.), 'The fasting girl of Schmidtweiler in the sixteenth century', *The Antiquary: A Magazine Devoted to the Study of the Past*, 37, 1901, 269–72 and 305–9.

*179 Krul, R. (1894), 'Drie singulieren: Frans van Dusseldorp, Bestje van Meurs en Engeltje van der Vlies', *De Tijdspiegel*, 3, 394–412.

*180 Lentulus, P. (1604), *Historia admiranda, de prodigiosa Apolloniae Schreierae, virginis in agro Bernensi, inedia*, Bern, Joannes Le Preux.

*181 Lossau, C.J. (1729), *Wahrhaffte und ausführliche Beschreibung eines* *besonderen und merckwürdigen Casus Inediae, welcher sich im Jahr 1728, mit eines Gärtners Tochter aus Steinbeck im Hollsteinischen bey Hamburg, nahmens Maria Jehnfels zugetragen*, Hamburg, C.W. Brandt.

*182 Mackenzie, A. (1777), 'An account of a woman in the shire of Ross living without food or drink', *Philosophical Transactions of the Royal Society of London*, 67, 1–11.

183 Martin, K. (1960), 'Das 'Wundermädchen' Margaretha Weiss aus Roth bei Speyer und die Silberstiftzeichnungen nach einem etwa zwölfjährigen krankhaften Mädchen von Hans Baldung Grien', *Pfälzisches Museum*, 58, 262–6.

*184 McNeill, D. (1882), 'An extraordinary fasting case', *British Medical Journal*, 1, 938.

*185 Millingen, J.G. (1839), *Curiosities of Medical Experience*, London, R. Bentley (second edn; first edn 1837).

186 Morgenthaler, W. (1915), *Bernisches Irrenwesen. Von den Anfängen bis zur Eröffnung des Tollhauses 1749*, Bern, G. Grunau.

187 Morgenthaler, W. (1926), 'Eine Hysterika zu Beginn des 17. Jahrhunderts', *Archiv für Geschichte der Medizin*, 18, 196–201.

*188 Philo-jatros (1774), *Merkwaerdig bericht wegens het zonderling geval eener nu zevenjarige spys-onthouding, plaats hebbende, volgens geloofwaardige getuigenissen, in Maria van Dyk, huïsvrouw van Jan de Groot, te Vleuten*, Arnhem, Nijhoff.

*189 Portio, S. (1551), *De puella germanica, quae fere biennium vixerat sine cibo, potuque*, Florence, Laurentius Torrentinus.

*190 Provanchères, S. de (1616), *Histoire de l'inappétence d'un enfant de Vauprofonde près Sens, de son désistement de boire et de manger, quatre ans onze mois et de sa mort*, Sens, George Niverd.

*191 Reusch, J. (1542), *Propositiones aliquot de fastidiosa Spyrensis puellae inediae*, Speyer, publisher not known.

*192 Reynolds, J. (1669), *A Discourse upon Prodigious Abstinence: Occasioned by the Twelve Moneths Fasting of Martha Taylor, the Famed Derbyshire Damosell*, London, R.W.

*193 Richmond, L. (1813), *A Statement of Facts, Relative to the Supposed Abstinence of Ann Moore, of Tutbury, Staffordshire: and a Narrative of the Circumstances which Led to the Recent Detection of the Imposture*, London, J. Croft.

*194 Riggs, B.H. (1882), 'Two cases of marvelous fasting, the result of nervous derangement', *Transactions of the Medical Association of Alabama (Montgomery)*, 371–4.

*195 Robin, P. (1587), *Histoire admirable et veritable d'une fille champestre du pays d'Anjou, laquelle a esté quatre ans sans user d'aucune nourriture que de peu d'eau*, Paris, Michel de Roigny.

*196 Robins, T. (1668), *Newes from Darby-shire or the Wonder of all*

Wonders. That ever yet was Printed, being a Perfect and True Relation of the Handy Work of Almighty God Shown upon the Body of one Martha Taylor . . . , This Maid as it hath Pleased the Lord, she hath Fasted Forty Weeks and more, which may very well be called a Wonder of all Wonders, London, T.P.

★197 Robins, T. (1669), *The Wonder of the World, being the Perfect Relation of a Young Maid, about Eighteen Years of Age, which hath no tasted of any Food this two and fifty Weeks*, London, publisher not known.

198 Rollins, H.E. (1921), 'Notes on some English accounts of miraculous fasts', *Journal of American Folklore*, 34 (134), 357–76.

★199 Royston, W. (1809), 'On a medical topography', *Medical and Physical Journal* (London), 21, 91–102.

★200 Schenckius a Grafenberg, J. (1665), *Observationum, medicarum rariorum*, Frankfurt, J. Beyer.

★201 Scheuchzer, J.J. (1733), 'De inedia diuturna Christinae Kratzerin', *Acta physico-medica academiae caesareae Leopoldino-Carolinae naturae curiosorum*, 3, 116–25.

★202 Schmidtmann, L.J. (1800), *Merkwürdige Geschichte eines jungen Mädchens im Hochstifte Osnabrück was bereits achtzehn Monate ohne Speisen und Getränke lebt, nebst physiologischen und pathologischen Betrachtungen darüber*, Hannover, Hahn.

★203 Schmidtmann, L.J. (1801), 'Über die Anna Maria Kienker zu Borgloh', *Journal der practischen Heilkunde* (Berlin), 12, 1–15.

★204 Sephton, R. (1876), 'The fasting girl in Lancashire', *British Medical Journal*, 1, 329.

205 Shaw, J.A. (1906), *The Best Thing in the World: Good Health, how to Keep it for Hundred Years. A Record of the Most Wonderful Fasts in the World's History*, Norwich (CT), C.C. Haskell.

206 Silverman, J.A. (1986), 'Anorexia nervosa in seventeenth century England as viewed by physician, philosopher and pedagogue: an essay', *International Journal of Eating Disorders*, 5, 847–53.

★207 Staravasnig, G.K. (1780), *Abhandlung von den ausserordentlichen Fasten der Maria Monika Mutschla zu Rothweil*, Freiburg (second edn, Vienna 1782).

★208 Steill, T. (1744), 'An extraordinary abstinence during fifty years', *Medical Essays and Observations* (Edinburgh), 5 (2), 477–80.

★209 Umfreville, T. (1743), *The Case of Mr. John Ferguson, of Argyleshire in Scotland, who hath Lived above Eighteen Years only on Water, Whey, or Barley-water*, London, W. Reason.

210 Van Deth, R. and W. Vandereycken (1991), 'Vastenwonderen en vlugschriften in Nederland', *Spiegel Historiael*, 26, 446–51.

211 Van Deth, R. and W. Vandereycken (1992), 'What happened to the 'fasting girls'? A follow-up in retrospect'. W. Herzog, H.-C Deter and W. Vandereycken (eds), *The Course of Eating Disorders:*

Long-term Follow-up Studies of Anorexia and Bulimia Nervosa, Berlin-Heidelberg-New York, Springer-Verlag, 348–66.

212 Van Deth, R. and W. Vandereycken (1993), 'Miraculous Maids? Self-starvation and fasting girls', *History Today*, (August), 43, 37–42.

★213 Van Wassenaer, N. (1629), *Historisch verhael aller ghedenckwaerdiger gheschiedenissen die in Europa, als Duytslandt, Vrankrijck etc. van den beginne des jaers 1621 voorgevallen sijn*, Amsterdam, Jan Jansz.

★214 Viverius, J. (1665), *Wintersche avonden of Nederlandsche vertellingen*, Amsterdam, Houthaak.

★215 Von Schafhäutl, K.E. (1885), *Ein physiologisch-medizinisches Räthsel. Die Wassertrinkerin Jungfrau Marie Furtner aus Frasdorf in Oberbayern, welche 50 Jahre hindurch ausschliesslich vom Wasser lebte*, Munich, L. Seitz.

★216 White, J.E. (1812), *The History of Ann Moor; with a Statement of the Evidence Substantiating the Fast of her Long Abstinence, who Died at Tutbury in Staffordshire, England, on the 20th of July, 1811*, Savannah, Seymour & Williams.

★217 Whiting, L.E. (1859), 'The woman who lives without eating', *Boston Medical and Surgical Journal*, 60, 109–11.

★218 Wier, J. (1577), *De lamiis liber: item de commentitiis jejuniis*, Basel, Oporinus.

★219 Wilkinson, W.M. (1870), *The Cases of the Welsh Fasting Girl [Sarah Jacob] & her Father. On the Possibility of Long-Continued Abstinence from Food*, London, J. Burns.

F. Literature for Chapter 5

★220 Anonymous (1620), *Symbolum Oenipontanum, Ynssprugger Warzaichen. Das ist der kranck oder krumme Tischler zu Ynnsprugg welcher über das fünffzehende Jahr in unerhörter Schwaichhait ligt und noch allhie lebendig zusehen ist*, Innsbruck, Daniel Baur.

★221 Anonymous (1825), 'Beschrijving en afbeelding van een levend menschelijk geraamte, thans te Londen zich bevindende', *Vaderlandsche Letteroefeningen*, 2, 716–24.

★222 Anonymous (1880), 'Dr Tanner's fast', *Medical Record (New York)*, 18, 55, 84, 112, 140, 158, 160, 256 & 352.

★223 Anonymous (1890), *Biography of Emma Schiller, the Greatest of all Living Skeletons*, no place or publisher known.

★224 Anonymous (1890), 'Lessons from the fasting mania', *Asklepiad*, 7, 236–9.

★225 Anonymous (1890), 'The fasting man', *British Medical Journal*, 1, 1444–6.

226 Binder, H. (1983), *Kafka: der Schaffensprozess*, Frankfurt, Suhrkamp.

227 Bogdan, R. (1988), *Freak Shows: Presenting Human Oddities for Amusement and Profit*, Chicago, University of Chicago Press.

228 Bouman, P.J. (1976), *Revolutie der eenzamen: spiegel van een tijdperk*, 34th edn, Assen-Amsterdam, Van Gorcum, 249.

*229 De Cissé, J. (1827), *Description intéressante de Claude-Ambroise Seurat appelé l'homme anatomique ou le squelette vivant*, Clermont, A. Veysset.

230 De Fonvielle, W. (c. 1900) *Mort de faim: étude sur les nouveaux jeûneurs*, Paris, Librairie Illustrée (s.d., ca. 1900).

231 De Moor, W.A.M. (1982), *J. van Oudshoorn*, vol 1, Amsterdam, Arbeiderspers, 445–51.

*232 De Varennes, M. (1814), 'Sur une fille qui a été près de onze ans sans prendre aucun aliment solide', *Bulletin de la faculté de Paris*, 151–3. Partially translated in *London Medical and Physical Journal* (1817), 38, 341–2.

233 Drimmer, F. (1976), *Very Special People: The Struggles, Loves and Triumphs of Human Oddities*, London-Toronto-New York, Bantam Books.

234 Dünnhaupt, G. (1978), 'The secondary literature to Franz Kafka's *Hungerkünstler*', *Modern Austrian Literature*, 11 (3/4), 31–6.

*235 Fabricius Hildanus, G. (1656), *Aanmerkingen rakende de genees ende heelkonst. Bestaande in zes deelen, yder deel in hondert geschiedenissen*, Dutch translation, Rotterdam, Arnout Leers.

236 Fetzer, L. and R.H. Lawson (1978), 'Den Tod zur Schau gestellt: Gogol und Kafkas Hungerkünstler', *Modern Austrian Literature*, 11, 167–77.

237 Fichter, M. (1987), 'The anorexia nervosa of Franz Kafka', *International Journal of Eating Disorders*, 6, 367–77.

238 Fiedler, L.A. (1978), *Freaks: Myths and Images of the Secret Self*, New York, Simon & Schuster.

*239 Gould, G.M., W.L. Pyle (1896), *Anomalies and Curiosities of Medicine*, Philadelphia, W.B. Saunders.

*240 Gunn, R.A. (1880), *Forty Days without Food! A Biography of Henry S. Tanner, M.D.*, New York, A. Metz.

241 Henel, I. (1964), 'Ein Hungerkünstler', *Deutsche Vierteljahrschrift für Literaturwissenschaft und Geistesgeschichte*, 38, 230–47.

*242 Huygens, C. (1672), 'Korenbloemen', quoted in J. ter Gouw, *De oude tijd*, vol 1, Haarlem, Kruseman, 1871, 278.

243 Joannon, P. (1981), '60 years before Bobby Sands: the hunger striker of Terence MacSwiney, mayor of Cork, Ireland', *Historia*, 418, 41–8.

244 Kafka, F. (1922), 'Ein Hungerkünstler', *Die neue Rundschau*, 33, 983–92. Translation: 'A fasting-artist'. M. Pasley (ed.), *The Trans-*

formation and Other Stories: Works Published during Kafka's Lifetime, London, Penguin Books, 1992, 210–19).

245 Kafka, F. (1958), *Briefe 1902–1924*, Frankfurt, S. Fischer.

246 Keyser, M. (1976), *Komt dat zien! De Amsterdamse kermis in de negentiende eeuw*, Amsterdam-Rotterdam, B. Israël & Donker.

*247 Lassignardie, H. (1897), *Essai sur l'état mental dans l'abstinence*, Bordeaux, Cassignol.

248 Lehmann, A. (1952), *Zwischen Schaubuden und Karussells: ein Spaziergang über Jahrmärkte und Volksfeste*, Frankfurt, P. Schöps.

*249 Lehmann, C., F. Müller, I. Munk, H. Senator and N. Zuntz (1893), *Untersuchungen an zwei hungernden Menschen*, Berlin, Georg Reimer (supplement to *Archiv für pathologische Anatomie und Physiologie und für klinische Medicin*, 131).

*250 Luciani, L. (1890), *Das Hungern: Studien und Experimente am Menschen*, Hamburg-Leipzig, Leopold Voss (original Italian ed. 1889).

251 Meige, H. (1936), 'Claude Seurat, le squelette vivant', *Aesculape*, 26 (11), 261–63.

252 Meislin, J. (1936), *Contribution à l'étude du jeûne prolongé*, Lausanne, Risold.

*253 Monin, E. and P. Maréchal (1887), *Stefano Merlatti, histoire d'un jeûne célèbre*, Paris, Marpon & Flammarion.

254 Morrison, J.A. (1963), *Kafka as Hungerkünstler*, Tulane University.

*255 Nielen, P.M. (1775), *Verhandeling over de oorzaaken van het bestaan des leevens zonder spysen, of selfs zonder spijs en drank, en over de oorzaaken, kentekenen, onderscheid, voorzegging en geneezing van de spijswalging, of afkeer tegen het gebruik van voedzels*, Utrecht, J.C. ten Bosch.

256 Rogers, E.N. (1976), *Fasting: The Phenomenon of Self-Denial*, Nashville, Nelson.

*257 Saltarino, S. (1895), *Fahrend Volk, Abnormitäten, Kuriositäten und interessante Vertreter der wandernden Künstlerwelt*, Leipzig, J.J. Weber.

*258 Salter, J.H. (1873), 'The "skeleton man"', *Lancet*, 2, 903.

259 Saxena, S.K. (1976), 'Fabric of self-suffering: a study in Gandhi', *Religious Studies*, 12, 239–47.

260 Scheugl, H. (1974), *Showfreaks und Monster: Sammlung Felix Adanos*, Cologne, M. DuMont Schauberg.

*261 Senator, H. et al. (1887), 'Bericht über die Ergebnisse des an Cetti aufgeführten Hungerversuchs', *Berliner klinische Wochenschrift*, 24, 290–2, 425–35.

262 Spann, M. (1959), 'Franz Kafka's leopard', *Germanic Review*, 34, 85–104.

263 Stallman, R.W. (1958), 'A hunger artist'. A. Flores and H. Swander (eds), *Franz Kafka Today*, Madison, University of Wisconsin Press, 61–70.

264 Van Geuns, H.A. et al. (1977), *Hongerstaking*, Baarn, Wereldvenster.

265 Van Oudshoorn, J. (1927), 'Laatste dagen'. *Verzamelde werken*, vol I, *Novellen en schetsen* (edited by W.A.M. de Moor), Amsterdam, Athenaeum, Polak & van Gennep (1976), 282–351.

266 Verbeek, E. (1984), *Loon voor duivelsdienst, over het verband tussen persoon en werk van Franz Kafka*, Assen, Van Gorcum.

267 Walsh, J.J. (1923), *Cures: The Story of the Cures that Fail*, New York-London, D. Appleton.

G. Literature for Chapter 6

268 Ackerknecht, E.H. (1970), *Therapie von den Primitiven bis zum 20. Jahrhundert*, Stuttgart, Ferdinand Enke. Translation: *Therapeutics: From the Primitives to the 20th Century*, New York, Hafner, 1973.

269 Ackerknecht, E.H. (1971), 'The end of Greek diet', *Bulletin of the History of Medicine*, 45, 242–9.

270 Allgeier, K. (1982), *Die geheimen Heilrezepte des Nostradamus*, Munich, Heyne.

★271 Bauhinus, C. (1604), *Disputatio possit ne homo aliquot annis absque cibo vivere*, Basel: publisher not known.

272 Benedict, F.G. (1915), *A Study of Prolonged Fasting*, Washington, DC, Carnegie Institute of Washington Publications.

★273 Blatchly, C.C. (1818), *An Essay on Fasting and on Abstinence*, New York, C.S. van Winkle, 10–13.

★274 Bourne (1808), 'Further account of the case of abstinence contained in our last, with the physiological and pathological remarks', *Medical and Physical Journal* (London), 20, 527–31.

275 Bray, G.A. (1990), 'Obesity: historical development of scientific and cultural ideas', *International Journal of Obesity*, 14, 909–26.

276 Carrington, H. (1908), *Vitality, Fasting, and Nutrition*, New York, Rebman.

★277 Casper (1844), 'Merkwürdiger Fall eines lange fortgesetzten Hungerns', *Wochenschrift für die gesamte Heilkunde*, 23, 361–7.

★278 Chossat, C. (1843), *Recherches expérimentales sur l'inanition*, Paris, Imprimerie Royale.

★279 De Valangin, F.J.P. (1768), *A Treatise on Diet, or the Management of Human Life*, London, J. & W. Oliver.

280 Dewey, E.H. (1900), *The No-Breakfast Plan and the Fasting Cure*, Passaic (New Jersey), Health Culture Company.

281 Granger, B. (1809), 'Some account of the fasting woman at

Titbury, who has at present lived above two years without food', *Edinburgh Medical and Surgical Journal*, 5, 319–26.

*282 Granger, B. (1813), 'On unusual cases of anorexy', *Edinburgh Medical and Surgical Journal*, 9, 157–9.

*283 Granger, B. (1813), 'Account of the second watch of the reputed fasting-woman', *Edinburgh Medical and Surgical Journal*, 9, 323–6.

284 Günther, H. (1930), *Die wissenschaftlichen Grundlagen der Hunger- und Durstkuren*, Leipzig, Hirzel.

*285 Harvet, I. (1597), *Discours par lequel est montré contre le second paradoxe de la première decade de M. Laur*, Niort, Thomas Portau. In appendix (83–116): Qu'il n'y a aucune raison que, quelques uns puissent vivre sans manger, durant plusieurs jours et années (a reprint of a Chapter from L. Joubert, *La première et seconde partie des erreurs populaires, touchant la médecine et le regime de santé*, Paris, 1578).

*286 Hays, I. (1834), 'Abstinence'. I. Hays (ed.), *The American Cyclopedia of Practical Medicine and Surgery*, vol 1, Philadelphia, Carey, Lea Blanchard, 125–34.

287 Heun, E. (1953), *Das Fasten als Erlebnis und Geschehnis*, Frankfurt, Klostermann.

288 Jung, C.G. (1950–51), 'Das Fastenwunder des Bruder Klaus', *Neue Wissenschaft*, 7. Reprinted in A. Jaffé (ed.), *C.G. Jung – Briefe, 1946–1955*, Olten-Freiburg, Walter (1972–73), II, 134–5. Translation in H. Read et al. (eds), *The Collected works of C.G. Jung*, vol 18, *Symbolic life and Miscellaneous Writings*, Princeton, Princeton University Press, 1978, 660–1.

289 Keys, A., J. Brozek, A. Henschel, O. Mickelsen and H.L. Taylor (1950), *The Biology of Human Starvation*, Minneapolis-London, University of Minnesota Press.

290 Klotter, C. (1990), *Adipositas als wissenschaftliches und politisches Problem. Zur Geschichtlichkeit des Übergewichts*, Heidelberg, Roland Asanger Verlag.

291 Kröner, W. (1927), *Das Rätsel von Konnersreuth und Wege zu seiner Lösung. Studie eines Parapsychologen*, Munich, Verlag der Aerztlichen Rundschau.

*292 Lipsius, D. (1611), *Demonstratio hominem non solum per aliquot dies et menses, sed et complures annos cibo et potu vitam transigere posse*, Frankfurt, publisher not known.

293 Lusk, G. (1906), *The Elements of the Science of Nutrition*, London-Philadelphia, W.B. Saunders.

294 Mannes, M. (1977), *Wissenschaftliche und soziale Aspekte der Ernährungslehre in der Mitte des vorigen Jahrhunderts*, Dissertation, University of Bonn.

*295 Petersen, J. (1897), 'Zur Geschichte der Ernährungstherapie'. E.

von Leyden (ed.), *Handbuch der Ernährungstherapie und Diätetik*, vol I, Stuttgart, Ferdinand Enke, 1–19.

*296 Poggio Bracciolini (1450), *Liber facetiarum*. G. Francesco (ed.), *Poggius Bracciolini, opera omnia*, Turin, Bottega d'Erasmo, 1964.

*297 Ritter, J.J. (1737), *De impossibilitate et possibilitate abstinentiae longae a cibo et potu; occasione puellae inediam longam fingentis*, Basel, J.H. Decker.

298 Rudolph, G. (1968), 'Histoire admirable d'une fille d'Anjou laquelle a été quatre ans sans user d'aucune nourriture que de peu d'eau commune. Anorexie mentale (?) au XVIe siècle', *Comptes rendus du quatre-vingt-treizième congrès national des sociétés savantes, Tours, 1968. Section des sciences*, vol II, *Histoire des sciences – biologie animale*, Paris, Bibliothèque Nationale, 17–29.

*299 Schmalz, E. (1829), 'Zwei Geschichten von Frauen, welche angeblich sehr lange ohne Nahrung zu sich zu nehmen ihr Leben fortgesetzt haben', *Journal der practischen Heilkunde*, 69 (Supplement), 216–35.

300 Sinclair, U. (1911), *The Fasting Cure*, Pasadena (California), published by the author.

*301 Stalpart van der Wiel, C. (1686), *Eerste deel van het tweede hondertgetal der zeldzame aanmerkingen, soo in de genees -als heel – en snykonst, meest by eygen ondervinding van tyt tot tyt vergadert*, The Hague, Daniël Geselle.

*302 Voltelen, F.J. (1777), *Diatribe medica aditialis memorabilem septennis apositiae historiam*, Leyden, S. & J. Luchtmans.

*303 Wadd, W. (1829), *Comments on Corpulency: Lineaments of Leanness. Mems on Diet and Dietetics*, London, John Ebers.

H. Literature for Chapter 7

*304 Abricossoff, G. (1897), *L'hystérie aux XVIIe et XVIIIe siècles (étude historique et bibliographique)*, Paris, G. Steinheil.

*305 Alexander of Tralles (sixth century), *Alexander von Tralles. Original-Text und Übersetzung nebst einer einleitenden Abhandlung*. German translation, Vienna, Wilhelm Braumüller, 1878–79.

*306 Aretaeus of Cappadocia (second century), *The Extant Works of Aretaeus, the Cappadocian*, London, Sydenham Society, 1856.

*307 Astruc, J. (1761), *Traité des maladies des femmes*, Paris, P.G. Cavelier.

*308 Aurelianus, Caelius (fifth century), *On Acute Diseases and on Chronic Diseases*. English translation, Chicago, University of Chicago Press, 1950.

309 Babb, L. (1965), *The Elizabethan Malady: A Study of Melancholia in English Literature from 1580 to 1642*, East Lansing, Michigan State University Press.

*310 Baglivi, G. (1723), *The Practice of Physick*, 2nd edn, London, Midwinter (1st edn 1704).

311 Baumann, E.D. (1934), 'Über die Magenkrankheiten im klassischen Altertum', *Janus*, 38, 241–65.

*312 Bergson, H. (1844), 'Über den Namen und das Vorkommen der Chlorosis bei Hippokrates', *Neue Zeitschrift für Geburtskunde*, 15, 97–109.

313 Bhanji S. and V.B. Newton (1985), 'Richard Morton's account of "nervous consumption"', *International Journal of Eating Disorders*, 4, 589–95.

314 Birchler, U.B. (1975), *Der Liebeszauber [Philtrum] und sein Zusammenhang mit der Liebeskrankheit in der Medizin, besonders des 16.–18. Jahrhunderts*, Zürich, Juris Druck & Verlag Zürich.

*315 Blache (1833), 'Anorexie'. *Dictionnaire de médecine ou répertoire général des sciences médicales*, vol 3, Paris, J. Béchet, 190–2.

*316 Boerhaave, H. (1745), *De geneeskundige onderwijzingen van de groote Herman Boerhaave*, Dutch translation, Amsterdam, Johannes Gysius.

*317 Boissier de Sauvages, F. (1768), *Nosologia methodica sistens morborum classes juxta Sydenhami mentem & botanicorum ordinem*, 2nd edn, Amsterdam, de Tournes (1st edn 1763).

318 Brammer, C. (1937), *Die Geschichte der Chlorose*, Dissertation, University of Düsseldorf.

319 Brumberg, J.J. (1982), 'Chlorotic girls (1870–1920): a historical perspective on female adolescence', *Child Development*, 53, 1468–77.

*320 Burton, R. (1621), *The Anatomy of Melancholy, What it is, with all the Kindes, Causes, Symptomes, Prognostickes, and Severall Cures of it*, Oxford, Henry Cripps.

*321 Castelli, B. (1713), *Lexicon medicum, graeco-latinum*, Leipzig, Thomas Fritsch.

*322 Celsus, A. Cornelius (first century), *Über die Arzneiwissenschaft, in acht Büchern*, German translation, Braunschweig, Friedrich Vieweg, 1906. Translation (in three volumes), *De medicina*, Cambridge, Harvard University Press, 1953–61.

*323 Cheyne, G. (1724), *An Essay on Health and Long Life*, London, George Strahan.

324 Consbruch, G.W. (1813), *Pathologisches Taschenbuch für practische Ärzte und Wundärzte*, Leipzig, J.A. Barth.

325 Crohns, H. (1905), 'Zur Geschichte der Liebe als 'Krankheit'', *Archiv für Kulturgeschichte*, 3, 66–86.

*326 Cullen, W. (1772), *Synopsis nosologiae methodicae in usum studiosorum*, Leyden, Van der Eyck & Vygh (1st edn 1769).

327 Daems, W.F. (1967), *Boec van medicinen in Dietsche: een middelneder-*

landse compilatie van medisch-farmaceutische literatuur, Leyden, Brill, 136.

★328 Darwin, E. (1796), *Zoonomia, or, the Laws of Organic Life* 2nd edn, London, J. Johnson (1st edn 1794).

★329 Diderot, D. and J. D'Alembert (1751–72), *Encyclopédie ou diction-naire raisonné des sciences, des arts et des métiers*, Paris, Briasson.

★330 *Encyclopaedia Britannica* (1771), Edinburgh, A. Bell & C. Macfar-quhar.

★331 Esquirol, J.E.D. (1838), *Des maladies mentales, considérées sous les rapports médicaux, hygiéniques et médico-légaux*, Paris, J.B. Baillière. Translation: *Mental Maladies, a Treatise on Insanity*, Philadelphia, Lea & Blanchard, 1845.

332 Fischer-Homberger, E. (1970), *Hypochondrie. Melancholie bis Neu-rose. Krankheiten und Zustandsbilder*, Bern-Stuttgart-Vienna, Hans Huber.

333 Fowler, W.M. (1936), 'Chlorosis: an obituary', *Annals of Medical History*, 8, 168–77.

★334 Galen, C. (second century), *Opera omnia*. (Greek text and Latin translation in 22 volumes), Leipzig, Cnobloch (1821–33).

335 Gallouin, F. and J. Le Magnen (1987), 'Évolution historique des concepts de faim, satiété, et appétits', *Réproduction Nutrition Dévelop-pement*, 27 (1B), 109–28.

336 Gee, S.J. (1907), *Medical Lectures and Clinical Aphorisms*, 2nd edn, London, Oxford Medical Publications (1st edn 1902).

337 Geist, H. (1959), 'Von mageren Leuten in der Antike', *Zahnärztli-che Praxis*, 10, 280.

338 Giedke, A. (1983), *Die Liebeskrankheit in der Geschichte der Medizin*, Dissertation, University of Düsseldorf.

339 Grigg, E.R.N. (1955), 'Historical and bibliographical review of tuberculosis in the mentally ill', *Journal of the History of Medicine*, 10, 58–108.

340 Hajal, F. (1982), Psychological treatment of anorexia: a case from the ninth century, *Journal of the History of Medicine*, 37, 325–8.

341 Hansen, A. (1931), 'Die Chlorose im Altertum', *Sudhoffs Archiv für die Geschichte der Medizin*, 24, 175–84.

★342 Harderus, J.R. (1703), *Disputatio inauguralis medica de anorexia*, Basel, publisher not known.

★343 Hippocrates (fifth century BC), *Oeuvres complètes d'Hippocrate*, Greek text and French translation in 10 volumes. Paris, J.B. Baillière, 1839–61. Translation: *Works of Hippocrates*, 4 volumes, Cambridge, Cambridge University Press, 1923–31.

344 Hudson, R.P. (1977), 'The biography of disease: lessons from chlorosis', *Bulletin of the History of Medicine*, 51, 448–63.

*345 Hufeland, C.W. (1836), *Enchiridion medicum oder Anleitung zur medizinischen Praxis*, Berlin, Jonas.

346 Hunter, R. and I. Macalpine (eds) (1963), *Three Hundred Years of Psychiatry, 1535–1860, A History Presented in Selected English Texts*, London-Oxford-New York, Oxford University Press.

347 Jackson, S.W. (1986), *Melancholia and Depression: From Hippocratic Times to Modern Times*, New Haven-London, Yale University Press.

348 Jarcho, S. (1944), 'Giuseppe Zambeccari: 'summary of the life of Maria Caterina Brondi', with the marginalia of an unidentified contemporary', *Bulletin of the History of Medicine*, 12, 400–19.

*349 Londe, C. (1829), 'Anorexie', *Dictionnaire de médecine et de chirurgie pratiques*, vol 1, Brussels, Lejeune, 270.

*350 Lorry, A.C. (1765), *De melancholia et morbis melancholicis*, Paris, P.G. Cavelier.

351 Loudon, I.S.L. (1980), 'Chlorosis, anaemia, and anorexia nervosa', *British Medical Journal*, 281, 1669–75.

352 Loudon, I.S.L. (1984), 'The diseases called chlorosis', *Psychological Medicine*, 14, 27–36.

353 Lowes, J.L. (1914), 'The loveres maladye of hereos', *Modern Philology*, 11, 491–546.

354 Mercer, C.G. and S.D. Wangensteen (1985), 'Consumption, heart-disease, or whatever: chlorosis, a heroine's illness, in *The Wings of the Dove*', *Journal of the History of Medicine*, 40, 259–85.

*355 Morton, R. (1689), *Phthisiologia seu exercitationes de phthisi tribus libris comprehensae. Totumque opus variis historiis illustratum*, London, Samuel Smith.

*356 Morton, R. (1694), *Phthisiologia, or, a Treatise of Consumptions. Wherein the Difference, Nature, Causes, Signs, and Cure of all Sorts of Consumptions are Explained*, London, Samuel Smith & Benjamin Walford.

357 Müller-Pychlau, I. (1940), *Über das Verschwinden der Chlorose*, Heidelberg-Dossenheim, Ludwig Lang.

*358 Naudeau (1789), 'Observation sur une maladie nerveuse, accompagnée d'un dégoût extraordinaire pour les alimens', *Journal de médecine, chirurgie et pharmacie* (Paris), 80, 197–200.

*359 Oribasius (fourth century), *Oeuvres d'Oribase*, French translation, Paris, J.B. Baillière, 1851–76.

360 Osler, W. (1904), 'The 'Phthisiologia' of Richard Morton, M.D.', *Medical Library and Historical Journal*, 2, 1–7.

*361 Paré, A. (1655), *De chirurgie ende opera van alle de wercken*, 4th edn, Amsterdam, Jan Frederickszoon Stam (Dutch translation; 1st Latin edn 1575).

362 Parry-Jones, B. (1991), 'Historical terminology of eating disorders', *Psychological Medicine*, 21, 21–8.

★363 Paul of Aegina (seventh century), *The Seven Books of Paul Aeginata*, English translation in three volumes, London, Sydenham Society, 1844–7.

★364 Pinel, P. (1818), *Nosographie philosophique ou la méthode de l'analyse appliquée à la médecine*, Paris, J.A. Brosson.

★365 Plutarch (first century), *Vita demetrii*, English translation: *Plutarch's lives*, vol 9, London, Heinemann 1914–26, 93–7.

★366 Raulin, J. (1758), *Traité des affections vaporeuses du sexe, avec l'exposition de leurs symptômes, de leurs différentes causes, et la méthode de les guérir*, Paris, J.F. Hérissant.

★367 Rostan, L. (1832), 'Abstinence', *Dictionnaire de médecine ou répertoire général des sciences médicales*, vol 1, Paris, J. Béchet, 283–308.

★368 Rufus of Ephesus (first century), *Oeuvres de Rufus d'Éphèse* French translation, Paris, J.B. Baillière, 1879.

369 Schwarz, E. (1951), *Chlorosis*, Brussels, Acta Medica Belgica.

★370 Selle, C.G. (1781), *Medicina clinica oder Handbuch der medicinischen Praxis*, Berlin, C.F. Himburg.

371 Shafii, M. (1972), 'A precedent for modern psychotherapeutic techniques: one thousand years ago', *American Journal of Psychiatry*, 128, 1581–4.

372 Shorter, E. (1980), 'Women's diseases before 1900'. M. Albin (ed.), *New Directions in Psychohistory*, Lexington, Lexington Books, 183–208.

373 Siddall, A.C. (1982), 'Chlorosis: etiology reconsidered', *Bulletin of the History of Medicine*, 56, 254–60.

374 Silverman, J.A. (1983), 'Richard Morton, 1637–1698, limner of anorexia nervosa: his life and times. A tercentenary essay', *Journal of the American Medical Association*, 250, 2830–2.

375 Silverman, J.A. (1987), 'Robert Whytt, 1714–1766, eighteenth century limner of anorexia nervosa and bulimia. An essay', *International Journal of Eating Disorders*, 6, 143–6.

376 Silverman, J.A. (1987), 'An eighteenth century account of self-starvation in a male', *International Journal of Eating Disorders*, 6, 431–3.

377 Silverman, J.A. (1988), 'Richard Morton's second case of anorexia nervosa: reverend minister Steele and his son', *International Journal of Eating Disorders*, 7, 439–41.

378 Starobinski, J. (1981), 'Chlorosis, the "green sickness"', *Psychological Medicine*, 11, 459–68.

379 Stone, M.H. (1973), 'Child psychiatry before the twentieth century', *International Journal of Child Psychotherapy*, 2, 264–308.

380 Stransky, E. (1974), 'On the history of chlorosis', *Episteme* (Milan), 8, 26–45.

381 Van Deth, R. and W. Vandereycken (1991), 'Was nervous consumption a precursor of anorexia nervosa?', *Journal of the History of Medicine*, 46, 3–19.

382 Veith, I. (1965), *Hysteria: The History of a Disease*, Chicago-London, University of Chicago Press.

*383 Von Haller, A. (1757–66), *Elementa physiologiae corporis humani*, Lausanne-Bern, M.M. Bosquet.

384 Von Hovorka, O. and A. Kronfeld (1908–09), *Vergleichende Volksmedizin: eine Darstellung volksmedizinischer Sitten und Gebräuche*, Stuttgart, Strecker/Schröder.

*385 Von Rein, (1834), 'Casus inediae, bei einem 19jährigen Mädchen beobachtet'. D.G. Kieser (ed.), *Klinische Beiträge*, vol 1, Leipzig, F.L. Herbig, 185–257.

386 Wack, M.F. (1990), *Lovesickness in the Middle Ages: The Viaticum and its Commentaries*, Philadelphia, University of Pennsylvania Press.

*387 Whytt, R. (1765), *Observations on the Nature, Causes, and Cure of those Disorders which have been commonly Called Nervous, Hypochondriac or Hysteric: to which are Prefixed some Remarks on the Sympathy of the Nerves*, 2nd edn, London-Edinburgh, T. Becket (1st edn 1764).

*388 Willan, R. (1790), 'A remarkable case of abstinence'. *Medical Communications* (London), 2, 113–21. Reprinted in A. Smith (ed.), *R. Willan: Miscellaneous Works*, London, T. Cadell, 1821, 437–45.

*389 Willerus, J. (1715), *Disputatio medica inauguralis de anorexia*, Leyden, Theodoor Haak.

*390 Winslow, L.S.F. (1880), 'Fasting and feeding: a detailed account of recorded instances of unusual abstinence from food and of cases illustrating inordinate appetite', *Journal of Psychological Medicine and Mental Pathology*, 6, 253–99.

*391 Winslow, L.S.F. (1881), *Fasting and Feeding Psychologically Considered*, London, Baillière, Tindall & Cox.

*392 Zedler, J.H. (1732–50), *Grosses vollständiges Universal Lexikon aller Wissenschaften und Künste*, Halle-Leipzig, publisher not known.

393 Zilboorg, G. and G.W. Henry (1941), *A History of Medical Psychology*, New York, W.W. Norton.

I. *Literature for Chapters 8 and 9*

★394 Adam, J. (1888), 'Sir William Gull on anorexia nervosa', *Lancet*, 1, 597.

★395 Allbutt, T.C. (1884), *On Visceral Neuroses*, London, Macmillan, 52–7.

★396 Astles, H.E. (1882), 'Anorexia in young girls accompanied with visceral disease', *Proceedings of the South Australian Branch of the British Medical Association (Adelaide)*, 31–2.

★397 Axenfeld, A. and H. Huchard (1883), *Traité des névroses*, 2nd edn, Paris, Germer Baillière, 1018–19.

★398 Briquet, P. (1859), *Traité clinique et thérapeutique de l'hystérie*, Paris, J.B. Baillière, 251–60.

★399 Brugnoli, G. (1875), 'Sull'anoressia. Storie e considerazioni', *Memorie della accademia della scienze dell'istituto di Bologna*, (series 3) 6, 351–61.

★400 Charcot, J.-M. (1885), 'De l'isolement dans le traitement de l'hystérie', *Progrès médical* 2 (1), 161–4. Translation: 'Isolation in the treatment of hysteria', *Clinical Lectures on Diseases of the Nervous System*, vol 3, London, The New Sydenham Society, 1889, 207–19.

★401 Charcot, J.-M. (1887), *Leçons du mardi à la Salpêtrière. Policliniques, 1887–1888*, Paris, Progrès médical/Delahaye-Lecrosnier, 354–6.

★402 Chipley, W.S. (1859), 'Sitomania its causes and treatment', *American Journal of Insanity*, 4, 2–9.

★403 Cleaves, M.A. (1889), 'Neurasthenia and its relation to diseases of women', *Transactions of the Iowa State Medical Society*, 7, 164–79.

★404 Collins, W.J. (1894), 'Anorexia nervosa', *Lancet*, 1, 203.

★405 De Berdt Hovell, D. (1873), 'Hysteria simplified and explained', *Lancet*, 2, 872–4.

★406 De Berdt Hovell, D. (1888), 'Sir William Gull on anorexia nervosa', *Lancet*, 1, 597.

★407 De Berdt Hovell, D. (1888), 'Anorexia nervosa', *Lancet*, 1, 949.

408 Decourt, J. (1954), 'L'anorexie mentale au temps de Lasègue et de Gull', *La presse médicale*, 62, 355–8.

★409 Deniau, L. (1883), *De l'hystérie gastrique*, Paris, A. Parent/A. Davy, 12–42.

410 Dowse, T.S. (1881), 'Anorexia nervosa', *Medical Press and Circular*, 32 (2), 95–7 147–8.

★411 Drummond, D. (1896), 'A case of anorexia nervosa', *Northcumberland and Durham Medical Journal* (Newcastle-upon-Tyne), 4, 7–8.

★412 Duncan, J.M. (1889), 'Hysteria, neurasthenia, and anorexia nervosa', *Lancet*, 1, 973–4.

413 Edge, A.M. (1888), 'A case of anorexia nervosa', *Lancet*, 1, 818.

*414 Fenwick, S. (1880), *On Atrophy of the Stomach and on the Nervous Affections of the Digestive Organs*, London, J. & A. Churchill, 98–123.

*415 Féré, C. (1892), *La pathologie des émotions: études physiologiques et cliniques*, Paris, Félix Alcan, 84–6. Translation: *The Pathology of Emotions: Physiological and Clinical Studies*, London, University Press, 1899.

*416 Féré, C. and F. Levillain (1883), 'Apepsie hystérique (Gull), anorexie hystérique (Lasègue), anorexie nerveuse (Gull, Charcot)', *Progrès médical*, 11 (7), 127–8.

*417 Freud, S. (1895), 'Manuskript G: Melancholie'. Translation: 'Draft G – Melancholia'. J. Strachey (ed.), *The Standard Edition of the Complete Psychological Works of Sigmund Freud*, vol 1, London, Hogarth Press, 1966, 200–1.

418 Freud, S. (1905), 'Über Psychotherapie'. Translation: 'On psychotherapy'. J. Strachey (ed.), *The Standard Edition of the Complete Psychological Works of Sigmund Freud*, vol VII, London, Hogarth Press, 1953, 257–68.

419 Freud, S. (1918), 'Aus der Geschichte einer infantilen Neurose'. Translation: 'An infantile neurosis'. J. Strachey (ed.), *The Standard Edition of the Complete Psychological Works of Sigmund Freud*, vol XVII, London, Hogarth Press, 1955, 3–135.

*420 Freud, S. and J. Breuer (1895), *Studien über Hysterie*. Translation: *Studies on hysteria*, J. Strachey (ed.), *The Standard Edition of the Complete Psychological Works of Sigmund Freud*, vol II, London, Hogarth Press, 1955.

*421 Garland, G.M. (1889), 'Gastric neurasthenia', *Transactions of the Association of American Physicians* (Philadelphia), 4, 204–21.

*422 Garry, T.G. (1888), 'Anorexia nervosa', *Lancet*, 1, 1002.

*423 Gilles de la Tourette, G. (1895), *Traité clinique et thérapeutique de l'hystérie*, vol 3, *Hystérie paroxystique*, II, Paris, E. Plon, Nourrit et Cie, 282–95.

*424 Gowers, W.R. (1888), *A Manual of Diseases of the Nervous System*, vol II, London, J. & A. Churchill, 928.

*425 Gull, W.W. (1868), 'The address in medicine delivered before the annual meeting of the British Medical Association, at Oxford', *Lancet*, 2, 171–6.

*426 [Gull, W.W.] (1873), 'Clinical society of London, Friday, October 24th, 1873. Anorexia hysterica' (apepsia hysterica)', *British Medical Journal*, 2, 527–9.

*427 [Gull, W.W.] (1873), 'Clinical society, Friday, October 24. Sir William Gull read a paper on anorexia hysterica (apepsia hysterica)', *Medical Times and Gazette*, 2, 534–6.

*428 Gull, W.W. (1874), 'Anorexia nervosa (apepsia hysterica, anorexia hysterica)', *Transactions of the Clinical Society of London*, 7, 22–8.

429 Gull, W.W. (1888), 'Anorexia nervosa', *Lancet*, 1, 516–17.

430 Habermas, T. (1989), 'The psychiatric history of anorexia nervosa and bulimia nervosa: weight concerns and bulimic symptoms in early case reports', *International Journal of Eating Disorders*, 8, 259–73.

431 Habermas, T. (1991), 'The role of psychiatric and medical traditions in the discovery and description of anorexia nervosa in France, Germany, and Italy, 1873–1918', *Journal of Nervous and Mental Disease*, 179, 360–5.

432 Habermas, T. (1992), 'Die Anorexia nervosa (Magersucht) in der deutschsprachigen medizinischen Literatur von 1900 bis 1945. Die Rolle der Magersucht in der Entstehung der Psychosomatik', *Sudhoffs Archiv*, 76, 37–62.

433 Habermas, T. (1992), 'Further evidence on early case descriptions of anorexia nervosa and bulimia nervosa', *International Journal of Eating Disorders*, 11, 351–9.

434 Habermas, T. (1992), 'Historical continuities and discontinuities between religious and medical interpretations of extreme fasting. The background to Giovanni Brugnoli's description of two cases of anorexia nervosa in 1875', *History of Psychiatry*, 3, 431–55.

*435 Hemmeter, J.C. (1898), *Diseases of the Stomach: Their Special Pathology, Diagnosis and Treatment*, London, H. Kimpton.

*436 Imbert, F. (1840), *Traité théorique et pratique des maladies des femmes*, Paris, Germer Baillière.

437 Inches, P.R. (1895). 'Anorexia nervosa', *Maritime Medical News (Halifax)* 7, 73–5.

438 Janet, P. (1894), *État mental des hystériques. Les accidents mentaux*, Paris, Rueff/Bibliothèque Médicale Charcot-Debove. Translation: *The Mental State of Hysterics*, New York, Putnam, 1901.

439 Janet, P. (1903), *Les obsessions et la psychasthénie*, Paris, Félix Alcan (two volumes, the second co-authored by F. Raymond).

440 Janet, P. (1907), *The Major Symptoms of Hysteria*, New York, Macmillan.

441 Janet, P. (1909), *Les névroses*, Paris, Ernest Flammarion.

442 Knight, S. (1976), *Jack the Ripper: The Final Solution*, London, Harrap.

*443 Lasègue, E.C. (1873), 'De l'anorexie hystérique', *Archives générales de médecine*, 21, 385–403. Translation: 'On hysterical anorexia', *Medical Times and Gazette* (2), 1873, 265–6, 367–9.

*444 Lasègue, E.C. (1881), 'De l'appétit en général et de l'appétit digestif en particulier', *Gazette des hôpitaux* (Paris), 54 (2), 10–11.

*445 Laycock, T. (1840), *A Treatise on the Nervous Diseases of Women; Comprising an Inquiry into the Nature, Causes, and Treatment of Spinal and Hysterical disorders*, London, Longmans.

*446 Lloyd, J.H. (1893), 'Hysterical tremor and hysterical anorexia (anorexia nervosa) of a severe type', *American Journal of the Medical Sciences*, 106, 264–77.

*447 Mackenzie, S. (1888), 'On a case of anorexia nervosa vel hysterica', *Lancet*, 1, 613–4.

*448 Marcé, L.-V. (1860), 'Note sur une forme de délire hypochondriaque consécutive aux dyspepsies et caractérisée principalement par le refus d'aliments', *Annales médico-psychologiques*, 6 (1), 15–28. Translation: 'On a form of hypochondriacal delirium occurring consecutive to dyspepsia, and characterised by refusal of food', *Journal of Psychological Medicine and Mental Pathology*, 13, 1860, 264–6.

*449 Marshall, C.F. (1895), 'A fatal case of anorexia nervosa', *Lancet*, 1, 149–50.

*450 Mitchell, S.W. (1877), *Fat and Blood, and How to Make Them*, Philadelphia, Lippincott.

*451 Mitchell, S.W. (1881), *Lectures on Diseases of the Nervous System, Especially in Women*, Philadelphia, Henry C. Lea's, 201–16.

452 Morgan, H.G. (1987), '[Comments on] Sir William Withey Gull MD Bart, Anorexia nervosa'. C. Thompson (ed.), *The Origins of Modern Psychiatry*, Chichester-New York, John Wiley, 25–47.

*453 Myrtle, A.S. (1888), 'Anorexia nervosa', *Lancet*, 1, 899.

*454 Osler, W. (1892), *The Principles and Practice of Medicine*, New York, Appleton.

*455 Playfair, W.S. (1888), 'Note on the so-called "anorexia nervosa"', *Lancet*, 1, 817–8.

*456 Preston, G.J. (1897), *Hysteria and Certain Allied Conditions*, Philadelphia, P. Blakiston, 177–80.

*457 Rist, A. (1878), 'Observation d'anorexie idiopathique', *Bulletin de la société médicale de Suisse Romande* (Lausanne), 12, 59–64.

458 Rosenthal, M. (1886), *Magenneurosen und Magencatarrh, sowie deren Behandlung*, Vienna-Leipzig, Urban & Schwarzenberg, 13–8.

459 Shorter, E. (1985), *Bedside Manners: The Troubled History of Doctors and Patients*, New York, Simon & Schuster.

460 Shorter, E. (1987), 'The first great increase in anorexia nervosa', *Journal of Social History*, 21, 69–96.

461 Silverman, J.A. (1988), 'Anorexia nervosa in 1888', *Lancet*, 1, 928–30.

462 Silverman, J.A. (1989), 'Louis-Victor Marcé, 1828–1864: anorexia nervosa's forgotten man', *Psychological Medicine*, 19, 833–5.

463 Silverman, J.A. (1992), 'Lasègue's editorial riposte to Gull's contributions on anorexia nervosa', *Psychological Medicine*, 22, 307–8

464 Silverman, J.A. (1992), 'The seminal contributions of Samuel Fenwick (1821–1902) to our understanding of anorexia nervosa: An historical essay', *International Journal of Eating Disorders*, 12, 453–6.

465 Simmonds, M. (1914), 'Über Hypophysisschwund mit tödlichem Ausgang', *Deutsche medizinische Wochenschrift*, 40, 322–3.

*466 Sollier, P. (1891), 'Anorexie hystérique (sitiergie hystérique): formes pathogéniques – traitement moral', *Revue de médecine*, 11, 625–50.

*467 Sollier, P. (1895), 'L'anorexie mentale', *Journal de médecine de Bordeaux*, 25, 429–32.

*468 Sollier, P. (1896), 'L'anorexie mentale', *Comptes rendus du congrès des médecins aliénistes et neurologistes de France* (Bordeaux), 2, 360–72.

*469 Sollier, P. (1897), *Genèse et nature de l'hystérie. Recherches cliniques et expérimentales de psycho-physiologie*, vol 1, Paris, Félix Alcan, 182.

*470 [Stephens, L.] (1895), 'Emsworth cottage hospital. Case of anorexia nervosa, necropsy (Under the care of Mr. Lockhart Stephens)', *Lancet*, 1, 31–2.

*471 Stichl, A. (1892), 'Beitrag zur Behandlung nervöser Störungen des Verdauungstractes'. H. Gugl and A. Stichl, *Neuropathologische Studien*, Stuttgart, Ferdinand Enke, 41–123.

*472 Stiller, B. (1884), *Die nervösen Magenkrankheiten*, Stuttgart, Ferdinand Enke, 68–75.

473 This, B. (1983), 'De Lasègue à Freud', *Le Coq Héron*, 86, 22–38.

474 Vandereycken, W., E. Kog and J. Vanderlinden (1989), *The Family Approach to Eating Disorders: Assessment and Treatment of Anorexia Nervosa and Bulimia Nervosa*, London–Costa Mesa (CA), PMA Publishing.

475 Vandereycken, W. and P.J.V. Beumont (1990), 'The first Australian case description of anorexia nervosa', *Australian and New Zealand Journal of Psychiatry*, 24, 109–12.

476 Vandereycken, W. and E.L. Lowenkopf (1990), 'Anorexia nervosa in 19th century America', *Journal of Nervous and Mental Disease*, 178, 531–5.

477 Vandereycken, W. and R. van Deth (1989), 'Who was the first to describe anorexia nervosa: Gull or Lasègue?', *Psychological Medicine*, 19, 837–45.

478 Vandereycken, W. and R. van Deth (1990), 'A tribute to Lasègue's description of anorexia nervosa (1873), with comple-

tion of its English translation', *British Journal of Psychiatry*, 157, 902–8.

479 Vandereycken, W., T. Habermas, R. van Deth and R. Meermann (1991), 'German publications on anorexia nervosa in the nineteenth century', *International Journal of Eating Disorders*, 10, 473–90.

480 Van Deth, R. and W. Vandereycken (1990), 'De eerste Nederlandstalige publikaties over anorexia nervosa', *Kind en Adolescent*, 11, 163–9.

*481 Wallet, G. (1892), 'Deux cas d'anorexie hystérique', *Nouvelle Iconographie de la Salpêtrière*, 5, 276–80.

*482 Wilks, S. (1888), 'Anorexia nervosa', *Lancet*, 1, 646–7.

*483 Worthington, L.S. (1875), *De l'obésité: étiologie, thérapeutique et hygiène*, Paris, Delahaye-Martinet, 176ff.

J. *Literature for Chapters 10 and 11*

484 Agras, W.S. and B.G. Kirkley (1986), 'Bulimia: theories of etiology'. K.D. Brownell and J.P. Foreyt (eds), *Handbook of Eating Disorders*, New York, Basic Books, 367–78.

485 Al-Issa, I. (1980), 'The beautiful female body: a key to mental health'. I. Al-Issa, *The Psychopathology of Women*, Englewood Cliffs (NJ), Prentice Hall, 285–306.

486 Altherr, T.L. (ed.), (1983), *Procreation or Pleasure? Sexual Attitudes in American History*, Malabar (FL), Krieger.

487 Altick, R.D. (1973), *Victorian People and Ideas*, New York, W.W. Norton.

488 Ariès, P. (1960), *L'enfant et la vie familiale sous l'ancien régime*, Paris, Plon. Translation: *Centuries of Childhood: A Social History of Family Life*, New York, Random House, 1962.

489 Ariès, P. & A. Béjin, (eds) (1982), *Sexualités occidentales*, Paris, Seuil. Translation: *Western Sexuality*, Oxford, Basil Blackwell, 1985.

490 Aron, J.-P (1973), *Le mangeur du XIX siècle. Une folie bourgeoise: la nourriture*, Paris, Robert Laffont.

491 Auerbach, N. (1982), *Woman and the Demon: The Life of a Victorian Myth*, Cambridge (MA), Harvard University Press.

492 Banks, C.G. (1992), ' "Culture" in culture-bound syndromes: the case of anorexia nervosa', *Social Science and Medicine*, 34, 867–84.

493 Banner, L.W. (1983), *American Beauty*, Chicago/New York, University of Chicago Press/Alfred A. Knopf.

494 Bennett, W. & J. Gurin (1982), *The Dieter's Dilemma: Eating Less and Weighing More*, New York, Basic Books.

495 Bertels, K. (1978), 'Gezinsgeschiedenis'. K. Bertels et al. (eds)

Vrouw man kind: lijnen van vroeger naar nu, Baarn, Ambo, 138–60.

496 Bhanji, S., F.E.F. Jolles and R.A.S. Jolles (1990), 'Goethe's Ottilie: an early 19th century description of anorexia nervosa', *Journal of the Royal Society of Medicine*, 83, 581–5.

497 Blanck, B. (1984), *Magersucht in der Literatur*, Frankfurt, R.G. Fischer.

498 Bokelberg, W. (ed.), (1980), *Sisis Schönheitenalbum*, Dortmund, Harenberg (with an introduction by B. Hamann).

★499 Brillat-Savarin, J.A. (1826), *La physiologie du goût*, Paris, A. Sautelet. Translation: *The Philosopher in the Kitchen*, Harmondsworth, Penguin, 1970.

500 Cameron, E. (1985), 'Femininity, or parody of autonomy: anorexia nervosa and *The Edible Woman*'. *Journal of Canadian Studies*, 20(2), 45–69.

501 Chernin, K. (1981), *The Obsession: Reflections on the Tyranny of Slenderness*, New York, Harper & Row.

502 Cohen, P.M. (1985), 'Christina Rossetti's *Goblin Market*: a paradigm for nineteenth-century anorexia nervosa', *University of Hartford Studies in Literature*, 17 (1), 1–18.

503 Cott, N.F. (1978), 'Passionlessness: an interpretation of Victorian sexual ideology, 1790–1850', *Signs, Journal of Women in Culture and Society*, 4, 219–36.

★504 Counihan, C.M. (1989), 'An anthropological view of western women's prodigious fasting: a review essay', *Food and Foodways*, 3, 357–75.

505 Dally, P. (1989), *Elizabeth Barrett Browning: A Psychological Portrait*, London, Macmillan.

506 Delamont, S. and L. Duffin (eds) (1978), *The Nineteenth-Century Woman: Her Cultural and Physical World*, London, Croom Helm.

507 De Mause, L. (ed.), (1974), *The History of Childhood*, New York, Psychohistory Press.

508 Demos, J. and V. Demos (1969), 'Adolescence in historical perspective', *Journal of Marriage and the Family*, 31, 632–8.

509 Dennis, W. (1949), 'Historical beginnings of child psychology', *Psychological Bulletin*, 46, 224–35.

510 Drinka, G.F. (1984), *The Birth of Neurosis: Myth, Malady, and the Victorians*, New York, Simon & Schuster.

511 Duffy, J. (1968), 'Mental strain and overpressure in the schools: a 19th century viewpoint', *Journal of the History of Medicine*, 23, 63–79.

512 Ehrenreich, B. and D. English (1978), *For Her Own Good*, New York, Anchor Press-Doubleday.

513 Featherstone, M., M. Hepworth and B.S. Turner (eds) (1991), *The Body: Social Process and Cultural Theory*, London, Sage.

514 Filene, P.G. (1974), *Him/Her Self: Sex Roles in Modern America*, New York, Harcourt Brace Jovanovich.

515 Fischer-Homberger, E. (1979), *Krankheit Frau und andere Arbeiten zur Medizingeschichte der Frau*, Bern-Stuttgart-Vienna, Hans Huber.

516 Fischler, C. (1990), *L'Homnivore: le goût, la cuisine et le corps*, Paris, Odile Jacob.

517 Flandrin, J.L. (1979), *Families in Former Times: Kinship, Household and Sexuality*, Cambridge, Cambridge University Press, 102.

518 Frank, K. (1990), *Emily Brontë: A Chainless Soul*, New York, Hamish Hamilton.

519 Freedman, R.J. (1984), 'Reflections on beauty as it relates to health in adolescent females', *Women and Health, The Journal of Women's Health Care*, 9 (2/3), 29–45.

520 Fried, R. and W. Vandereycken (1989), 'The Peter Pan syndrome: was James M. Barrie anorexic?', *International Journal of Eating Disorders*, 8, 369–76.

521 Furst, L.R. and P.W. Graham (eds), (1992), *Disorderly Eaters: Texts in Self-Empowerment*, University Park, Pennsylvania University Press.

522 Garner, D.M. and P.E. Garfinkel (1980), 'Cultural expectations of thinness in women', *Psychological Reports*, 47, 483–91.

523 Gay, P. (1984), *The Bourgeois Experience, Victoria to Freud*, vol I: *Education of the Senses*, Oxford-New York, Oxford University Press.

524 Gay, P. (1986), *The Bourgeois Experience, Victoria to Freud*, vol II: *The Tender Passion*, Oxford-New York, Oxford University Press.

525 Gilbert, S.M. and S. Gubar (1979), *The Madwoman in the Attic: The Woman Writer and the Nineteenth-Century Literary Imagination*, New Haven, Yale University Press.

526 Gillis, J.R. (1974), *Youth and History: Tradition and Change in European Age Relations 1770-present*, New York-London, Academic Press.

527 Goody, J. (1982), *Cooking, Cuisine and Class: A Study of Comparative Sociology*, Cambridge, Cambridge University Press.

528 Gordon, R.A. (1990), *Anorexia and Bulimia: Anatomy of a Social Epidemic*, Oxford-Cambridge (MA), Basil Blackwell.

★529 Grand, S. (1893), *The Heavenly Twins*, London, George Heinemann.

530 Grauer, A. and P.F. Schlottke (1987), *Muß der Speck weg? Der Kampf ums Idealgewicht im Wandel der Schönheitsideale*, Munich, Deutscher Taschenbuch Verlag.

531 Green, H. (1986), *Fit for America: Health, Fitness, Sport, and American Society*, New York, Pantheon Books.

532 Haller, J.S. (1972), 'From maidenhood to menopause: sex education for women in Victorian America', *Journal of Popular Culture*, 6, 49–70.

533 Haller, J.S. and R.M. Haller (1974), *The Physician and Sexuality in Victorian America*, Urbana, University of Illinois Press.

534 Hamann, B. (1989), *Elisabeth: Kaiserin wider Willen*, Munich, Piper. Translation: *Elisabeth, Reluctant Empress*, New York, Knopf, 1986.

535 Hartmann, M. and L.W. Banner (eds), (1974), *Clio's Consciousness Raised: New Perspectives on the History of Women*, New York, Harper & Row.

536 Hawes, J.A. and N.R. Hines (eds), (1985), *American Childhood: A Research Guide and Historical Handbook*, Westport (CT), Greenwood Press.

537 Heer, F. (1975), *Werthers Weg in den Untergrund: Geschichte der Jugendbewegung*, Munich, Bertelsmann Verlag.

538 Himmelfarb, G. (1986), *Marriage and Morals Among the Victorians*, New York, Alfred A. Knopf.

539 Hines, N.R. and J.M. Hawes (eds), (1985), *Growing Up in America: Children in Historical Perspective*, Urbana-Chicago, University of Illinois Press.

★540 Hoffman, H. (1845), *Struwwelpeter*. Translation (with original illustration) reprinted in P.S. Powers, *Obesity: The Regulation of Weight*, Baltimore-London, Williams & Wilkins, 1980, 217.

541 Hollander, A. (1975), *Seeing through Clothes*, New York, Viking Press.

542 Hymowitz C. and M. Weissman (1978), *A History of Women in America*, New York, Bantam Books.

543 Kaplan, J.R. (ed.), (1980), *A Woman's Conflict: The Special Relationship between Women and Food*, Englewood Cliffs (NJ), Prentice Hall.

544 Keniston, K. (1976), 'Stranded in the present'. G.M. Kren and L.H. Rappoport (eds), *Varieties of Psychohistory*. New York, Springer, 251–6.

545 Kern, S. (1973), 'Explosive intimacy: psychodynamics of the Victorian family', *History of Childhood Quarterly*, 1, 437–62.

546 Kern, S. (1975), *Anatomy and Destiny: A Cultural History of the Human Body*, Indianapolis, Bobbs-Merrill.

547 Kett, J.F. (1977), *Rites of Passage: Adolescence in America 1790 to the Present*, New York, Basic Books.

548 Key, E. (1899), *Das Jahrhundert des Kindes*, Berlin, S. Fischer. Translation: *The Century of the Child*, London-New York, G.P. Putnam, 1909.

549 Kren, G.M. and L.H. Rappoport (eds), (1976), *Varieties of Psycho-history*, New York, Springer.

550 Kunzle, D. (1982), *Fashion and Fetishism: A Social History of the Corset, Tight-lacing and Other Forms of Body Sculpture in the West*, Totowa (NJ), Rowman/Littlefield.

551 Lakoff, R. Tolmach and R.L. Scherr (1984), *Face Value: The Politics of Beauty*, Boston-London, Routledge & Kegan Paul.

552 Leach, W. (1980), *True Love and Perfect Union: The Feminist Reform of Sex and Society*, New York, Basic Books.

553 Lewis, C.R. (1982), 'Elizabeth Barrett Browning's 'family disease': anorexia nervosa', *Journal of Marital and Family Therapy*, 8, 129–34.

554 Marwick, A. (1988), *Beauty in History*, London, Thames & Hudson.

555 Mazur, A. (1986), 'US trends in feminine beauty and overadaptation', *Journal of Sex Research*, 22, 281–303.

556 McGuinn, N. (1978), 'George Eliot and Mary Wollstonecraft'. S. Delamont and L. Duffin (eds), *The Nineteenth-Century Woman: Her Cultural and Physical World*, London, Croom Helm, 188–205.

557 McSherry, J.A. (1985), 'Was Mary, queen of Scots, anorexic?', *Scottish Medical Journal*, 30, 243–5.

558 Mennell, S. (1985), *All Manners of Food: Eating and Taste in England and France from the Middle Ages to the Present*, Oxford, Basil Blackwell.

559 Modell, J., F.F. Furstenberg and T. Hershberg (1976), 'Social change and transitions to adulthood in historical perspective', *Journal of Family History*, 1, 7–32.

560 Money, J. (1985), *The Destroying Angel: Sex, Fitness and Food in the Legacy of Degeneracy Theory, Graham Crackers, Kellogg's Corn Flakes and American Health History*, Buffalo, Prometheus Books.

561 Monin, E. (1924), *L'Hygiène de la beauté: guide rituel de la femme*, Paris, Albin Michel, 153.

562 Moulin, J. (1975), *L'Europe à table: introduction à une psychosociologie des pratiques alimentaires en occident*, Paris, Elsevier-Sequioa.

563 Musgrove, F. (1964), *Youth and the Social Order*, Bloomington, Indiana University Press.

564 Neuman, R.P. (1975), 'Masturbation, madness, and the modern concept of childhood and adolescence', *Journal of Social History*, 8, 1–27.

565 Newton, S.M. (1974), *Health, Arts and Reason: Dress Reformers of the 19th Century*, London, John Murray.

566 O'Brien, J. (1937), *The Novel of Adolescence in France: The Study of a Literary Theme*, New York, Columbia University Press.

567 Paterson, W. (1982), 'Was Byron anorexic?', *World Medicine*, 17, 35–8.

568 Perrot, P. (1984), *Le travail des apparences, ou les transformations du corps féminin XVIIe-XIXe siècle*, Paris, Seuil.

569 Poovey, M. (1987), "Scenes of an indelicate character': the medical 'treatment' of Victorian women'. C. Gallagher and T. Laqueur (eds), *The Making of the Modern Body: Sexuality and Society in the Nineteenth Century*, Berkeley, University of California Press, 137–68.

570 Rampling, D. (1985), 'Ascetic ideals and anorexia nervosa', *Journal of Psychiatric Research*, 19, 89–94.

571 Rampling, D. (1988), 'The asceticism of anorexia nervosa'. D. Hardoff and E. Chigier (eds), *Eating Disorders in Adolescents and Young Adults: An International Perspective*, London, Freund Publishing House, 47–54.

★572 Rossetti, C. (1862), *Goblin Market* (new edn, illustrated by A. Rackham), London, Harrap, 1984.

573 Russett, C. Eagle (1989), *Sexual Science: The Victorian Construction of Womanhood*, Cambridge (MA), Harvard University Press.

574 Rutschky, K. (ed.), (1977), *Schwarze Pädagogik: Quellen zur Naturgeschichte der bürgerlichen Erziehung*, Frankfurt, Ullstein.

575 Ryle, J.A. (1939), 'Discussion on anorexia nervosa', *Proceedings of the Royal Society of Medicine*, 32, 735–7.

576 Sabom, W.S. (1985), 'The gnostic world of anorexia nervosa', *Journal of Psychology and Theology*, 13, 243–54.

577 Schütze, G. (1980), *Anorexia Nervosa*, Bern-Stuttgart-Vienna, Hans Huber.

578 Schwartz, H. (1986), *Never Satisfied: A Cultural History of Diets, Fantasies and Fat*, New York/London, Free Press/Collier Macmillan.

579 Schwartz, H. (1989), 'The three-body problem and the end of the world'. M. Feher, R. Naddaff and N. Tazi (eds), *Fragments for a History of the Human Body*, Part 2, New York, Urzone, 407–65.

580 Schwartz, M.A. (1984), 'Expansionary America tightens the belt: social scientific perspectives on obesity', *Marriage and Family Review*, 7 (1/2), 49–63.

581 Seid, R. Pollack (1988), *Never too Thin: Why Women are at War with Their Bodies*, New York, Prentice Hall Press.

582 Shorter, E. (1975), *The Making of the Modern Family*, New York, Basic Books.

583 Shorter, E. (1982), *A History of Women's Bodies*, New York, Basic Books.

584 Shorter, E. (1992), *From Paralysis to Fatigue: A History of Psychosomatic Illness in the Modern Era*, New York, Free Press.

585 Showalter, E. (1985), *The Female Malady: Women, Madness and English Culture, 1830–1980*, New York, Pantheon Books.

586 Silverstein, B., L. Perdue, B. Peterson, L. Vogel and D.A. Fantini (1986), 'Possible causes of the thin standard of bodily attractiveness for women', *International Journal of Eating Disorders*, 5, 907–16.

587 Silverstein, B., B. Peterson and L. Perdue (1986), 'Some correlates of the thin standard of bodily attractiveness for women', *International Journal of Eating Disorders*, 5, 895–905.

588 Skultans, V. (1979), *English Madness: Ideas on Insanity, 1580–1890*, London-Boston, Routledge & Kegan Paul.

589 Smith-Rosenberg, C. (1985), *Disorderly Conduct: Visions and Gender in Victorian America*, New York, Alfred A. Knopf.

590 Sokolow, J.A. (1983), *Eros and Modernization: Sylvester Graham, Health Reform, and the Origins of Victorian Sexuality in America*, London-Toronto, Associated University Presses.

591 Spacks, P. Meyer (1981), *The Adolescent Idea: Myths of Youth and the Adult Imagination*, New York, Basic Books.

592 Steele, V. (1985), *Fashion and Eroticism: Ideals of Feminine Beauty from the Victorian Era to the Jazz Age*, Oxford-New York, Oxford University Press.

593 Stone, L. (1977), *The Family, Sex and Marriage in England 1500–1800*, New York, Harper & Row.

594 Strong, B. (1973), 'Toward a history of the experiential family: sex and incest in the 19th-century family', *Journal of Marriage and the Family*, 35, 457–66.

595 Suleiman, S.R. (ed.), (1986), *The Female Body in Western Culture: Contemporary Perspectives*, Cambridge (MA), Harvard University Press.

596 Tannahill, R. (1973), *Food in History*, London, Methuen.

597 Tanner, J.M. (1981), *A History of the Study of Human Growth*, Cambridge, Cambridge University Press.

598 Thomas, H.K. (1988), 'Emily Dickinson's "renunciation" and anorexia nervosa', *American Literature*, 60, 205–25.

599 Tickner, L. (1988), *The Spectacle of Women: Imagery of the Suffrage Campaign 1907–14*, Chicago/London, University of Chicago Press/Chatto & Windus.

600 Tufte, V. and B. Myerhoff (eds), (1979), *Changing Images of the Family*, New Haven-London, Yale University Press.

601 Turner, B.S. (1984), *The Body and Society: Explorations in Social Theory*, Oxford-New York, Basil Blackwell.

602 Turner, B.S. (1992), *Regulating Bodies: Essays in Medical Sociology*, London-New York, Routledge.

603 Vandereycken, W. and R. van Deth (1990), 'What happened to the

growth spurt of nineteenth-century adolescents? An essay on the history of a scientific omission', *Psychological Medicine*, 20, 767–71.

604 Van Ussel, J.M.W. (1968), *Geschiedenis van het seksuele probleem*, Meppel, Boom.

605 Vicinus, M. (ed.), (1972), *Suffer and Be Still: Women in the Victorian Age*, Bloomington, Indiana University Press.

606 Welter, B. (1966), 'The cult of true womanhood: 1820–1860', *American Quarterly*, 18, 151–74.

607 Wettley, A. (1959), *Von der Psychopathia Sexualis zur Sexualwissenschaft*, Stuttgart, Enke.

608 Whorton, J.C. (1982), *Crusaders for Fitness: The History of American Health Reformers*, Princeton (NJ), Princeton University Press.

609 Wintle, J. (ed.), (1982), *Makers of Nineteenth-Century Culture 1800–1914*, London, Routledge & Kegan Paul.

610 Wolf, N. (1990), *The Beauty Myth*, London, Chatto & Windus.

Index